The Religious Life of

THOMAS JEFFERSON

The
Religious Life
—— of ——
Thomas Jefferson

CHARLES B. SANFORD

UNIVERSITY PRESS OF VIRGINIA

Charlottesville

THE UNIVERSITY PRESS OF VIRGINIA
Copyright © 1984 by the Rector and Visitors
of the University of Virginia

Fifth paperback printing 2002

Library of Congress Cataloging in Publication Data
Sanford Charles B.
  The religious life of Thomas Jefferson.

  Bibliography: p.
  Includes index.
  1. Jefferson, Thomas, 1743–1826—Religion.   I. Title.
E332.2.S255 1984   973.4′6′0924   83-21649
ISBN 0-8139-1131-1

Printed in the United States of America

Contents

Preface

This work on the religious thought of Thomas Jefferson grew out of a study of Jefferson's reading interests, particularly in religious and ethical subjects as reflected in his library holdings and literary comments.[1] In examining the literature about Thomas Jefferson, it soon became apparent that comparatively little study had been done of Jefferson's personal religious beliefs. Even scholars who are familiar with Jefferson's deism, Unitarianism, and enthusiasm for Bible study do not seem to appreciate the importance of his religious beliefs to his political philosophy and career.

Previous studies of Jefferson's religion were short and superficial[2] or lacked objectivity.[3] Only recently have scholarly studies of Jefferson's religion appeared, and these usually have followed a special interest or stressed a particular theme.[4] There is need for a comprehensive, objective, and well-documented study of Jefferson's religious thought.

Such a study is by no means easy, for Jefferson's statements on religion are scattered throughout his vast correspondence and literary compositions. His writings, moreover, are imperfectly indexed.[5] For this reason, it has seemed wise to provide extensive documentation from Jefferson's writing in this study. It is hoped this work, nine years in the making, will help meet the need for a deeper understanding of the spiritual side of this great American.

For encouragement and help in preparing this work grateful acknowledgment is made to James A. Bear, Jr., Resident Director of the Thomas Jefferson Memorial Foundation, Professors Norma Jones and Redmond Burke of the University of Wisconsin—Oshkosh, and Professor Winthrop Hudson of Colgate-Rochester Divinity School.

The Religious Life of
THOMAS JEFFERSON

CHAPTER I

THOMAS JEFFERSON
AS A RELIGIOUS PERSON

For a variety of reasons a considerable amount of confusion and controversy has swirled about Thomas Jefferson's religion. Because of Jefferson's work for political and social freedom, most Jeffersonian scholars view him as one of America's foremost democratic liberals in his philosophy of government and society, but little attention has been paid to the place of religion in this philosophy.[1]

Even such writers as Norman Cousins and Elbert Thomas who recognized the importance of religion in the thinking of Jefferson have tended to see his religion in the political context of human rights and freedom.[2] Others who have been concerned with Jefferson's religion have seen it as a social force, rather than a body of personal convictions. Even those who have praised Jefferson's religion have done so because of his political actions to protect the religious freedom of the individual conscience rather than from an understanding of Jefferson's inner religious life.[3]

Attacks on Jefferson's Religion

On the other hand, Jefferson was fiercely attacked for his lack of religion during his lifetime and for many years after his death. The attacks originated with Jefferson's political opponents when he ran for president in 1800. Upwards of a hundred pamphlets and many newspaper articles were published attacking Jefferson as a "French infidel and atheist." Alexander Hamilton called Jefferson an "atheist and fanatic."[4] Numerous sermons were preached warning that if Jefferson was elected he would discredit religion, overthrow the church, and destroy the Bible. People in New England actually hid their Bibles to save them when Jefferson was elected president.[5]

The idea that Jefferson was an irreligious atheist pursued him all his life. Daniel Webster, after a visit to Monticello, commented on Jefferson's "preference for French opinions, morals and religion," as well as sour French wine. Even after his death Jefferson's irreligious reputation persisted. As late as 1830, the Philadelphia public library refused a place on its shelves for books about Jefferson for this reason.[6] To this day many people insist that Jefferson was an atheist.[7]

Jefferson has also incurred opposition from religious leaders for his championing of the complete separation of church and state. During his lifetime Jefferson believed that most of the attacks upon his religious reputation came from church leaders who wanted "their form of Christianity established through the United States," something he resolutely opposed.[8] In fact, when president he refused even to proclaim a national Thanksgiving Day, in order not to influence religious practices of the country's people.[9]

Over the years since Jefferson's death those who have favored official religious observances by governmental bodies and the public schools, as well as governmental aid to religious organizations, have often perceived Thomas Jefferson as the one most responsible for America's deplorable lack of religion.[10] In the continuing debate about the place of religion in American society, however, Jefferson's reputation has grown to such a place that his statements have now been used by those arguing on both sides of the issue.[11] It is always possible in Jefferson's voluminous writings to find statements on various sides of many issues.

Jefferson wisely chose not to make public answer to the personal attacks upon himself and his religion, for he always felt that arguing in the newspapers was a futile thing. Instead, in a private letter to his friend Dr. Benjamin Rush, he declared: "I have sworn, upon the altar of God, eternal hostility against every form of tyranny over the mind of man." As Dumas Malone has commented, "Time has largely relegated those pamphlets [attacking Jefferson's religion] to oblivion, while painting in bold letters on the walls of his national monument what is perhaps this most characteristic of all his single utterances."[12]

In Defense of Jefferson's Religion

If Jefferson has had many detractors because of his religion over the years, he also has had many defenders. Malone has called Jefferson's faith "the religion of a reasonable man." Merrill Peterson, from his study of Jefferson's life, has concluded that Jefferson "wished for himself, for all his countrymen, not freedom from religion but freedom to pursue religion wherever reason and conscience led." Although the clergy of the formerly established churches in New England and Virginia attacked Jefferson's religion, there were many ministers of the less favored sects who defended him.[13] Leslie Hall in 1913 had little use for Jefferson as a religious thinker, criticizing his ideas as "undigested, . . . ignorant, . . . and unworthy of serious consideration," but Henry Wilder Foote, a scholarly Unitarian minister of the twentieth century, believed Jefferson's "knowledge of and admiration for the teachings of Jesus have never been equaled by any other president."[14]

It is in Henry Randall's early biography of Jefferson with its many recollections by family and friends, however, that we find the most convincing evidences of Jefferson's personal religion. Jefferson remembered being taught his prayers by his mother, and he and his brothers and sisters were baptized as infants into the Church of England. This early training in the Scriptures and prayers of the church influenced him all his life, his family believed. A granddaughter recalled receiving her first Bible as a gift from her grandfather.[15]

There are many examples of Jefferson's reverence for the Bible. Jefferson wrote to a friend in his later years, "I never go to bed without an hour's reading of something moral, whereon to ruminate in the intervals of sleep."[16] The book he chose most often for these devotions was a Bible he had made himself by cutting out his favorite passages from the New Testament and pasting them in a bound volume. In times of crisis, Jefferson turned to the Bible. When his daughter Polly died leaving only his oldest daughter Martha surviving of all his six children, he was found with the Bible in his hands seeking consolation. When he was dying, Jefferson was heard by his family to pray from the Bible, "Lord, now lettest thou thy servant depart in peace." He was buried with the Episcopal service by his own parish minister. Although Jefferson wrote some harsh words about the bigotry of the priesthood over the centuries, he numbered many clergymen among his personal friends, including Joseph Priestley, prominent Unitarian minister and writer; Ezra Stiles, president of Yale; and Jared Sparks, president of Harvard. He was always on good terms with his own local minister. Despite his opposition to any form of civil religious observances,

Jefferson believed that the symbol of the country's seal should contain a public profession of Christianity by the nation.[17]

Claude Bowers, defending Jefferson against the charge of being opposed to religion and the Bible, concluded that Jefferson's greatest contribution to his fellow men was that "he separated the church and the state in the interest of both and made it possible for men to worship God according to the dictates of their conscience."[18]

Jefferson's Church Membership

What church, if any, Jefferson belonged to, and even if he was a Christian at all, has been widely disputed. As late as 1913 Hall attacked Jefferson as being at best only a nominal church member. He claimed there was no proof to support the tradition that Jefferson was a member and officer of the Charlottesville Episcopal church and that, in any case, his views were certainly not Episcopalian. Although Jefferson's personal convictions were hardly orthodox Anglican, they were no more extreme than those of other educated men of his time. He and John Adams agreed on the nature of "true religion as being the moral precepts taught by Jesus."[19]

From his intimate knowledge of Jefferson's family life, Randall cited many instances of Jefferson's church interest. He attended church services regularly, using his own well-worn prayer book. He and his family were baptized, married, and buried by the Anglican church. It is true that, on occasion, he refused to be a godfather at the baptism of friends' children because he could not honestly "profess before God and the World" belief in the doctrine of the Trinity contained in the Apostles' Creed that was part of the Anglican service. He was spared this difficulty in the case of the baptism of his own children, since the baptismal service in use at that time required the godparents, not the real parents, to make the vows of belief.[20]

As to the lack of records of Jefferson's church membership referred to by Hall, there are the records of birth, baptisms, and deaths written into the family Bible preserved by Jefferson. Moreover, anyone who has had occasion to seek after church records knows how imperfectly they are kept and preserved, particularly in the partly frontier area of Virginia served by traveling, missionary pastors where Jefferson lived as a child. It would be surprising if accurate records could be found after all these years.[21] Like many other young people away at college for the first time, young Thomas Jefferson's early letters show more interest in his studies and social activities than in church, but it is probable that he attended Bruton Parish Church in Williamsburg, worshiping with other William and Mary students in their gallery sections of the church.[22] Both Jefferson and his father were elected vestrymen of their local Episcopal church, as was often the case for the neighborhood gentry, and Jefferson's own financial records testify to his support of his church. He was, in fact, always generous in contributing to churches. He wrote in his account book, "I have subscribed to the building of an Episcopal church, two hundred dollars; a Presbyterian, sixty dollars; and a Baptist twenty-five dollars." Jefferson probably drew the plans for the new Episcopalian church in question, although only a few pictures of the building are now left.[23]

While president, Jefferson not only referred to God frequently in his public addresses and studied the Bible in private but took pains to attend divine services in the House of Representatives. His enemies sourly termed this "political expediency." After his retirement to Monticello, Jefferson continued to attend church services, riding into town on horseback carrying a small folding chair of his own invention. He described these services in a letter to Thomas Cooper: "The court house is our common temple. Here Episcopalian and Presbyterian, Methodist and Baptist, meet together, join in hymning their Maker, listen with attention and devotion to each other's preachers and all mix in society in perfect harmony."[24]

Conclusions

From the evidence of his life, we may safely conclude that Jefferson remained a member in good standing of his local Episcopal church all his life, in outward form at least. His inward convictions were another matter, however. His great-grandson described Jefferson's religion as that of a "conservative Unitarian. . . . He did not believe in the miracles, nor the divinity of Christ, nor the doctrine of the atonement, but he was a firm believer in Divine Providence, in the efficacy of prayer, in a future state of rewards and punishments, and in the meeting of friends in another world."[25]

Although in public he was always respectful of other religions, in private he could wield a sharp pen. He found points both to admire and to criticize in such varied religious groups as Presbyterians, Quakers, Baptists, Roman Catholics, and Jews. Peterson believes that Jefferson was unique in his beliefs, "a sect to himself" as he himself said, "but he belonged to no church." Peterson is here confusing inner conviction with outward church membership and is wrong in saying Jefferson was not a church member. All the evidence points to the fact that Jefferson more than met all the church requirements for the time and place.[26]

On the other hand, he might well have become a Unitarian church member if there had been such a society in his area for him to attend instead of being "an Unitarian by myself," as he wrote to a friend. He was a lifelong friend and admirer of Joseph Priestley, eminent Unitarian theologian and scientist, and attended Priestley's church while living in Philadelphia.[27]

The sincerity of Jefferson's religion and moral character was misunderstood by many people, even some of his friends and neighbors. He was called "atheist, deist, or devil," according to his own admission. This rejection was a source of sadness to him,[28] but it is clear that most of the criticisms came from those who knew neither Jefferson nor his religious beliefs. With unusual understanding and tolerance, Jefferson remarked that the attacks were not really against his real self and beliefs but against a hated, imaginary figure his opponents mistook for Thomas Jefferson.[29] The vilification of Jefferson's religion continued even after his death. In the mid-nineteenth century, church leaders were still calling Jefferson a "French infidel propagandist." It was not until 1947 at special services at the Jefferson Memorial in Washington that Unitarians were proud to read from Jefferson's Bible and acknowledge the "debt Unitarian principles owe to the free religious faith of Thomas Jefferson."[30]

Jefferson, then, has been studied and admired quite universally for his contributions as a democratic liberal and champion of the political, social, and religious rights of man. His religious beliefs, however, have aroused much controversy and disagreement. They deserve more study and understanding than they have yet received.

CHAPTER II

JEFFERSON'S
RELIGIOUS IDEAS

Introduction

Over the years, Jefferson's religious ideas and character have been subject to much misunderstanding and misinterpretation. A recent scholar has even termed his religion "radical if not revolutionary." What is the truth about Jefferson's religion? Was he more unorthodox than most of his fellow Americans?

To answer these and other questions, Jefferson's early religious experiences and studies must be considered, and some of his religious convictions examined. It is also important to indicate the development of Jefferson's religious beliefs over the years. Except in a few notable cases, however, Jefferson was not one to change his ideas with rapid facility. In most cases his ideas in later years show a continuing development and further refinement of those he held earlier.[1] At various times in his life, however, Jefferson's career and experiences led him to consider various aspects of religion. Usually he explored thoroughly the subject of his interest, ordering and studying books on the topic and occasionally sharing the results of his studies in letters to friends.[2]

One of Jefferson's earliest childhood recollections was of being called upon to say the Lord's Prayer for company before dinner. He also remembered being taught his prayers by his mother and the sung Psalms of the Anglican church by a loved older sister, Jane. This early training gave him a lifelong appreciation of devotional religion.[3]

When Jefferson went away from home to college at William and Mary, according to most of his biographers he was challenged by stimulating teachers and the deistic writers of the Enlightenment, lost the pious faith of his Anglican upbringing, and, after a period of doubt and crisis, developed a new rational religion. The idea that Jefferson had a crisis of faith in college, such as many students have known, makes him seem more human and accounts for some of the facts of his intellectual life. Unfortunately, it does not adequately explain all the facts, and the evidence for such a crisis is scanty and weak.[4]

In a letter to Thomas Cooper which was cited by Gilbert Chinard as evidence of Jefferson's loss of orthodox faith, Jefferson recalled his "bold pursuit of knowledge" as a youth and his eagerness to "beard every authority which stood in the way of truth and reason." But he gives no indication of any emotional crisis over old beliefs that were being shaken. The whole tone, instead, is that of an enthusiastic iconoclast gleefully shaking the establishment, an attitude Jefferson retained to the end of his days although tempered in later years by the politeness and wisdom of age. Rather than showing a shaken religious faith, Jefferson's recollection of his student days indicated a student who was enthusiastically responding to new intellectual stimulation and unfolding horizons.[5]

Jefferson's feelings and attitudes toward the study of religion are well shown in a letter he wrote to his nephew Peter Carr to guide him in his college studies of religion. He urged Carr to examine fearlessly all the ideas of Christianity before the "tribunal of reason." In urging this searching examination of religion upon one whom he regarded much as he would have his own son, Jefferson surely would have warned young Carr of any emotional dangers or pitfalls. It would have been natural for Jefferson to mention any emotional crisis that he had experienced as a young student himself. He did not. In fact, it is quite clear such a possibility never entered his mind. He wrote, "Do not be frightened from this inquiry by any fear of its consequences." Reason results in a stronger religion than faith and revelation, he argued.[6]

The only emotional danger that Jefferson recalled from his college days was the temptation to fall in with the wrong companions, those who spent more time fox hunting and in the taverns than at their studies. He warned his grandson when he went away to college of this danger, which Jefferson had experienced himself. Stuart Brown, one Jeffersonian scholar who has recognized Jefferson's fondness for "rational religion," does not believe Jefferson ever had any violent emotional religious experience.[7]

The most that can be said from Jefferson's own recollections of his college days is that when he was a student, he had a period of religious speculation and questioning while he was seeking new religious and spiritual ideas. "When I was young," he wrote to the Reverend Isaac Story, "I was fond of speculations which seemed to promise some insight into the country of spirits, but observing at length that they left me in the same ignorance in which they had found me, I have ceased to read concerning them." This youthful interest accounts for the quotations on fate, death, and immortality in the literary notebook kept by Jefferson during his college days.[8]

Jefferson had little in his religious upbringing to be disturbed when he came into contact with deistic thought at college. His childhood religious training had not been rigorous, and the Anglican church of colonial Virginia was less strict than the Calvinistic sects or New England Puritan churches.

Religion Is Known by Reason

When he urged Carr to "fix reason in the judgment seat" and use it as a guiding "oracle given by heaven," Jefferson struck a favorite theme. He often stated that reason was the guide to his own religious thought and believed that reason was the means by which others could know religious truth. "Every man's reason," he wrote, "is his own rightful umpire." To give up thinking for oneself was "the last degradation of a free and moral agent."[9]

In this high confidence in reason and intellect in all matters, including religion, Jefferson was a true disciple of the Enlightenment. Isaac Newton, Francis Bacon, and John Locke were the heroes of the age. While displaying a prized painting of his heroes to Alexander Hamilton on one occasion, Jefferson expressed his belief that they were the three "greatest men that have ever lived, having laid the foundation of the physical and moral sciences." Hamilton typically replied that he regarded Julius Caesar as the greatest man who ever lived.[10]

Francis Bacon was honored because he was one of the first to champion the modern scientific method of detailed observation of facts and logical thinking instead of the medieval method of theological synthesis, and Jefferson early developed a knack for observation, as Bacon recommended. All his life he kept extensive records and observations of the weather and the progress of his plants and crops. His first published book, *Notes on the State of Virginia,* is filled with detailed observations of the flora and fauna of Virginia, as well as reports on the people and social and religious customs. All his life he was eager to learn the facts of such varied fields as agriculture, science, architecture, political science, and sociology. His reading interests were broad, and his library covered many fields.[11]

Jefferson valued Isaac Newton as the great thinker who pioneered the laws of the physical sciences and unlocked the secrets of the movements of the stars. Previously men had been at the mercy of the unknown forces of nature. Now they could understand the laws by which the forces of nature operated and be forever freed from fear and superstition, a proof, Newton believed, of "the greater glory of God." Many educated religious thinkers, from John Adams to Cotton Mather, were inspired by Newton to see more of the power and purpose of God in his universe. Other deistic and agnostic writers had used Newton's discoveries to dispense with God altogether. Jefferson was an interested student of all these schools of thought.[12]

Jefferson was influenced by John Locke not so much because he agreed with Locke's religious and social ideas—he wanted to "go beyond" Locke in many cases—but because Locke had wanted to apply to the social and political arena the same principles of thought and knowledge that Newton and Bacon had applied to the physical world. Jefferson, as a social philosopher and statesman, was interested in finding moral and social laws similar to the laws of nature which would help overcome the social and moral problems that impeded progress. Jefferson studied Locke thoroughly and used his ideas freely in formulating his own philosophy of the nature of moral man in society, as reflected in the Declaration of Independence and the Virginia Act for Establishing Religious Freedom.[13]

The important element in the thinking of all three of his intellectual heroes, Bacon, Newton, and Locke, was reason. Reason was banishing ignorance and superstition and leading to knowledge and the advancement of progress in both science and religion. "Reason and experiment have been indulged," Jefferson wrote, "and error has fled before them." He commented to a clergyman friend: "Truth and reason are eternal. They have prevailed, and they will eternally prevail." In religion, reason and free inquiry would guard against error and oppression, for, he said, "they are the natural enemies of error and of error only." In later years Jefferson came to see that the insight of reason which was given to each person "by their Creator for the investigation of truth" varied; hence truth and religious opinion could also vary.[14]

Reason also was important because it protected the religious inquirer from fanaticism. Jefferson relied on the reason bestowed on each person by God as the final "umpire of truth" in an argument with Miles King, who wrote to him trying to "save him from his atheism." To William Carver he commented wryly on his experience with the battle between religious fanatics and "those who refuse blindly to abandon their own reason" in matters of religion.[15] The chief question in this conflict over religion, which pursued Jefferson all his life, was the basis of authority in religion. The medieval church had stressed faith and revelation; the new world of Newton, Bacon, and Locke stressed reason. The argument persists to this day.

Early in his religious thinking Jefferson perceived that religion was a matter of inner reflection and conviction. "No man can form his faith to the dictates of another," he wrote. "The essence of religion consists in the internal persuasion of the mind."[16] In public Jefferson always extended this freedom of "inner belief of the mind" to those who differed from himself, but in private he found it difficult to be sympathetic with those of mystical or philosophical bent or those who followed blind faith. Reason was necessary as a protection against "an indulgence in speculations that disquiet the mind, . . . plunging into the fathomless abyss of dreams and phantasms," he argued, and was the only means of "determining between what really comes from God and the phantasms of deluded imagination." Reason was also valued by Jefferson because it was the gift of God to man. "For the use of reason," he wrote, "everyone is responsible to the God who planted it in his breast, as a light for his guidance."[17]

One of the chief philosophers to blame for influencing people into the abyss of dreams and phantasms and useless speculations, in Jefferson's opinion, was Plato. Jefferson frequently criticized "the whimsies of Plato's own foggy brain." It was particularly unfortunate, Jefferson felt, that Christianity had been influenced by Platonic mysticism and revelation, which had hindered progress ·and freedom, instead of keeping to the simple teachings of Christ.[18] The need to reform the church and society by the light of reason and to clear away the accumulated rubbish of religious superstition was one of the main convictions of the Enlightenment.[19]

Another favorite author of Jefferson, whom he praised in later years and copied from at great length while a student, was the eighteenth-century deist philosopher, Henry St. John, Viscount Bolingbroke. It seems clear that it was largely from Bolingbroke that Jefferson learned his skepticism of religious truth that depended upon "revelation" and "accepting by faith" beliefs which were contrary to reason. Influenced by Bolingbroke, Jefferson came to a lifelong conviction that the God whom nature revealed and the religion which reason indicated were more believable than the God and doctrines of biblical revelation and dogma.[20]

Reason was important also because, without it, religion became quarrelsome and divisive, for, as Jefferson put it, "every individual of every religious sect believes all wrong but his own!" Jefferson's later writings indicate that he hoped for the spread of a religion of reason and morality and believed that this rational belief in the one God of nature could be a unifying factor among the religious pluralism of America.[21] As Jefferson wrote to Ezra Stiles, the Calvinistic president of Yale, they might differ in their theology and dogma, but they could agree on morality and their admiration for Jesus' teachings, for "no doctrines of his lead to schism."[22]

Thomas Jefferson, thus, early came to believe that the "God of nature" had given the inner "oracle of reason" to each person as the true guide to religious insight. He worshiped this God and followed that oracle all his life.

Religion Is Personal and Private

Another of Jefferson's lifelong convictions was that religion was a personal and private matter. He confided to a close friend, "I not only write nothing on religion, but rarely permit myself to speak on it, and never but in a reasonable society . . . [or in private] conversation." So strong was Jefferson's desire for privacy about his religion that his immediate family did not know he had compiled his own version of the New Testament until after his death.[23]

Early in his studies of society, Jefferson came to the conclusion that religion was essentially an inner and private matter between "every man and his Maker" in which no outside agency, not even the church and certainly not the government, should interfere. He was therefore, he wrote, "most scrupulously reserved on the subject." He went so far as to believe one should not try "to change another's creed." So he opposed sending missionaries "to make converts" and distributing Bibles outside of America.[24]

Freedom of conscience was one of the most important of the rights of man, Jefferson believed, and he was one of the most influential of the American founding fathers in establishing religious freedom as the law of the land. The right to hold varied personal opinions, especially about religion, needed to be defended constantly, even against the "tyranny of public opinion." If necessary, the right to "choose error" must be protected.[25]

As Jefferson indicated on various occasions, the "malignant perversions, misrepresentations and calumies" that he endured about his religion made him more zealous in protecting his privacy. He sometimes cautioned his many correspondents to keep his letters private because "the public papers" caused "so much malignant distortion and perverted construction" of his words. When, despite his best efforts, his private opinions were leaked to the press, the Virginian was greatly "mortified."[26]

Such experiences go far to explain his desire to keep his religious views private and the consequent lack of understanding of his religion by the public. His pride prevented him from making public explanations. He insisted that people must judge his virtue by his character, declaring, "It is in our lives, and not from our words, that our religion must be read." The most that he would do in his own defense was to prepare a "Syllabus of the Doctrines of Jesus" defending his religious beliefs "from that anti-Christian system imputed to me by those who know nothing of my opinions."[27] This outline of his religion he quietly shared with his close friends and family.[28] He did not want his thoughts made public, however, and only consented to have his work published in far-off Edinburgh if it was done anonymously, explaining, "I was unwilling to draw on myself a swarm of insects, whose buzz is more disquieting than their bite." He dreaded "all the hewing and hacking . . . [of the] dogmatizing, venal jugglers," he said. As he explained, "I am now at the age of quietism, and wish not to be kicked by the asses of hierophantism."[29]

Jefferson's article on the New Testament led to more unwelcome public discussion of his religion. He mentioned his study of the Bible to a friend, Charles Thomson, and word got out that Jefferson the atheist had changed his views and was publishing a book on religion.[30] He hastened to inform his friends that he had no intention of publishing a book on so controversial a subject and certainly had not changed his views. He was especially provoked by a would-be biographer who asked him if his change of religion was "authentic." He tartly replied that he answered for his religion "only to one Being." "Say nothing of my religion," he instructed. "It is known to my God and myself alone; its evidence before the world is to be sought in my life; if that has been dutiful to society the Religion which has regulated it cannot be a bad one."[31]

Religion, then, for Jefferson was an inner, personal belief and a private matter between a man and his God. While still a young man he exclaimed: "I never submitted my opinions to the creed of any party of men in religion or in politics. . . . If I could not go to heaven but with a party, I would not go there at all!"[32]

Jefferson's "Theology"

In summary, we may conclude that Jefferson, in his college years, began an involvement with Enlightenment and deistic writers which deeply influenced him toward a liberal, intellectual, moralistic, personal, and humanitarian view of government, society, and religion. This study continued all of his life and is reflected in his choice of favorite quotations and the books in his extensive library.[33]

Jefferson, however broad his intellectual interests, was not an organized philosopher. He was at most, as Adrienne Koch has argued, a philosophe whose writings have philosophical content. Nor was Jefferson a theologian in a systematic sense, and his religious writings have been criticized as "undigested and lacking in order and consistency."[34] This kind of criticism did not disturb Jefferson, for he was not interested in developing a theology; he had too much trouble all his life with the theological system-builders to look with favor on the idea.

Nevertheless, Jefferson's wide-ranging thought led him to study thoroughly all of the varied ideas of Christianity at one time or another. His writings can easily be grouped around the main subjects of Christian theology, and he had well-reasoned and firmly held convictions on all of them.

Any Christian theology will be concerned with ideas of God, ideas of man, ideas of Jesus Christ, and ideas of the nature of life after death. Jefferson was concerned with all of these subjects. The succeeding chapters consider them in much the same order that Jefferson became involved with them during his life.

CHAPTER III

JEFFERSON'S

RELIGIOUS IDEAS OF MAN:

THE RIGHTS OF MAN

After completing his college studies, Jefferson took up the study and practice of law under the guidance of George Wythe and became increasingly involved in colonial and national politics. In his continuing religious development, he soon passed from his youthful questionings about God and speculations about life and death to a systematic study of the nature of man.

His commonplace notebooks show that he was reading widely in literature, political philosophy, the classics, law, and history to learn the nature of man and the origin of human government and society. He was laying the groundwork for his religious, political, and social convictions that were to be the basis of his inner life and career and preparing himself for his role as one of the political and philosophical leaders of the American Revolution.[1]

A Summary View of the Rights of British America

Jefferson soon showed himself to be one of the most articulate philosophers of the American Revolution. Although young, he was elected to represent his home area in the colonial legislature at Williamsburg, where he distinguished himself by his diligent study and committee work. Content to let others do the orating and debating, he turned to his pen for drafting proposals. One of the first of these was a "draft of instructions to the Virginia delegates in the Continental Congress," published as *A Summary View of the Rights of British America,* which set forth the "rights which god and the laws have given equally to all." In this paper Jefferson drew a parallel between the settlement of America and that of Britain by their "Saxon ancestors who, in like manner, left their native wilds and woods in the North of Europe, to possess themselves of the island of Britain" and establish a free and happy society. Jefferson argued that Americans had the same basic rights as their Saxon ancestors, including the right to their lands, which the king could not take away.[2] To the end of his life Jefferson was a firm believer in the "Saxon myth," as Peterson has termed it. He was convinced that the English people lived with more freedom and happiness under Anglo-Saxon common law and customs than they had under English law after the Norman Conquest.[3]

In this, his first, state paper, Jefferson not only brought forth important ideas from his studies for the consideration of his fellow delegates but set the theme for major ideas about man and society that he was to develop further in later documents. He mentions, for example, "rights," "freedom," and "equality" that "God," "nature," and "law" have given to all men. Although Jefferson's carefully drafted paper was not adopted, it gained him a reputation which led to his being chosen to write an even more important and famous paper.[4]

Declaration of Independence

It was surprising enough that Jefferson, while still comparatively young and little known, should be chosen to be on the committee to draw up the Declaration of Independence with such famous leaders as John Adams, Benjamin Franklin, Roger Sherman, and Robert Livingston. It was still more surprising that he should be the one chosen to compose the actual draft for the others to consider. John Adams remembered the incident: "The sub-committee met. Jefferson proposed to me to make the draft. I said, 'I will not.' 'You should do it.' 'Oh, no!' 'Why will you not?' . . . 'Reason first—You are a Virginian, and a Virginian ought to appear at the head of this business. Reason second—I am obnoxious, suspected, and unpopular. You are very much otherwise. Reason third—You can write ten times better than I can' 'Well,' said Jefferson, 'If you are decided, I will do as well as I can' "[5]

Jefferson, working with his usual diligence after the sessions of debate of the Continental Congress in his rented quarters on the second floor of a brick house at Seventh and Market streets of Philadelphia, composed the document that was to become not merely a political and diplomatic state paper but a creed for the American people. In it Jefferson crystalized the ideology of the new nation around four beliefs: the equality of men, the natural rights of man, the sovereignty of the people, and the right of revolution.[6]

The purpose of the Declaration of Independence was to set forth the reasons that had led the American colonies to "dissolve the political bands which had connected them" with Great Britain and to "assume among the powers of the earth the separate and equal station" to which they were entitled. Much of it was filled with a long enumeration of the grievances of the colonists against King George III which the passing years have made of little interest.[7] What made the Declaration great was just one sentence at the beginning of the second paragraph in which Jefferson managed to compress a cosmology, a political philosophy, and a national creed.[8] In these inspired words Jefferson expressed his deepest convictions about life and the nature of man based upon what he believed to be "the laws of nature and nature's God." The sentence states: "We hold these truths to be self-evident: that all men are created equal; that they are endowed by their creator with *inherent and* [changed by debate in Congress to *certain*] inalienable rights; that among these are life, liberty, and the pursuit of happiness: that to secure these rights, governments are instituted among men, deriving their just powers from the consent of the governed; that whenever any form of government becomes destructive of these ends, it is the right of the people to alter or abolish it. . . ."[9] Familiar as these words are to most people, it is often overlooked that Jefferson based his argument for human rights upon his religious beliefs about the nature of God and man. All men had rights that were endowed in their very humanity by their Creator. For Jefferson, this was a "self-evident" truth upon which all other arguments depended.[10]

Just what books and sources may have influenced Jefferson in formulating the Declaration of Independence has long been a matter of debate, not only among scholars but among Jefferson's friends and foes. James Wilson, John Locke, Lord Kames, and others from Jefferson's readings in history have all been suggested.[11] Whatever unconscious influence his reading may have had upon him, Jefferson testified nearly fifty years later to his friend James Madison that the Declaration was original and that he had "turned to neither book nor pamphlet while writing it." Actually, the point at issue is not the exact sources of the ideas of the Enlightenment from the "various elementary books of public right," as Jefferson termed them, that influenced him. The idea of natural rights was in the air and accepted by everyone. Jefferson could hardly have avoided it.[12]

It was his moral conviction about human life that made the Declaration of Independence so important, not only for America but for all people everywhere. Politically, the gaining of independence by thirteen British colonies was not overly important. It was the moral purpose and humanitarian ideals of the Declaration of Independence that influenced history and began an age of revolution that continues to the present time[13]

The "Natural" Rights of Man

The central premise upon which the whole argument of the Declaration of Independence was based was that God had created all men with a common intrinsic nature and certain "natural" rights that could not properly be abridged or taken away without the agreement of the groups of people formed into societies. This line of reasoning was not original with Jefferson and the American founding fathers or with the later French revolutionists. It had been developed in England over the years by Locke, William Blackstone, Lord Kames, and others during the long struggles between the various royal factions and the people and Parliament.

What the philosophers of the American Revolution were searching for was an argument that would undercut the old theory of "the divine right" of kings and cardinals to rule over the common people, which had been the foundation of medieval society. Jefferson put the argument against this "divine right" of kings and nobles to rule in ringing terms near the end of his life in a letter written to be read for the fiftieth anniversary celebration of the signing of the Declaration of Independence: "All eyes are opened, or opening, to the rights of man. . . . The mass of mankind has not been born with saddles on their backs, nor a favored few booted and spurred, ready to ride them legitimately, by the grace of God."[14]

In opposing the idea that God had given certain royal families or religious leaders a divine right to rule over other people at a certain period in history, the defenders of the American Revolution, such as Jefferson and Thomas Paine, went back to the creation of all men, free and equal, by the hand of God as the source of authority. The argument was not that men were born equal, but that they had been created equal by God. In private, deists like Jefferson and Paine had some reservations about the Old Testament and did not hesitate to correct the biblical account of creation in the light of Newtonian science and emerging anthropology. They were, however, in general agreement with the biblical idea of a first creation, and the more they learned of the flora and fauna of the world, the more they saw the marvels of God's creation and the basic similarity of the human species.[15]

From these proven facts, they went on to elaborate the rights men had by the fact of their creation-given human nature, their "natural" rights. Such rights, John Locke theorized, were the rights to hold on to one's life, to individual liberty, and to hold property improved by one's labor. It will be noted that Jefferson changed Locke's list of rights from "life, liberty, and property" to "life, liberty, and the pursuit of happiness," a more inclusive and suggestive phrase which, for good or ill, has characterized the American dream ever since.[16]

According to the Whigs, men soon came to see the advantages of living in society in order to protect their natural rights. Locke thought that early man formed society and government both to protect the group from outside attack and to protect the less assertive members from the aggressions of the stronger. Government was the result of a "social contract" to protect the natural rights of men, but if the contract was broken by the king, the people had the right to overthrow him as Parliament did James II. Jefferson used the same argument against King George III in the Declaration of Independence.[17]

Jefferson, however, was never convinced by the social contract theory of society, especially as presented by Thomas Hobbes, that life for man was nasty and brutish until the selfishness of people was restrained by strong government.[18] Jefferson believed man was fundamentally good, that his life in a primitive state, while different from that in more advanced civilizations, was happy, and that most of the difficulties for the common man came from oppression and bad government, of which he had seen much in America, England, and France. Politically, he believed men had the right to enjoy the fruits of their own labors, to form their own governments, and to change them if they grew oppressive.[19]

With Jefferson's interest in people and his legal interest in government and social institutions, it is not surprising that he devoted his life to the political and social reforms he saw as necessary to enhance man's free enjoyment of his natural rights. He worked for the extension of the vote to more people and the protection of their rights under the United States Constitution and through reform of the state laws of Virginia.[20] He reformed the laws of inheritance to discourage the establishment of a landed aristocracy in Virginia patterned after the English gentry.[21] He favored better education to encourage the true aristocracy of "virtue and talents" instead of that of "wealth and birth." The "artificial aristocracy" of class was "a mischievous ingredient in government," he argued, while the "natural aristocracy of virtue and talents" was "the most precious gift of nature for the . . . government of society."[22]

This political philosophy of Jefferson was based on a moral view of man and life. He always believed in the fundamental goodness and rationality of men, in contrast to those who believed that the mass of men were foolish, evil, and not to be trusted with self-government. He wrote John Adams that he thought men and leaders all through history could be divided into "Whigs," or democrats, and "Tories," or aristocrats, on this basis. As he explained to another friend, "The doctrines of Europe were that men can not be restrained within the limits of order and justice but by forces wielded over them by . . . kings, hereditary nobles, and priests. . . . We believed . . . that man was a rational animal, endowed with rights, and with an innate sense of justice; and that he could be restrained from wrong and protected in right, by moderate powers, confided to persons of his own choice, and held to their duties by dependence on his own will."[23]

Jefferson had no high opinion of the aristocracy. He once wryly commented that he had not observed that wealth increased a man's intelligence. After close observation at the courts of England and France, he concluded that kings were like barn animals, pampered, overfed, and taught never to think, so that "in a few generations they become all body and no mind. . . . Kings—from all of whom the Lord deliver us!"[24] Jefferson's lifelong belief in the ability of the common man in contrast to that of the aristocracy and his

championship of the equal rights of men may well reflect his boyhood experiences of the worth of ordinary people on the Virginia
frontier.[25]

Conclusions

It is not surprising that Jefferson became the leader of this new
republic of the people, championing their rights, believing in their
abilities, and striving to enlarge their opportunities. His political
and social philosophy, in the last analysis, was rooted in his religion.
The common man had basic rights and could be safely entrusted
with political power because of the way he had been created by an
all-wise and perfect God. It was the selfish interests of special groups
that had caused the mischief history recorded. The cure was to
enlarge the scope for man to exercise his "natural rights." Jefferson
thus developed his theories of government from his faith in the
goodness of man, which in turn grew out of his basic optimistic
nature and his belief in God, the good Creator of all mankind.[26]

CHAPTER IV

JEFFERSON'S
RELIGIOUS IDEAS OF MAN:
MAN'S NEED FOR RELIGIOUS FREEDOM

Although Jefferson spent much of his life fighting for the political and social rights of men, he was just as zealous in his defense of their religious rights. He vowed to Edward Dowse "never" to "bow to the shrine of intolerance" and always "to maintain the common right of freedom of conscience." It was his efforts to defend religious freedom that involved him in the most bitter conflicts of his political career.[1]

Importance of Religious Freedom

For a variety of reasons Jefferson regarded religious freedom as the most important of the rights of man. In the first place, religious freedom involved more than the government or even the church. It involved God and the human conscience. People are "accountable for their principles," he wrote, not to creed or party, priest or state, but to "God alone." Moreover, man also received from God the inspiration for his religious beliefs. "God is the only rightful and competent Judge of creeds," he wrote to an intolerant critic.[2]

Jefferson put the idea that religious freedom was rooted in God's purposeful creation of man in more polished form in his bill for establishing religious freedom in Virginia when he wrote: "Almighty God hath created the mind free, and manifested his supreme will that free it shall remain by making it altogether insusceptible of restraint; that all attempts to influence it by temporal punishments, or burthens, or by civil incapacitations, tend only to beget habits of hypocrisy and meanness, and are a departure from the plan of the holy author of our religion."[3] Religious freedom was for Jefferson, then, the most important of the rights of man. The course

Jefferson took in developing his ideas on the subject is instructive to trace, for it shows his own emerging religious convictions.

Doctrine of Toleration

Jefferson began his development of the belief in religious freedom by emphasizing the importance of toleration. He repeatedly stated that it was essential to practice religious toleration in society since people would inevitably differ in their religious beliefs just as they differed in tastes, talents, and appearances. It was "absurd," he declared, for some people to tell the Almighty he should make all people think or look alike.[4]

In his *Notes on the State of Virginia,* Jefferson developed the argument for tolerance at some length. "Reason and free inquiry are the only effectual agents against error," he wrote. "Give a loose to them, they will support the true religion by bringing every false one to their tribunal. . . . They are the natural enemies of error, and of error only." To illustrate the foolishness of intolerance, he pointed to the former laws of France prohibiting the eating of potatoes and the teaching of the discoveries of Galileo. He concluded, "Subject opinion to coercion: whom will you make your inquisitors? Fallible men. . . . And why subject it to coercion? To produce uniformity. But is uniformity of opinion desireable? No more than of face and stature." As Jefferson the lawyer saw it, it was an error to believe "that the operations of the mind as well as the acts of the body, are subject to the coercion of the laws. . . . The rights of conscience . . . we could not submit. . . . We are answerable for them to our God." Jefferson was indebted to his wide reading, particularly from John Locke, Lord Shaftesbury, and John Milton, for many of these ideas on toleration.[5]

Locke had argued that no one had a right to punish his neighbor by the civil law for different religious practices, even if they were in error, since the neighbor injured no one but himself by his error.[6] Jefferson used the same argument in *Notes on the State of Virginia* when he wrote that it did no injury to him for his neighbor to believe in twenty gods or no god, a statement for which he was roundly attacked by his religious opponents.[7] Jefferson copied approvingly in his notes Locke's statement "I can not be saved by a worship I disbelieve and abhor" and used this thought when he wrote indignantly: "Millions of innocent men, women and children, since the introduction of Christianity, have been burnt, tortured, fined, imprisoned. . . . What has been the effect of coercion? To make one half the world fools, and the other half hypocrites."[8]

Among the forces that had worked against religious freedom and human progress, Jefferson concluded from his Enlightenment studies, were the clergy and the church. He wrote, "In every country and in every age, the priest has been hostile to liberty. He is always in alliance with the despot, abetting his abuses in return for protection to his own." From his observations while minister to France, Jefferson wrote to George Wythe of the ignorance, superstition, and oppression of the French people, who were "loaded with misery by kings, nobles and priests, and by them alone." He did make an exception of the curés who ministered to the poor people in the villages of France, but not the higher clergy.[9]

It is plain that Thomas Jefferson shared something of the aversion to the Roman Catholic church that most writers of the Enlightenment had. During his stay in France he placed his daughter in a French convent school because of the good education that it provided for girls. He was quick to withdraw her, however, when, under the influence of the sisters, she wrote Papa to see if she could become a Catholic.[10] In his old age, Jefferson wrote John Adams in unflattering terms of the "bigotry of Jesuitism."[11] On the other hand, Jefferson aided in the estabishment of Catholic churches in America as freely as he did Protestant ones, and he wrote more often in a bitter tone against the narrowness of the sects and the New England clergy who sought favored positions of power than he did against the Catholic church.[12] Jefferson did, however, view with disfavor episcopal power in the church, in line with his general convictions favoring more power for the common people and less for people of privilege in all human institutions.[13]

If there was need for greater religious toleration in Europe in the eighteenth century, there was also a need for it in America, as Jefferson was well aware. Even in the New World the record for religious toleration was none too good, as Jefferson pointed out in his history of the Virginia colony, where the Presbyterians and Quakers, seeking freedom in America, had been persecuted by "the reigning sect." They could be deported for assembling together for services, and their children could be taken away from them if they did not have them baptized in the Anglican church.[14]

Even when there were no laws concerning religious practices on the books, it had long been argued by English judges that the tenets of Christianity were part of English common law and hence enforceable by the courts. Jefferson the lawyer undertook legal studies that convinced him that this was a mistaken interpretation of *"ancien scripture"* to mean all Holy Scripture when what was actually meant to fall under the law was "Ecclesiastical law."[15] By this "pious fraud," he wrote, "the Bible, Testament and all [was] ingulphed into the common law without citing any authority."[16]

Not only the Quakers but the Jews excited Jefferson's sympathy because of the persecution that they had endured, especially because they were "the parent sect and basis of Christendom." Jefferson was proud that America was the first country "to prove that religious freedom is most effectual and to restore to the Jews their social rights," he wrote to the rabbi of the Jewish synagogue in Savannah, Georgia.[17] The United States, he wrote to John Adams, is an example to "old Europe" and is "destined to be a barrier against the return of ignorance and barbarism." He admitted to another Jewish correspondent, however, that "public opinion needs reformation [of] the prejudices still scowling on your religion."[18]

Toleration, in the last analysis, is not a political problem at all. It is a matter of public opinion and individual conviction, and Jefferson all his life argued eloquently for a wide toleration of different religious opinions. As Christians, he wrote, "let us not be uneasy about the different roads we pursue [to heaven] . . . but, following the guidance of a good conscience, . . . we shall all meet in the end." The very differences emphasized by different religious sects meant that people must choose from among them the one to which they would conform. "But if we chuse for ourselves," he argued, "we must allow others to chuse also. . . . This establishes religious toleration."[19]

Jefferson was always much disturbed by human intolerance, since he was the target of many intolerant attacks by his religious and political opponents. He argued against the "tyranny" of "public opinion" and those who would "toll us back to the times when we burnt witches." After the bitter presidential campaign of 1800,

Jefferson warned the nation: "Let us reflect that having banished from our land that religious intolerance under which mankind so long bled and suffered we have yet gained little, if we countenance a political intolerance, as despotic[,] as wicked and capable of as bitter and bloody persecution."[20]

The difficulty, as Jefferson early saw, is that toleration is not enough. Religious toleration was an advance over the religious wars of the preceding centuries, but there was an inherent arrogance when the established church proclaimed that it would tolerate the mistaken doctrines of some sects that were not too objectionable but not those of others. As Jefferson pointed out, when John Locke advocated toleration by the Anglican church of other Protestant sects but not of Catholics (who supported a foreign prince) or of Jews and Quakers (who did not believe in the Trinity), his position marked an advance over earlier bigotry but left more to be accomplished.[21]

As a result of these convictions, Jefferson was one of the first and most determined of the American founding fathers to advocate a new and complete separation of church and state in order to ensure complete religious freedom in the new republican government on the American continent.

Religious Freedom and Separation of Church and State

Jefferson's first struggle for religious freedom in America was in his home state of Virginia. In his *Notes on the State of Virginia* he gave much of his rationale for seeking to separate the Anglican church in Virginia from its favored governmental position, and in his "Autobiography" he described the situation. The first royal grant to Sir Walter Raleigh specified that the colony of Virginia was to favor "the true Christian faith, now professed in the church of England." The colony was early divided into parishes with an established Anglican minister in each who received a yearly salary in tobacco and a glebe house and land paid for by the taxes of all in the parish. Despite much persecution, other sects, especially the Presbyterians, gradually gained a foothold, partly, Jefferson believed, because the established clergymen were too busy with their farms and the classical day schools they conducted to attend to their pastoral functions. But the dissenters "were still obliged to 'pay contributions to support pastors and teachers of what they deemed religious errors. . . . The first republican legislature, which met in '76, was crowded with petitions to abolish this spiritual tyranny. These brought on the severest contests in which I have ever been engaged."[22]

As Jefferson summarized the struggle, opinion in the legislature was so evenly divided that a series of compromises were reached in this and succeeding legislatures. The laws enforcing religious opinions and church attendance were repealed, and taxes to support the established church were suspended from year to year. Some leaders, including Patrick Henry, then governor of Virginia, favored a checkoff tax to be divided among the religious groups, but Jefferson wanted the public to be free to support voluntarily whatever "teacher of religion won their approbation."[23]

After the Revolution, Jefferson was on the committee charged with revising Virginia's colonial laws to a code suitable for a democratic state. One of his aims in revising the laws was "to establish religious freedom on the broadest bottom." As he wrote in his notes on Locke's policy of toleration, "Where he stopped short we may go on." In his draft of a constitution for Virginia in 1776, for example, Jefferson proposed that "all persons shall have full and free liberty of religious opinion: nor shall any be compelled to frequent or maintain any religious institution."[24]

By far his most famous proclamation of religious liberty, however, was Jefferson's bill for establishing religious freedom, which was adopted by the Virginian legislature in 1786 after several years of effort with the help of James Madison. By this time, Jefferson was in France serving as American minister. Jefferson was jubilant, not only for the political victory in Virginia but even more for the enhancement of the cause of the Enlightenment abroad and the reputation of America among European intellectual libertarians.[25]

The enactment of the Virginia Act for Establishing Religious Freedom was a milestone in human progress because it went beyond Locke's policy of toleration and enacted complete religious freedom, not only of all Christian groups but of all religious opinions whatsoever, including "the Jew, the Mahometan, and the Hindoo."[26] Jefferson had purposely drafted the law in brief but sweeping words: "No man shall be compelled to frequent or support any religious worship, place, or ministry whatsoever, nor shall be enforced, restrained, molested, or burthened in his body or goods, or shall otherwise suffer, on account of his religious opinions or belief; . . . all men shall be free to profess . . . their opinions in matters of religion."[27]

Jefferson's Act for Establishing Religious Freedom is important for the way that it cogently summarized the arguments for religious and intellectual freedom. It also expressed Jefferson's own intellectual and religious odyssey. Briefly, Jefferson argued for religious freedom on the following grounds.

1. "Almighty God hath created the mind free, and" willed "that free it shall remain." The mind of man, and for Jefferson that also meant the spirit of man, was, by the intrinsic free-ranging nature and individual variety created in it by God, not intended to be forced into one mold. Religious and intellectual freedom was one of the God-created rights of man.

2. To attempt to enforce religious uniformity by "temporal punishments" or "civil incapacitations" was doomed to failure, Jefferson argued, because it violated God's plan for encouraging religion by the "influence" of "reason alone," set up "fallible and uninspired men," "civil as well as ecclesiastical," in "dominion over the faith of others," "established and maintained false religions over the greatest part of the world and through all time," and resulted, not in true agreement, but in "hypocrisy and meanness."

3. It was "sinful and tyrannical" to force a man to support a religion "which he disbelieves and abhors." It was even an infringement on his freedom of choice to force him to support a "teacher of his own religious persuasion," since it prevented the free encouragement of the most able and diligent pastor.

4. It was as foolish to penalize a citizen for his religious opinions as for his ideas of science or education, and it deprived him of his "natural right."

5. Religious establishment was bad because "it tends . . . to corrupt the principles of that very religion it is meant to encourage, by bribing with a monopoly of worldly honours and emoluments, those who will externally profess and conform to it."

6. It was wrong to use the civil magistrate to suppress the propagation of opinions and principles, even of supposedly false ones, because "truth is great and . . . has nothing to fear from the conflict . . . [with] error . . . unless by human interposition disarmed of her

natural weapons, free argument and debate." It was time enough
for the magistrate to act "when principles break out into overt acts
against peace and good order."

7. Freedom of religion was one of "the natural rights of mankind," and any infringement of it was "an infringement of natural
right."[28]

As a lawyer, Jefferson was much concerned with the legal basis
of religion and the church. He agreed with Locke that neither civil
penalties nor "the right of the sword by the magistrate" had any
place in religious instruction. Jefferson wrote, "Our Savior chose
not to propagate his religion by temporal punishments or civil
incapacitations," but "by it's influence on reason."[29] But it was in
the writings of the political philosopher Montesquieu, which he
studied thoroughly and copied extensively in his commonplace book
on law and government, that Jefferson found justification for his
belief favoring the separation of church and state and in religious
freedom as a "natural right" of man.[30]

In the passage dealing with religious freedom that Jefferson copied, Montesquieu made a distinction between "natural law," which
was concerned with the "grand principles of justice and law"; "religious law," which was concerned with the "goodness of the person
who observes it"; and "civil law," which was concerned with the
welfare of society and the protection of property. He believed that
the law of nature was thus of the highest order, but religious and
civil law each had its proper place. However, religious or civil law
must never override the principles of justice determined by the law
of nature. As Montesquieu declared, "The public good is never
that which deprives a private individual of his rights."[31]

Jefferson agreed with Montesquieu's propositions but went on
to urge the end of any government establishment of religion and
the abolition of the entire realm of religious law. Because America's
situation was different from that of France and because he was
determined to avoid the evils of French society in America, Jefferson
resolved to prevent the church in America from ever having any
civil power and law of its own. Therefore, he recognized only "natural law" and "civil law" and reduced "religious law" to the status
of voluntary agreements between church members regulating themselves alone. As he wrote in his notes, a church was a "voluntary
society," and a person "should be as free to go out as he was to

come in." Jefferson also endorsed the argument that "each church being free, no one can have jurisdiction over another one, not even when the civil magistrate joins it."[32]

Despite the fact that Jefferson's convictions on religious freedom and the disestablishment of the church were thus of long duration and firmly based on his study and reflection, many of his friends among the Virginian gentry did not understand or share them. Dr. James Currie probably expressed the opinion of many planters when he wrote Jefferson from Richmond, "The other Religionists are damned mad at the Establishment and Anathematise the Assembly, . . . but I don't care who preach or pray." John Page, Jefferson's best friend when they were college students at William and Mary, wrote of the problem that disestablishment was producing for the Episcopal church. Ministers were having trouble supporting themselves by "voluntary contributions." Preachers were less independent of large contributors, and "enthusiastic bigotry" was flourishing.[33] Many churchmen also felt that disestablishment seriously weakened the church. Bishop William Meade, who wrote an early history of the Episcopalian church, however, felt that disestablishment made the church stronger. Merrill Peterson has suggested that disestablishment encouraged the more intolerant sects in Virginia and injured its reputation for liberality and enlightenment.[34] Many of Jefferson's aristocratic friends also agreed with Page, and Jefferson always felt that his part in pushing through the disestablishment of the Episcopal church in Virginia alienated many friends and the clergy who longed for "a whiff of union between church and state." In the violent writings of his enemies, there is evidence that he was right. Randall relates several incidents of such biased attacks upon Jefferson.[35]

It should be emphasized, however, that even those friends who disagreed with Jefferson about disestablishment were confident of his interest in the welfare of the church. In the same letter in which he argued with Jefferson on the need for tax support of the clergy, Page reported the results of a church convention in Philadelphia, confident of Jefferson's interest. Francis Hopkinson promised to send Jefferson a copy of the "new Book of Common Prayer," and Dr. Currie also sent Jefferson news of church meetings. Jefferson's close friends took for granted his interest in the church and solicited his help and advice. Only later did enemies attack his religion and, in turn, incur his bitter comments. Jefferson did, in fact, aid and support the church in its voluntary establishment all his life.[36]

What Jefferson's Anglican friends failed to realize was that disestablishment was not for him a practical matter of whether it would aid or hinder the growth of the church, religion, and public morality but a deep, philosophical conviction. It was not that Jefferson did not love the church but that he loved freedom more. He believed that disestablishment would make the church strong and the pastors more zealous, but even if the reverse should prove to be the case, disestablishment was still necessary because the danger of religious oppression and tyranny outweighed the danger of religious indifference and public immorality. This difference of opinion over the relative importance of civil rights versus public morality has continued down through American history and has earned for Jefferson a continuing hostility from some religious leaders and the approbation of others.[37] In his own time, however, the battle for religious freedom was still in doubt, and Jefferson threw his influence behind the complete separation of church and state in order to ensure the basic rights of religious freedom.

When the adoption of the Constitution of the United States was being considered, the lack of a Bill of Rights "providing clearly for freedom of religion" was one of the things that disturbed Jefferson. He was influential in establishing the Bill of Rights. Throughout his political career, Jefferson strongly defended the constitutional guarantees of religious freedom. After he became president, he continued his belief that the government had no proper jurisdiction over religious beliefs, as he stated in his second inaugural address. He went so far as to maintain that the government should not proclaim Thanksgiving day on the grounds that it was a religious function.[38]

While president, he frequently defended religious freedom in corresponding with various religious groups. It was in one such greeting to the Danbury Baptist Association that Jefferson first promulgated what has become a basic doctrine of the United States: the Constitution, he wrote, had wisely erected "a wall of separation between Church and State." Many other religious groups that had felt the sting of persecution in America wrote to thank Jefferson for his efforts to protect religious freedom and received courteous replies from him reiterating his firm belief in the importance and value of religious freedom.[39]

However much opposition and abuse from influential people and former friends Jefferson received, it is clear that his "severe struggle" for disestablishment and religious freedom earned him the appreciation and support of many of the ordinary citizens. Jefferson, being an astute politician, marshaled this support into an important political force to support his policies. This cultivation of political power was not so much for personal purposes as for the development of his vision of a free, enlightened, progressive republic in the New World. It was this cause which Jefferson shared with the "free" church and the more "bigoted" sects. Although he was too polite and clever to say so, his liberal Unitarianism differed widely from their conservative theology, and he had more in common with liberal Unitarians such as Joseph Priestley and Thomas Cooper, with whom he frequently corresponded. Nevertheless, in the common cause of religious and civil liberty, they found in Jefferson a powerful champion, and he found in them useful allies and welcome friends.

Jefferson spoke from his heart when he thanked the Methodist Society of New London for their "approbation" and wrote, "The approving voice of our fellow citizens for endeavors to be useful is the greatest of all earthly rewards."[40] The idea that men had a duty to society and must use their abilities to serve their fellow citizens occurs frequently in Jefferson's thought and deeply motivated him. It most probably came from his early religious upbringing and from his study of Roman Stoic philosophers.[41]

Conclusions

It is clear that religious freedom was a deep and cherished belief of Thomas Jefferson all of his life and that he was influenced toward this belief by his wide reading of Enlightenment philosophers, by political writers of the English Reformation, by his college studies of literature, and by his studies of English law, especially the roots of common law in Anglo-Saxon codes.[42] From the beginning, Jefferson used his considerable political talents, even at the risk of his own career and some of his friendships, to fight for the disestablishment of favored churches and the complete separation of church and state in America. He was one of the most outspoken and persistent of those Americans who advocated and defended the first enactment of complete religious freedom as the policy of a major nation of the world.

His actions were due to his deep conviction that man's right to religious freedom apart from any coercion by society was the most important of the God-given "rights of men" and the most needed of social reforms. After seeing the poverty and exploitation in Europe's cities, Jefferson feared the development of urbanization and industrialization in America with their accompanying social and moral problems.[43] In these early days, however, he deemed the danger of religious persecution more pressing than the need for inculcating public morality. Hence the "wall of separation between church and state."

The depth of Jefferson's commitment to personal freedom and religious liberty is seen in the fact that, of all the many accomplishments of his life and career for which he wanted to be remembered by his fellow citizens, among the ones that he directed be carved on his tombstone were that he was "AUTHOR OF THE DECLARATION OF AMERICAN INDEPENDENCE" and "OF THE STATUTE OF VIRGINIA FOR RELIGIOUS FREEDOM."[44]

CHAPTER V

JEFFERSON'S RELIGIOUS IDEAS OF MAN: THE DUTIES OF MAN

Jefferson's great popularity with Americans today rests largely on his championing of religious and civil liberties and his proclamation of the American dream of the pursuit of happiness. It is usually overlooked, however, that he also stressed the duties of man.

The Proper Pursuit of Happiness

Happiness, Jefferson believed, was to be found by each person working, studying, and developing his talents and abilities in order to fulfill his duty to society. He was constantly urging his young friends and relatives to be studious and make good use of their opportunities. He deplored the charming indolence of many of his aristocratic, horse-racing friends.[1] He worked for social and political reforms so that people might not be prevented from developing their abilities because of the circumstances of their birth, wealth, class, or religion. For the same reason he worked tirelessly for broader public education through public schools, public libraries, and universities. He was one of the first social reformers to stress the importance to society as well as to the individual of the encouragement of such self-development. Government, he wrote to John Adams, should encourage an "aristocracy of virtue and talents" to manage "the concerns of society" instead of the "artificial aristocracy of wealth and birth," which hindered, rather than improved, society.[2]

Jefferson had his own ideas of what constituted a really good and happy man. He wrote to his friend and secretary William Short, "As you say of yourself, I too am an Epicurian."[3] Most scholars have noted both a stoical, ascetic strain in Jefferson's character and an epicurean appreciation of the finer things of life.[4] In his eating habits, for example, Jefferson did not indulge in rich foods but he did insist on the finest of French wines.[5] The fact that he quietly walked to his own inauguration as a democratic protest against the royal ostentation of his predecessors has been noted by those who admire his plebian instincts. It has not been so widely noticed that he spent a large sum of money to replace the ordinary horses used by thrifty John Adams to draw the president's carriage with the finest Virginian thoroughbreds because he could not abide inferior horses. The epicureanism of Jefferson was more an intellectual philosophy than the sybaritic habits of an epicure. Stuart Brown sees a similarity, for example, between Jefferson and the twentieth-century epicurean George Santayana, who epitomized epicureanism as "Eat, drink, and be merry for tomorrow we die, but moderately and with much art, lest we die miserably and die today." Jefferson's interest in art, music, literature, and science attests to his devotion to the pursuit of happiness in the higher sense generally valued during the Enlightenment.[6]

"Happiness," Jefferson wrote, "is the aim of life, but virtue is the foundation of happiness." Men practiced virtue, he argued, because it gave them personal satisfaction to help those in distress, as did the good Samaritan. Upon the proposition that happiness was based upon the highest self-development and virtue, Jefferson and other Enlightenment writers developed an elaborate theory of society based upon liberal religious beliefs. Jefferson wrote, "God has formed us moral agents . . . that we may promote the happiness of those with whom He has placed us in society by acting benevolently towards all." "Nature hath implanted in our breasts a love of others," he continued, "a sense of duty to them, a moral instinct, in short, which prompts us to succor their distresses."[7]

Jefferson's confidence in man's ability to govern himself and to develop a better society for all was based, then, on his belief in the fundamental goodness of man, which in turn depended upon the conviction that man was a creation of an all-wise, benevolent God who had "destined man for society and endowed him with a sense of right and wrong relative to this." Jefferson thus balanced the pursuit of individual happiness against the greater good of society, flavored an epicurean appreciation of the finer things of life with a dash of Christian morality, and advocated both the rights of men for free, individual self-development and the duties that responsible people owed to their society. Those who by talent and educational opportunities composed the "aristocracy of virtue and talents" owed special service and leadership to society. Jefferson wrote a revealing and chiding letter to his friend Edward Rutledge on this point: "There is a debt of service due from every man to his country, proportioned to the bounties which nature and fortune have measured to him. . . . There is no bankrupt law in heaven by which you may get off . . . from paying your own debts."[8]

Jefferson was himself the best example of an aristocrat of talent devoting himself to the cause of the common man. When political abuse was beating upon him, he longed wistfully for the peaceful life of a gentleman farmer and scholar. But he dedicated his life to his fellow man in political leadership.[9]

So strong was Jefferson's sense of duty that he tended to reduce all religion to the study of morality. In his library he classified religion as a division of "moral philosophy."[10] He frequently wrote in both private letters and official addresses about the necessity that moral men fulfill their duties to society.[11] Jefferson, indeed, made no secret of the fact that he much preferred the study of morality, "which is the same in all religions," to that of religious doctrine, in which "all differ." "We all agree," he wrote to a friend, "in the obligation of the moral precepts of Jesus, and nowhere will they be found delivered in greater purity than in his discourses." Jefferson blamed religious wars and persecutions on differences over religious dogmas, but he excepted the study of moral principles from this indictment. Instead of causing argumentation and conflict, religion should "regulate" a person's conduct and create "honest and dutiful" people, Jefferson believed. "We should all be of one sect, doers of good, and eschewers of evil," he wrote to a Calvinist friend.[12]

The Classical Moral Influence on Jefferson

Jefferson came by his interest in morality instead of sectarian religion naturally, for this theme was common in the Enlightenment. People were seeking an end to religious strife and authoritarian coercion and a larger inspiration for political and intellectual freedom. To meet this need, the Enlightenment, especially in France and America, turned to the "golden age" of Athens and republican

Rome for guidance. There was a revival of interest in the classical period. Slaves, ships, and towns were given Latin and Greek names, as seen in such American cities as Syracuse, Cicero, and Cincinnati, and many authors assumed classical pseudonyms. So strong was the emphasis on the classics in the eighteenth century that not only was the college curriculum filled with their study, but many courses in the academies and colleges were taught in Greek or Latin.[13]

Jefferson was well versed in the classics. As a child he was taught by the Reverend William Douglas, a clergyman from Scotland who taught boys in his home "the rudiments of Latin, Greek and French." Then he studied with the Reverend James Maury, "a correct classical scholar," and attended the College of William and Mary. All his life Jefferson valued his reading of the classics in "all the beauties of their originals" as one of the greatest "luxuries" his father had provided for him."[14]

A study of the classical authors was especially valuable to Jefferson and the writers of the Enlightenment because it provided an alternative authority for morality to that of the medieval church and its authoritarian teachings. Adrienne Koch believes Jefferson's interest in the philosophies of Roman Stoicism and Epicureanism was due to the fact that they provided systems of morality independent of both church and state.[15] Just as the medieval theory of the divine right of kings to rule had as a corollary the theory of nobelesse oblige, that the nobility had an obligation to govern benevolently and responsibly, the new Enlightenment theory of the God-given right of men to rule themselves had offsetting it a belief in the duty of men to live morally in society. It was natural, then, for Jefferson to find, in his college classical studies, codes of morality and ethical standards to support his social and religious theories. The Greek poets and dramatists were the first writers to reveal to him the great moral issues of human life, and they continued to inspire him all his life.[16]

Epicureanism

In his letter to William Short praising the Epicurean philosophy, Jefferson stated, "I consider the genuine (not the imputed) doctrines of Epicurus as containing everything rational in moral philosophy which Greece and Rome have left us." He went on to characterize

Cicero as "enchanting," Plato as an "incomprehensible mystic," and Seneca as "a fine moralist. . . . But the greatest of all reformers . . . was Jesus of Nazareth."[17]

Jefferson made an estimate of the strengths and weaknesses of his favorite classical moralists in a "syllabus" which he sent to Rush, Priestley, and other friends with whom he discussed religion, mentioning by named Epictetus, Seneca, Antonius, Socrates, and Epicurus. He concluded that the "ancient moral philosophers were really great" in teaching people to govern "those passions which, unrestrained, would disturb our tranquility of mind." But they were "short and defective in developing our duties to others." They taught "benevolence in the circles of kindred and friends" and stressed "love of country," but they neglected "peace and charity toward our neighbors . . . and still less the whole family of mankind." The greatest of moral philosophers, Jefferson concluded, was Jesus of Nazareth because "his moral doctrines . . . inculcated universal philanthropy, not only to kindred and friends, but to all mankind, gathering all into one family, under the bonds of love, charity, peace, common wants and common aids."[18]

Although Jefferson knew Epicurean philosophy from original sources, it is significant that he mentioned *The Syntagma of Gassendi* as an influential source for his ideas of Epicureanism.[19] Pierre Gassendi was a French priest and professor much admired during the Enlightenment who had rescued the ideas of Epicurus from libertine misinterpretations by stressing that while happiness was the aim of life, it could be attained only through self-discipline and noble living, not by self-indulgence.[20] This favorite idea Jefferson used in admonitions to friends and relatives all his life.[21]

Stoicism

There is some difference of opinion among students of Jefferson's thought as to the relative importance that he placed upon Stoicism and Epicuranism. Gilbert Chinard has argued that Jefferson was attracted by Stoic writers in his youth and later became more interested in Epicurean philosophers. Koch thinks that Jefferson adopted Stoic discipline as the method for attaining Epicurean goals of life. Merrill Peterson has contended that Jefferson chose what he liked from both Stoic and Epicurean thought. Jefferson's letters indicate no conflict in his mind between Stoicism and Epicureanism. Perhaps the most that can be said is that Stoic ideals made a stronger emotional appeal to him in his youth, and the Epicurean philosophy had a greater intellectual appeal for him in his later years.[22]

The strongest evidence of the Stoic influence upon Jefferson is to be found in the passages that the young Jefferson copied in his commonplace book from Homer, Euripides, Herodotus, Vergil, Ovid, Horace, Cicero, and Seneca.[23] From Cicero, for example, he copied this significant passage: "He is the happy man to whom nothing in this life seems intolerable enough to depress him; nothing exquisite enough to transport him unduly." From Horace he copied a passage defining the "free and wise man" as one who "rules his passions, scorns honors, and is afraid neither of poverty, death or prison."[24] That such ideas influenced Jefferson all his life is indicated by the fact that the same quotation from Homer's *Iliad* not only had a place in his youthful commonplace book but was used by him in his old age in a letter to John Adams:[25]

> Two urns by Jove's high throne have ever stood,
> The source of evil one, the one of good;
> From thence the cup of mortal man he fills.
> Blessings to these, to those distributes ills;
> To most, he mingles both.[26]

Jefferson was wont to turn to quotations from the classics to express his deepest feelings. While he was courting his wife, he copied from Euripides, "Happy is the life of those whose marriages have come to good issue, but those to whom they fall out ill both at home and abroad are unfortunate." This quotation proved a happy omen, for Jefferson found a love and happiness in his home and family strong enough to survive even the death of his wife. From the pain of his grief for her, he found comfort in the classics, and had this favorite verse from the *Iliad* engraved on her tombstone, in the full beauty of the Greek:

> If in the house of Hades men forget their dead,
> Yet I even there will remember my dear companion.[27]

Jefferson's Classical Life

Jefferson found in his favorite classical authors more than fitting quotations. He discovered and appropriated congenial values and life-styles that reinforced the influence of classical morality upon his thinking. Horace's epode glorifying the rural life of a Roman country villa appealed to Jefferson, the Virginian planter.[28] The idea of building on a hill with a view; the style and arrangement of the master's house and the service quarters for the slaves; the simple, mathematical lines and proportions that Jefferson developed so beautifully at Monticello all reveal the classical influence upon Jefferson's life.[29]

All of his life Jefferson favored the Roman and Greek style of architecture. He was responsible for modeling the Virginia Capitol on the Roman Maison Carrée at Nîmes, which Jefferson thought "the best morsel of ancient architecture now remaining" and had "studied, enraptured," when he visited it in France. After his retirement he designed the University of Virginia around a central space in the classical way. He called it an "academical village," made up of halls of learning of classical design. Jefferson's fondness for classical beauty thus influenced countless state capitols and college campuses that followed.[30]

Jefferson studied and used classical authors for practical work. In designing and carrying out architectural work he used the works of Palladio and Vitruvius. Visitors to Monticello were surprised to see Jefferson consulting his books by Cato and Varro for guidance in agricultural work on his farms along with more modern works. In a sense, it is not too much to say that Thomas Jefferson lived in the classical world, adopting its ideals and virtues and adapting what was appropriate and pleasing of the classical life to his own experiences and needs. John Adams remarked that Jefferson was "the best brusher off of dust" he had ever known.[31]

There were, indeed, many lessons that could be learned from the world of ancient Greece and Rome. The struggle for American independence in which Jefferson had participated could be compared with the epic struggles of Homer's heroes.[32] From the failures of Cicero's republican Rome, lessons could be drawn for the present struggle to establish democratic government in America. Similarly, the mobs of the French Revolution produced the tyrant Napoleon just as those of Rome had produced the wicked Caesars.

There were also striking similarities between Jefferson's life and the lives of the Romans whom he admired. Varro, Cicero, Horace, and Pliny the Younger were all men whose values and traditions were shaped by the rural living they admired and enjoyed, but whose work and careers kept them much in the city. So it was with Jefferson, Washington, Madison, and other American leaders, especially those from the South. In the North, especially in New England, the prevalence of villages modified the sharp difference between city and rural life, but it was different on southern plantations. The details of daily living—planning the crops, supervising the work of the slaves, studying, reading, corresponding with friends, or visiting their homes for conversation and musicales—all were nearly the same for Jefferson and Pliny, and the daily life described by Jefferson after his retirement to Monticello reads like one of Pliny's letters.[33]

Since, for both Jefferson and the Romans, limited means of transportation and communication made impossible the modern suburban life of homogenized culture, Monticello was an attempt to combine the best of both worlds, the urban and the rural. All his life Jefferson admired the wholesome effect of rural living and deplored the degrading effect of life in cities and the disillusionments of politics. As he saw it, "those who labour in the earth" on their own fields have the largest "deposit of genuine virtue from God," while those who work in trade and manufactures in crowded cities are subject to greed, "subservience and venality so the germ of virtue . . . is suffocated." Moreover, "the mobs of great cities" were easily misled by unscrupulous leaders and could sap the strength of a republic. In America, Jefferson believed, the presence of "vacant lands" for poor people from the cities "to resort to for laboring the earth" had prevented the development of slums, but he feared that the experiences of European and Roman history might someday be repeated in the United States, which, he was convinced, was the world's best hope for republican democracy.[34]

From his study of classical authors, Jefferson gained a lifelong attachment to the ideals of the noble Romans whom he admired. His reading notes are filled with such sentiments as the importance of duty, honor, and faithful service to one's country whatever the sacrifice.[35] Loyalty and friendship were highly valued by the Romans and by Jefferson.[36] He deplored the separation and alienation of friends that resulted from the changes brought by the years and by diverging political beliefs. "Some friends have left me by the way," he wrote. "It is a satisfaction to me that I was not the first to leave them." His daughter Martha always said that her father would not give up a friend or an opinion.[37]

Serving one's country as a politician, Jefferson found, could result in more than the loss of friends. It could provoke the abuse of enemies and the crowd. A Stoical virtue was needed. He wrote to a fellow Republican under attack, "The patriot, like the Christian, must learn that to bear revilings and persecutions is a part of his duty." When he retired after long years of service, he was glad to leave the battle to his younger friends Madison and Monroe. "I pray to be permitted to depart in peace," he wrote, "and like the superannuated soldier, to hang my arms on the post."[38]

Jefferson used his extensive reading of the great classical writers not only as an early guide to high morality and noble virtue but also as an inspiration and solace in times of testing over the years. The classical life, with its lessons of virtue and its warnings of social vices, deeply affected Jefferson's religious views of man and society.

Man's Sense of Morality

It is evident from his studies of the ancient classics and of congenial Enlightenment authors and from statements of his own convictions as statesman, essayist, and aristocratic Virginian planter that Jefferson placed a primary emphasis on morality in both the personal and social life of men. In his thoughts and writings he devoted as much attention to the duties as to the rights of men. He wrote that man's "moral instinct is the brightest gem with which the human character is studded, and the want of it more degrading than the most hideous of bodily deformities."[39]

Jefferson's ethical philosophy shows a definite development in complexity and sophistication over the years. It began with the ethical standards of his class and upbringing that Jefferson accepted as a matter of course. His moral beliefs were next influenced by the ethical presuppositions of justice and jurisprudence coming from his legal studies and further developed into a highly evolved philosophy of man, government, and society with a profoundly ethical emphasis.

The Moral Law

In its simplest formulation, Jefferson's moral philosophy took the form of listing ethical beliefs and maxims collected from his reading and favorite moralists that he recommended to his family and friends. In his old age, for example, at the request of the parents of two boys who had been named for him, he wrote to each of them a short letter containing exactly the same ethical advice: "Adore God. Reverence and cherish your parents. Love your neighbor as yourself and your country more than yourself. Be just. Be true. Murmur not at the ways of Providence." He also quoted his favorite psalm in a favored translation: "The happy man that may to God's blest courts repair, 'tis he whose every thought and deed by rules of virtue moves."[40]

When his grandson Thomas Jefferson Randolph went away from home to school for the first time, Jefferson eased his anxiety by writing these admonitions: "Never do what is wrong. . . . Avoid taverns, drinkers, smokers, idlers, and dissipated persons, and you will find your path more tranquil." In this same letter, Jefferson shared some revealing experiences of the hazards of his own maturing. He was left on his own resources at fourteen years of age by the death of his father, he recalled, and "was often thrown into the society of horse racers, card players, fox hunters, and scientific and professional men." He was "astonished" that he did not "become as worthless as they were" and believed the reason was the good moral example of other older men that he admired.[41]

Indeed, "the prudent selection and steady pursuit of what is right" guided by wise "rules of virtue," as Jefferson summed up his beliefs, was a lifelong motivating force which appears repeatedly throughout his writings. It is evident in his discussions with adults as well as in his advice to children and young people. While living in France he wrote of the "corruption of morals" found in Paris and warned against "a European education for our youth" because of the danger that a young man might "form a connection, as is the fashion here . . . where beauty is begging in every street."[42] Jefferson was too prudent a man to form such an attachment himself. He must have presented something of a contrast to Benjamin Franklin in French social life. The nearest he ever came to such a relationship was in a mild flirtation with a charming married woman, Mrs. Maria Cosway, who clearly intrigued him. Jefferson wrote of the happy times that they shared in visiting the French countryside and neglecting other obligations for the pleasure of each other's company.

Over ten pages in length, and written laboriously while he had a broken wrist, Jefferson's "love letter" to Maria Cosway must have been as strange a one as his bewildered charmer ever received. It took the form of a dialogue between "head" and "heart," following eighteenth-century literary style, but it really was a long, revealing essay on the importance of love, friendship, sorrow, and grief in human life from the viewpoint of one emotional Virginian and convinced Stoic, Thomas Jefferson. It clearly showed the restraint of his good judgment and moral standards upon emotional impulses. With some penetration Jefferson advised, "Do not bite at the bait of pleasure till you know there is no hook beneath it." He continued, "We have no rose without its thorn; no pleasure without alloy."[43]

In his ideas on social standards Jefferson was moderate in his approach. He deplored "the poison of whiskey," which was "desolating" American homes, but approved of wine as a moderate drink. He agreed with a doctor who denounced the abuses of tobacco and wine. As for dancing, he wrote, "Every affectionate parent would be pleased to see his daughter qualified to participate with her companions in dancing, drawing, and music."[44]

When he became a statesman, Jefferson extended his belief in moral codes to the nation, which, he believed, should be "most exact in its moral conduct towards other nations."[45] A revealing incident occurred while he was president of the United States. A courier of the British government offered to turn the British minister's dispatches over to the United States. Jefferson refused the offer: "My answer was that . . . moral duties . . . and a character of good faith was of as much value to a nation as an individual and was that by which it would gain most in the long run." He wrote to Madison, "No nation, however powerful, any more than an individual, can be unjust with impunity." Morality was clear-cut for

Jefferson: "He who says I will be a rogue when I act in company with a hundred others, but an honest man when I act alone, will be believed in the former assertion, but not in the latter."[46]

Perhaps the most elaborate exposition of Jefferson's ideas of the moral obligations of nations occurred in the opinion he wrote as a member of President Washington's cabinet to refute the argument of Alexander Hamilton that the United States should repudiate its treaties of friendship with France after it changed from a monarchy to a republic. Jefferson argued that the treaties were between the nations of France and the United States, and "tho' both of them have since changed their forms of government, the treaties are not annulled by these changes." What most aroused Jefferson's ire was Hamilton's argument that a government could suspend its treaties "whenever they became dangerous, useless, or disagreeable." Jefferson's Roman sense of honor and duty was affronted, and he appealed to the moral sense of "every rational and honest man" to decide whether the moral law gave anyone "permission to annul his obligations for a time, or forever, whenever they became 'dangerous, useless, or disagreeable.' "[47]

Behind all of these varied instances of Jefferson's urging of moral standards upon his family, friends, and fellow statesmen was implicit his lawyer's faith in the efficacy of law in shaping human conduct by restraining evil and encouraging good. Even with children, Jefferson believed that the laws of morality should prevail. He wrote to his young daughter Martha: "If ever you are about to say anything amiss or to do any thing wrong, consider . . . your conscience, and be sure to obey it. Our Maker has given us all this faithful internal Monitor." Writing to his nephew away at college, he further developed his ideas about conscience: "The moral sense, or conscience, is as much a part of man as his leg or arm. It is given to all human beings in a stronger or weaker degree. . . . It may be strengthened by exercise. . . . Lose no occasion of exercising your dispositions to be charitable, humane, true, just, firm, courageous." To George Washington, he wrote, "Conscience is the only sure clew which will eternally guide a man clear of all doubts and inconsistencies."[48]

As a lawyer, Jefferson knew full well that people often disobeyed the law. Some people even seemed to have no sense of right and wrong, but Jefferson argued that "the want . . . of the moral sense in some men, like the want . . . of the sense of sight and hearing in others, is no proof that it is [lacking in] the species." When people lacked a conscience, Jefferson argued, they must be taught to do the right by "education," by appeals to their reason or self-interest, by social pressure, by "penalties established by the laws, and ultimately by the prospects of a future state of retribution." In this passage it is possible to see Jefferson the lawyer, teacher, psychologist, social reformer, and moralist at work. In his eager battle to reform men and society, he was willing to use every possible weapon, including those of religion and the prospects of heaven and hell, even though he had some personal doubts about their existence.[49]

Beginning, then, with simple lists of maxims for good behavior and a lawyer's belief in the importance of law and justice in society, Jefferson moved to a belief in human conscience and man's sense of morality as entities in their own right established by God when he created humanity. In this belief in the moral law within human beings, he was reflecting his studies of Enlightenment writers. Isaac Newton had shown the marvelous place of law in nature's wondrous order;[50] Bacon and Locke had laid the foundations of law and understanding of the processes of man's thinking and social organization that Destutt de Tracy, Dugald Stewart, P. J. G. Cabanis, Helvétius, and Hume elaborated in various ways.[51] What was more natural to believe than that there was a moral law governing the behavior of people and society similar to the law of gravity? The church of the Middle Ages had failed miserably to improve the lot of the common man by its religious laws. Perhaps if men could use their reason to discover the moral law and bring their conduct and societies into harmony with it, progress would be faster.[52]

Such, clearly, was the belief of Jefferson. He suggested the growth of his thinking in a letter to Pierre Samuel Dupont de Nemours: "I believe with you that morality, compassion, generosity are innate elements of the human constitution . . . and that justice is the fundamental law of society." It was this sense of right and wrong in every human being which made possible both primitive and advanced society, he argued. "Man was destined for society. . . . He was endowed with a sense of right and wrong, . . . [which] is the true foundation of morality [and society]." And just as the wonders of Newton's heavens offered proof of a Divine Creator, so the fact that men lived peaceably together in human society proved the existence of the moral law. He often declared, "The Creator would indeed have been a bungling artist had he intended man for a social animal without planting in him social dispositions." In his state paper for President Washington, Jefferson wrote his most careful formulation of his ideas on human morality: "Nature has written her moral laws . . . on the head and heart of every rational and honest man, . . . where every man may read them for himself. Man has been subjected by his creator to the Moral law of our nature or . . . Conscience as it is sometimes called." Both individuals and nations are subject to "the same moral duties."[53]

Sister M. Rosaleen Trainer, in a study on conscience, has argued that when Jefferson talked about a "moral sense or faculty" in man, he was reflecting Enlightenment thought, but when he accepted the view that the moral law was promulgated in man's being by the Creator he was following the "moral law" concept of Locke and Thomas Hooker going back to Thomas Aquinas, Saint Augustine, and Plato. However, she offers no proof that Jefferson actually was indebted to the medieval tradition for his belief in moral law.[54] In fact, Jefferson often stated his aversion to Plato and medieval mystics as corrupters of true Christianity. Far from seeing any good in the medieval tradition, Jefferson blamed a return to the ideas of the Inquisition for the moral retrogressions of the Napoleonic era.[55] It is true that Jefferson was trained in the classics and knew the writings of the church fathers, but when he used these sources it was to support his belief that the medieval church distorted and depraved the teachings of Christ.[56] His own thinking was uninfluenced by church theologians. If there was any medieval influence upon his concept of moral law, he was unconscious of it.

Daniel Boorstin is closer to the truth than Trainer when he emphasizes that Jefferson and the American deists took man's relation to nature rather than to God as their starting point. After all, their task was to subdue a raw frontier and build a new society. They sought to see and follow the plan of the Creator implicit in nature in order to build the City of God in human society.[57] It is quite evident that Jefferson, in developing his belief in man's moral nature based on God's moral law, was more influenced by his study of Enlightenment writers; his admiration for Greek and Roman ideals of duty, justice, and morality; his appreciation of law and justice gained from his legal studies rooted in English common law;

and his own religious and family background than by any philosophical tradition.

The Moral Sense

Jefferson's belief that all human beings had a natural sense of right and wrong was at the foundation of all his work, whether as a parent raising his children, an elder advising youths, or a statesman recommending governmental policies. Although Jefferson stressed the importance of admonitions and education, it should not be concluded that he thought the moral sense was just the sum of the codes and beliefs which an individual had learned. It was deeper than that. There was "a moral instinct . . . [which] nature hath implanted in our breasts." Evidence of the moral instinct was to be found everywhere, for both children and adults had it.[58]

Jefferson had observed a sense of justice and good judgment on the Virginian frontier and wickedness and stupidity in the French court. So he argued: "State a moral case to a ploughman and a professor. The former will decide it as well, and often better than the latter, because he has not been led astray by artificial rules."[59] Jefferson discovered evidences of the sense of right in all societies, including the primitive, as did the French Encyclopedists, whom he found congenial and encouraged.[60] Although he did not idealize "the noble savage" as Rousseau did, he did idealize rural life rather than city life, and his knowledge of the Indians of his own area gave him a profound respect for the dignity and morality of their tribal councils and social customs.[61]

As Jefferson and the Enlightenment thinkers studied various cultures, however, the problem of different moral standards prevailing in other societies arose. They were puzzled by the fact "that the same actions are deemed virtuous in one country and vicious in another." As an example, Jefferson pointed out that in America horse-stealing was punished much more severely than in Europe because American horses were kept in unenclosed lands rather than in closely guarded confinement, while stealing fruit from orchards was a serious offense in Europe, but merely a prank in this country. Customs make a difference, but justice was still justice. He concluded, "The answer is that nature has constituted utility to man the standard and test of virtue."[62] Jefferson thus followed the utilitarianism of David Hume and Francis Hutcheson, which held that the greatest good for the greatest number was the guide to morality.[63] Jefferson's concept of utility, however, was richer than the term implies. He was not just thinking of what was sensible or practical in a certain society, but of what actively promoted men's happiness and welfare because of a deep sense of goodwill. He wrote to John Adams on the problem: "Virtue does not consist in the act we do, but in the end it is to effect. If it is to effect the happiness of him to whom it is directed, it is virtuous, while in a society under different circumstances and opinions, the same act might produce pain, and would be vicious. The essence of virtue is in doing good to others." In defining the basic ingredient of the moral sense for all peoples as "doing good to others," it is plain that Jefferson went beyond his Enlightenment philosophers and classical moralists to the teachings of Jesus, whom he termed the greatest moralist of them all.[64]

Since Jefferson found in all cultures and civilizations evidences of the moral sense that was necessary for men to live together in society, he disagreed with "the principles of Hobbes . . . that the sense of justice is founded on convention only" and that early man made a compact to form society giving up some of his rights and freedoms for the sake of protection and security. "I believe, on the contrary," he wrote, "that every human mind feels pleasure in doing good to another, as a wise creator must have seen to be necessary in an animal destined to live in society."[65]

It made no difference whether man lived in a primitive or advanced society; human rights and duties were basically the same, however much they might vary in detail. "No man has a natural right to commit aggression on the equal rights of another," he wrote. "This is all from which the laws ought to restrain him; every man is under the natural duty of contributing to the necessities of the society; and this is all the laws should enforce on him. The idea is quite unfounded, that on entering into society we give up any natural right."[66]

Jefferson's respect for human rights thus led him to believe that the best government was one that governed least in all societies, because all men had a natural sense of right and duty which could be safely trusted. Some people in primitive society may have murdered and stolen from their fellows, just as some had in modern society, but the majority in both societies knew murder was wrong. As Jefferson argued in his legal opinion for President Washington, "The moral duties which exist between individual and individual in a state of nature, accompany them into a state of society."[67]

Jefferson's ideas of government and society stood upon the firm foundation of his belief in the moral nature of man, which, in turn, was rooted in his belief in God, the Master Creator of both the world of nature and the world of man. His argument was short and simple: "Man was created for social intercourse; but social intercourse cannot be maintained without a sense of justice; then man must have been created with a sense of justice."[68] Jefferson did not say which came first, his belief in God the Creator of human morality or his belief in man's goodness, which suggested a moral God as Creator. Since Jefferson was a religious person as well as a diligent student of man and society, it is probable that he always held both ideas and found continuous evidence to reinforce them mutually. One thing he was sure of: without a belief in God and morality, human life in society would be impossible. He said as much in reply to a skeptical question raised by John Adams as to whether religion had helped or hindered man's happiness. "Sectarian dogmas," Jefferson argued, had made the world worse, but "the moral precepts innate in man and taught us by Jesus of Nazareth" had prevented the human world from becoming a "Hell."[69]

In the universal agreement about morality, which contrasted so sharply with the divisiveness of dogmas, Jefferson perceived the guiding hand of an all-wise Creator. The varieties of religious dogma reflected differences in human thought, but moral beliefs showed a divinely created unanimity. "We all agree in the obligation of the moral precepts of Jesus," he wrote. "The practice of morality being necessary for the well-being of society, our Creator has taken care to impress its precepts so indelibly on our hearts that they shall not be effaced by the subtleties of our brain."[70]

Although Jefferson was too much of an intellectual to repudiate entirely the role of reason in formulating human conduct, he feared the easy rationalizations many people employed to excuse wrong conduct; so he depended on the feelings of the heart, rather than the reasonings of the head, to motivate man for his own good and that of society. As proof he pointed to the fact that "morality, compassion, generosity are innate elements of the human constitution." "The existence of a moral sense in man and the connection which the laws of nature have established between his duties and his interests" were signs of the wise provision of God for the good of human society. It was part of God's perfect plan "that every human mind feels pleasure in doing good to another." "God has formed us moral agents . . . that we may promote the happiness of those with whom He has placed us in society." The trait that was most necessary to enable men to live peacefully together in society was the very one that gave them the deepest happiness. So the moral law showed the glory of God in human society as Newton's law showed the glory of God in the heavens.[71]

Jefferson submitted some interesting examples of why he believed that the feelings of the heart were more important than the thinking of the head in guiding moral actions in the dialogue between "Head" and "Heart" which he wrote to Maria Cosway. "The feelings of sympathy, of benevolence, of gratitude, of justice, of love, of friendship," he wrote her, "were too essential to the happiness of man to be risked on the uncertain combinations of the head." He recalled a time when he met "a poor wearied soldier" who asked for a ride in his carriage. His head, Jefferson said, led him to refuse since the load might tax the horses, but his heart then led him to turn back to help the soldier. It was his head, Jefferson said, that led him to do selfish things but the heart that prompted him to do generous acts. So Jefferson's "Heart" indicted his "Head" for its guidance in moral matters. Yet in his own temptation concerning Maria Cosway, he was guided by his prudent good judgment instead of by the wayward impulses of his heart. Perhaps the answer lies in the fact that the moral feelings that Jefferson praised were altruistic ones concerned with the good of all people rather than selfish ones seeking personal pleasure.[72]

In a long essay on morality written to Thomas Law, Jefferson discussed various traits that had been suggested by Enlightenment writers as the basis of morality and his own reactions to them. William Wollaston made truth the foundation of morality, he wrote. The thief did wrong because he acted out a lie toward another person's property. Truth was an important part of ethics, Jefferson conceded, but it was the result, not the cause, of morality. The second theory that Jefferson raised made "the love of God the foundation of morality." Duties to God were but one branch of morality, he objected, and what about atheists, such as his friends Diderot and d'Holbach, who were "the most virtuous of men?"

Another theory which Jefferson rejected was that morality was based on the aesthetic sense. Man did have "an innate sense of what we call beautiful" which applied to the subjects of "fancy or imagination" through the arts and literature, but that was "a faculty entirely distinct from the moral one," he argued. Jefferson also rejected "self-love or egoism" as a factor governing man's conduct toward others. In fact, "self-gratification" often led a person to violate his moral duties, he argued. Self-love could be the basis of morality, Jefferson contended, only when understood in the broad sense "that we feed the hungry, clothe the naked, bind up the wounds of the man beaten by thieves . . . because we receive ourselves pleasure from these acts."

Jefferson acknowledged his indebtedness to the writings of his friend Helvétius as the source of this idea. He disagreed with Helvétius, however, when the latter argued that no one could really love evil. Most people loved good "because nature hath implanted in our breasts a love of others, . . . a moral instinct which prompts us irresistibly to feel and to succor their distresses," Jefferson agreed. But some few men did love evil for the sake of evil, he argued. In the case of these rare morally "deformed" people who lacked a moral sense, society must supply the want by education and the restraints of law and order.[73] This essay on morality by Jefferson, incidentally, furnishes a good example of the influence of his reading, for he clearly was quoting and remembering many of the works he had read from his library.[74]

Scholars who have studied Jefferson's philosophical thought have been interested to trace the influence of various philosophers that he read upon him. Koch has studied the influence of British Enlightenment authors, while Karl Lehmann emphasized the importance of Jefferson's historical and classical studies.[75] Trainer is intrigued with the varied and sometimes contradictory strains in Jefferson's writings on human conscience. She suggests that Jefferson eclectically chose whatever appealed to him from various philosophies of the British, French, and medieval traditions. In the end, she declares Jefferson's ideas of conscience as both a "distinct, innate, moral faculty" and as a "function of reason" to be irreconcilable. She follows these two trends to their ultimate conclusions, perhaps going further than Jefferson would have gone, and concludes that Jefferson accepted the medieval idea of man as a rational, social person subject to the moral law of God and also the contradictory Enlightenment idea that man had a moral sense organ by which he instinctively knew right from wrong.[76]

It is true that there are ambiguities in Jefferson's writings. Some may be due to the fact that his thought has come down to us in scattered fragments from letters and essays written at widely spaced intervals to different friends in response to a variety of discussions. Some discrepancies may be due to the fact that Jefferson recognized that there were perplexities in life and in man's understanding of it that could only partially be explained, sometimes by one theory, other times best by another. Jefferson was more interested in accounting for particular cases than in building a comprehensive system of philosophy. Moreover, some of Jefferson's inconsistencies may be in the eye of the beholder.

Conclusions

Although much scholarly attention and popular acclaim have been paid to Thomas Jefferson's emphasis on the common man's God-given rights to "life, liberty, and the pursuit of happiness," Jefferson's writings and his studies of favorite authors reveal that he placed an equal emphasis on the duties which responsible men owed to their society and the question of what constituted the highest pursuit of happiness. The neglect of Jefferson's emphasis on morality and duty in concentrating on his ideas of human rights is unfortunate, for it results in a biased view of both Jefferson's philosophy and human society.

The philosophy that Jefferson developed in his pursuit of happiness based on refined Epicureanism and disciplined Stoicism has the advantage of giving logical and satisfying answers to the purpose of life and of being beneficial to society. Jefferson harmonized what has seemed to some scholars to be two contradictory traditions of morality: the moral law concept that morality was based on the law of God perceived by man's reason and the moral sense philosophy that morality was based on moral feelings or the impulse to do good. He did it by the unifying factor of his belief in God, the Creator of man, who, intending man for the joys of social living, implanted in him both his reason by which he could perceive the moral law and his moral sense by which he would desire to obey it.

One of the surprising results of studying Jefferson's beliefs is the discovery of how greatly his political and social philosophy was based on his religious convictions. Jefferson championed the rights of man because they were given to each person by God. He believed that the common man could be trusted with political power because God had provided the necessary wisdom and talents scattered among all sorts of leaders whom the people would recognize by their own God-given judgment. He believed that, despite the temporary set-backs which history revealed, God had deposited in human nature sufficient impulse toward the good to make progress in human relations possible. It is only in the light of Jefferson's religious convictions that his social and political beliefs are understandable or even believable.

A study of Jefferson's ideas also reveals abundant evidence of the influence of Jefferson's wide reading on his thought. Few men of his age—or any other, for that matter—read as widely and remembered as much as he did. He studied both the works of ancient Greek dramatists and the works of Shakespeare, as well as the latest Enlightenment writers. One is constantly amazed not only by the number of authors and titles in his library but by the extensiveness of his selections in different languages. He read Homer in the Greek and Pliny in the Latin. He read also in Italian and French.[77]

Jefferson yearned for the scholarly life, but destiny used him in a life of political action. His reading and study, however, furnished him with the tools of thought from which he formed the convictions that directed his life of service. Not the least of these guiding inspirations was his religious faith. It was his moral conviction that made Jefferson an inspiring and moving leader of men.

CHAPTER VI

JEFFERSON'S
RELIGIOUS IDEAS OF MAN:
THE NATURE OF MAN

Thomas Jefferson had much to say about man, his rights and duties, freedoms and obligations, social and political organizations, and morals and religion. Jefferson's interests always encompassed many facets of human nature and human society. It is not easy, however, to determine what Jefferson believed about the essential nature of man. What was man really like? Was he good or bad, saint or sinner? Did he have a soul, was he only an animal, or, even more disturbing to contemplate, was he just a machine? Jefferson said that he was a "materialist not a spiritualist," but his idea of materialism was very broad. He saw wonder in material man with his faculty of thought and in the sun with its faculty of gravitation. He attributed both mysteries to an all-wise God.[1]

If man was a creation of God, what kind of creation was he? How could the various complexities of human behavior and the ambiguous record of social progress that history revealed be explained? With characteristic, studious zeal and wide-ranging interest, Jefferson addressed himself to the problem of the nature of man.

Man's Dual Nature

Even a casual reading of his writings reveals Jefferson's optimism about human nature. He believed that the majority of men were endowed with basic goodness and morality and so could govern themselves. He maintained that the drift of history, despite temporary setbacks, was upward and that science was making for increasing progress. As he wrote to John Adams, "I think with you that it is a good world on the whole, that it has been framed on a principle of benevolence, and more pleasure than pain dealt out to us. . . . My temperament is sanguine, I steer my bark with Hope in the head, leaving fear astern."[2]

Despite his determined optimism, however, Jefferson was aware of another, darker side to human nature. His work as a lawyer made him well acquainted with the selfish and criminal side of men. As a statesman and politician, he knew only too well the injustice and treachery of which political foes, and even friends, were capable. As a student of history, he was aware of the evils and cruelties that existed in even the Greek and Roman civilizations which he admired.[3] What could account for this dual aspect of human nature? This puzzling question remains implicit and largely unanswered in Jefferson's writings on the nature of man.

Man Is Good

Although Jefferson did not address himself very much to the question of why he believed man was good, he frequently testified to his belief in the basic goodness of people. Discussing philosophy with Dupont de Nemours, he declared, "I believe with you that morality, compassion, generosity are innate elements of the human constitution; . . . that justice is the fundamental law of society." John Adams, discussing political science with Jefferson, argued that people were not equal and so more power should be given to the better educated aristocrats. Jefferson replied that God had broadly scattered "virtue and wisdom" among all the people when he "formed man for the social state." Hence, the people could be trusted. Jefferson's belief in the goodness of man was encouraged by the great development in science, commerce, the arts, and human wisdom in America since the colonial days when witches had been burned. He was sure there would be even more development in the future. The progress of the Enlightenment delighted Jefferson, for he saw it as a flowering of the seeds of virtue and goodness that a wise Creator had placed both in human nature and in the physical world.[4]

Basic to Jefferson's faith in the goodness of man was his faith in man's Creator, God. It was this religious belief on Jefferson's part that nourished his conviction of man's goodness despite the wars and personal disappointments he had experienced and even led Adams, the cynic, to seek encouragement in Jefferson's reasoned optimism.[5]

Man Is Bad

Jefferson was too keen a student of human behavior and had too wide an experience of human affairs, however, not to recognize that there were widespread exceptions to the basic goodness of people. For the most part, he observed with equanimity the foibles of the human race and was not upset when he discovered evils in men. He always regarded these as exceptions from the norm of the moral and the good. Only the more serious infractions aroused his concern, and he always felt that even these problems could be handled satisfactorily by improving education and adopting social reforms. At the same time, he felt much misery had been caused by "morally deformed" leaders, such as Napoleon and the Caesars. He recognized that "seeds of moral decay" were within all people. Man's "self-love often seduced him from the right," he wrote.[6]

In government especially, it was necessary to guard against "human weakness, corruption, and wickedness" by spreading power broadly to many people. Greed for money was another source of moral corruption in man, Jefferson believed. He wryly commented, "I have not observed men's honesty to increase with their riches."[7]

Another evil trait of human nature that caused Jefferson much distress was the tendency of people to lie, slander, and gossip, especially about those in public office. He was troubled by the popularity of exposés, and slander in the newspapers and "the abandoned prostitution to falsehood" of the press. For the most part, Jefferson counseled avoidance of public name-calling. He refused to be "baited by these political bull-dogs," he wrote, and he advised his political followers to do their duty steadfastly despite the lies of their opponents. Lies were such cheap and easy weapons that they would surely be used. The truth would eventually come out, he believed, and the issue could be safely left to "the scourge of public opinion." Occasionally, however, he ventured a reply when sufficiently provoked. On one such occasion he wrote that he was unable "passively to receive the kick of an ass."[8]

It is clear from his writings that Jefferson combined a somewhat cynical and skeptical view of human nature with an optimistic belief in the future of human society. From his study of Enlightenment philosophy and scientific progress he drew hope for human development, but his study of history and the ancient classics taught him caution about individual virtue.[9]

As well as recognizing individual weaknesses and evils, he thought special problems arose when populations were crowded together in cities. He was troubled by the poverty, ignorance, and superstition he noticed everywhere in Europe. He wondered why such a rich country as France with such "amiable" people should be "loaded with so much misery." He blamed it on their "kings, nobles, and priests." He thought England was not oppressed as badly as France, but he feared that the English love of pomp, nobility, and wealth made them susceptible to despotism.[10]

His experience in Europe's courts had not taught Jefferson admiration for royalty. He wrote: "Louis the XVI was a fool, of my own knowledge. . . . The King of Prussia was a mere hog in body as well as mind, and George of England was in a straight waistcoat." He blamed their incompetence on their life-style and lack of moral education: "Take any race of animals, confine them in idleness, whether in a stye or a state-room, gratify all their appetites, and banish whatever might lead them to think, and in a few generations they become all body and no mind."[11]

Jefferson also blamed the priests and the church for many social evils. "Christ's principles were early departed from by those who professed to be his special servants," he wrote, "and perverted into an engine for enslaving mankind, a mere contrivance to filch wealth and power to themselves." He reiterated this conviction in various forms to friends throughout his life.[12] In blaming much of humanity's misery upon bad governing by inept kings, upon economic exploitation by selfish nobles, and upon fears and superstitions fostered by power-hungry clergy, Jefferson was influenced not only by his own observations but by his Enlightenment readings.[13]

History indicated that even in free, democratic societies, the lure of power, the praise of the crowd, and the insidious temptation that the end justified the means were corrupting influences that plagued all governments. Corruption was so easy that special safeguards of checks and balances were needed to protect democratic government.[14]

History was full of examples of human evil. Jefferson told John Bernard that his experience as a lawyer and his study of history continually reminded him of the "dark side of humanity." Many of the histories written in the eighteenth century followed the theme of the evils that had resulted from religious and political benightedness. Jefferson was much impressed with Edward Gibbon's monumental study of the weaknesses that led to the fall of the Roman Empire.[15]

From his studies and experiences of life, then, Jefferson was convinced that there were dangers of weakness and corruption that constantly threatened mankind. While most people were basically moral and good, there were seeds of evil in all, and in some more than others, which might quickly get out of hand if legal and social safeguards were not erected to encourage the good and prevent the evil. As to the future, the best protection was to place power in the hands of the masses of humanity, who would be too good and too many to be easily corrupted and would possess too much common sense and good judgment to be long misled. Jefferson was more optimistic about the goodness of man and had higher hopes for the future than his friend John Adams, who was more of a New England skeptic. Even Jefferson, however, found that he had been too sanguine, writing, "I fear, from the experience of the last twenty-five years, that morals do not of necessity advance hand in hand with the sciences."[16]

Man and Sin

From his comparative silence on the subject, it would seem that Jefferson was relatively untroubled by the question of what caused the dual nature of man. For the most part he simply accepted as fact that, although the good predominated, there was a "dark side to humanity" which had to be guarded against. He spent so much of his life overcoming human evils, whether in his grandchildren by gentle admonitions or in society by sweeping reforms, that he had little time for theological speculations concerning the origins of evil.

He did, however, have some strong convictions about evil and sin based on his religious beliefs and studies and did not hesitate to voice them. Jefferson's writings indicate that he had well-reasoned ideas about the place of sin in human nature and social life.

Man Not a Sinner

In the first place, Jefferson was much opposed to the orthodox, Calvinistic theological position of preachers of his day who insisted that man was so totally depraved by original sin that only God's grace could save him. He wrote heatedly to a liberal friend against Calvin's doctrines of predestination and eternal damnation. When John Adams mischievously wished Jefferson good health and long life until he became as good a Calvinist as Adams was, Jefferson wrote back an indignant attack on Calvin, arguing that Calvin worshiped a "malignant daemon" and "blasphemed God by the atrocious attributes" that he gave to God. In other letters Jefferson attacked what he called the "five demoralizing dogmas of Calvin," which he identified as believing in "three Gods," denying the importance of "good works and love of neighbor," exalting "incomprehensible faith," denying the "use of reason in religion," and believing that "God elected certain individuals to be saved and others to be damned, and that no crimes of the former can damn them and no virtues of the latter save."[17]

Jefferson also attacked Saint Paul, rightly deducing that it was Pauline theology which was the chief basis of Calvinism. He frequently wrote with indignation of the "corruptions" of Jesus' pure doctrines by Paul and by the later "speculations of crazy theologists which have made a Bable of a religion, the most moral and sublime ever preached to man." He often identified Plato's "foggy mysticism" as the source of the intangible speculations of the medieval church that had distorted Jesus' simple doctrines.[18] Athanasius was another villain, according to Jefferson, for his part in establishing the Trinitarian Nicene Creed as authoritative in Christianity and defeating the more reasonable Arian beliefs in one God.[19]

Jefferson's notes on his reading provide further evidence of his opposition to religious orthodoxy. He copied down Bolingbroke's attack on "the god of Moses who is unjust, cruel, and delights in blood" and on the God of Paul who "elects some of his creatures to salvation, and predestinates others to damnation, even in the womb of their mothers." From Bolingbroke, he also found the seed of the idea that Plato's philosophy had corrupted Christ's original teachings with its "polytheistical notions of divine nature." Jefferson was also impressed with Bolingbroke's attack on the doctrine of the atonement as being barbaric.[20] Jefferson noted John Locke's argument about the need for both "faith and works" for Christian salvation as well as "repentance and a reformation of life."[21] In his literary notebook, Jefferson included several passages from Milton's poetry but little of the sweeping theology of *Paradise Lost*. There was just this one passage about the evil in men:

> But of this be sure
> To do ought Good never will be our Task
> But ever to do Ill our sole Delight,
> As being contrary to his high Will
> Whom we resist.[22]

Aside from this one quotation from Milton, and the one from Locke on man's need for repentance, there are few, if any, statements in Jefferson's writings to support a belief in the sinfulness of man, while there is a great preponderance of writing by Jefferson opposed to this idea. Jefferson acknowledged the evil in man, but he refused to call man a sinner. As a convinced Enlightenment liberal, he disliked the church's doctrine of original sin and the blood atonement. Such medieval teachings, he argued, had kept people bound in fear and superstition too long and were preventing them from advancing into a world of progress and enlightenment ruled by reason.[23]

Man's Lost Garden of Eden

Since Jefferson and the Enlightenment philosophers rejected the doctrine of original sin, how did they explain the presence of evil in people and what did they think about the fall of man in the Garden of Eden? Needless to say, they did not take the account in Genesis literally. Conyers Middleton, who was very influential in Jefferson's religious thinking, called the story of the fall of man a fable or allegory.[24]

There is a sense in which the men of the Enlightenment took the story of Adam and Eve being driven out of the Garden of Eden as an allegory explaining their own interpretation of history.

Romanticists like Rousseau looked back to the time of the "noble savage" when man lived an idyllic life, uncorrupted by civilization.[25] Over the centuries human institutions became depraved. The masses of ordinary people were exploited by kings and priests, and people lost much of their goodness. Their original, innocent "self-love" degenerated into "selfish love" that delighted in tyrannizing over others. But there was hope that reason could overcome superstition, reform could overcome exploitation, and nature's harmonious ways could be rediscovered and reestablished. Then man could hope to regain his lost paradise in a new Garden of Eden by forming a new political and ethical community based on a new, free, and just social contract.[26]

Although Jefferson was too knowledgeable of frontier life to accept the idea of the noble savage uncritically, he was touched by the idea. Based on his own experience of frontier Virginia, he always spoke highly of the American Indians.[27] There is no evidence that he accepted Rousseau's idea of the "noble savage," but he did accept the idea of the "Saxon myth." His extensive studies of English common law convinced him that the Saxons of Great Britain had enjoyed greater freedom and democracy before the coming of the Normans and that their institutions and freedoms had degenerated under the medieval laws that the Normans instituted. Jefferson believed American democracy was an opportunity to regain this better life. He thought that the greater economic opportunities in America and the better practical education and ability of the American people to make decisions for themselves offered an unparalleled opportunity to establish a new life of freedom and happiness in the New World. To this extent, in his own way, Jefferson may be said to have allegorized the story of man's fall from the Garden of Eden and his attempt to regain it and given it an American setting.[28]

There was another school of thought among Enlightenment writers, however, which saw the Garden of Eden story not as a symbolic allegory but as a pleasant fable with little real meaning for the enlightened person. All the story of the Garden of Eden and man's loss of it really said, according to this interpretation, was that man was basically good but also human and subject to evil. He needed to work and keep busy in order to avoid temptation. The "moral sense" needed to be cultivated and the "weeds of evil" uprooted.[29] Jefferson was influenced by such writers as Rush and Priestley to

believe that the good seeds of morality, implanted in man by the
God of nature, could be encouraged to grow by the proper teachings
of virtue and that the weeds of evil habits could be discouraged.[30]

Sin, according to the moral sense view, was a disease of the moral
faculties akin to the diseases of the body such as yellow fever. Both
were to be overcome by good health and good "sensibilities" and
the encouragement of good virtues and good moral feelings. Excesses
of tobacco, liquor, passionate feelings, and violent actions were all
to be avoided.[31] Just as bodily diseases and the cruelties of nature
were deplorable but had their purposes in the total scheme of things,
so uses might be found for the evils and sorrows of people, as
Jefferson's favorite Stoic philosophers were fond of pointing out.
Only for grief, Jefferson plaintively wrote to Adams, could he find
no useful purpose.[32] So Jefferson and the men of the Enlightenment
largely explained away human sin and the fall of man from the
Garden of Eden.

The moral sense theory gave Jefferson the advantage of a long-
range view of human evils and the ups and downs of history. Human
sin was, after all, only one small part of God's good creation. Moreover, the theological invention of sin led man to regard himself as
an outcast from his Creator, so that he lost his sense for true religion.
The Puritan, according to the Enlightenment writings of Thomas
Paine admired by Jefferson, "calls himself a worm, and the fertile
earth a dunghill; and all the blessings of life by the thankless name
of vanities."[33] The Calvinist was, in short, a moral hypochondriac.
Overcoming evil was not a metaphysical war with sin as the Puritan
believed but a simple adjustment of a few faults in nature's creation.

Man's "Salvation" by Education

Instead of theology, the followers of the Enlightenment placed great
hope in education to improve humankind and eradicate evil, as well
as in the advance of science and progress to reform society.[34] Jefferson was inclined by his own nature to scholarly study and scientific observation. He also had a practical interest in the promotion
of education and the increase of man's knowledge,[35] since he believed
these were the real means for the salvation of men from moral
wrongs and for the redemption of society from evil and corruption.

Education, in the first place, was the means to save the common man from the ignorance, superstition, and misery fastened upon him by kings, priests, and nobles so prevalent in Europe, Jefferson believed. A second and related reason for Jefferson's interest in public education was that he realized that the power to govern could not be entrusted to ignorant citizens. When endowing all men with the freedom to rule themselves, nature's god obligated them with the duty to learn how to make democracy work. Writing from Europe, Jefferson urged a friend to "preach a crusade against ignorance." A democracy must educate the common people, and taxes for education were a small price to pay compared with what "kings and priests" would exact from ignorant followers, he continued. He proved to be an uncanny prophet concerning the dangers of lack of education in South America: "The revolution of South America will succeed against Spain. But ignorance and superstition will chain their minds and bodies under religious and military despotism."[36]

Jefferson was interested both in the education of youth for the future and of adults for the present. He often commented on the importance of books and libraries to train citizens for freedom, and he made proposals for the establishment of public libraries as well as public schools. He wrote: "The light which has been shed on mankind by the art of printing has eminently changed the condition of the world and . . . continues to spread. While printing is preserved, it can no more recede than the sun return on his course."[37]

Because of his compelling faith in education as a means of salvation for the enlightened person, Jefferson early in his public career devised a plan for public education which he advocated all his life. He hoped that Virginia would follow the good example of New England where an educated and influential citizenry had resulted from its early development of town schools. Geography, which caused New England people to live in towns, was against him in Virginia, where people lived scattered on plantations. Jefferson's plan for public schools was not adopted until the 1870s, long after his death.[38]

Jefferson, accordingly, turned his attention to salvaging what he could from his plan for public education and devoted the last years of his life to establishing a state university for Virginia. He had originally hoped to make his alma mater, the College of William and Mary, into such a university, but because of religious jealousies—William and Mary was an Episcopalian school—he had to give up the idea. He did succeed, however, in establishing a new university at Charlottesville, the University of Virginia, created after his own vision. This university was the great accomplishment of his old age. So proud of it was he that he had "FATHER OF THE UNIVERSITY OF VIRGINIA" inscribed on his tombstone.[39]

He had written various proposals for a state-supported university for many years. After his retirement he revised these plans, had them shepherded through the legislature, and repeatedly wrung funds from it for the establishment of the university. He was the architect and building superintendent for the grounds and buildings; he drew up the curriculum and hired the professors; he selected the books and set up the library. Although every stage of the development of the university involved Jefferson in argument, the greatest controversy developed over the choice of curriculum and professors, especially as those choices affected the teaching of religion. Jefferson wanted his university to be a beacon of enlightenment and liberalism in the New World. Accordingly, he emphasized science and government and deemphasized theology. He chose, as one of the professors, his friend Thomas Cooper, who was eminently qualified but was also an outspoken proponent of Unitarianism and foe of Calvinism. The choice of Cooper aroused vehement opposition from the Calvinists and finally had to be rescinded. Further opposition developed because Jefferson made no provision for the teaching of religion, insisting that the separation of church and state prohibited the teaching of the beliefs of any one sect in a state institution. He did compromise to the extent that he offered space where different denominations might establish their own seminaries adjoining the university grounds.[40]

He also provided for the teaching of morality and philosophy along the same lines as those he had often advised family friends to follow in their studies. His aim was an institution that would foster the development of the ideals of the Enlightenment by which he had lived all of his life. The rights and duties of men and the pure teachings of Jesus upon which all people agreed could and should be taught, but the dogmas of religion that divided friends, thwarted religious freedom, and led to tyrannies of church and state should be avoided, he believed.[41]

Jefferson was consistent to the end of his life in believing in the importance of education as the means of salvation of humanity from both individual sins and social evils. If some people were deficient in the moral sense, education could supply the lack, and education would lead all men to exercise better morals. He had seen this progress in America. "I have observed this march of civilization advancing from the seacoast, passing over us like a cloud of light, increasing our knowledge and improving our condition," he wrote. "Barbarism has been receding, and will in time disappear from the earth." The enlightenment of the masses of mankind provided by education would lead to the overthrow of tyranny and help science to solve social problems. Even the retrogressions of the Napoleonic Wars could not stop the progress of education. "The art of printing alone, and the vast dissemination of books, will maintain the mind where it is, and raise the conquering ruffians to the level of the conquered," he wrote to Adams. "Even should the cloud of barbarism and despotism again obscure the science and liberties of Europe, this country remains to preserve and restore light and liberty to them." Thus education was helping man to find again in a new and more complicated social setting the paradise that he had lost when he grew out of the simpler societies of nature, Jefferson believed.[42]

Jefferson's life marked an end and a fulfillment of the eighteenth-century Enlightenment, but it also marked a beginning and a fore-shadowing of the problems of the modern age. The "Cooper controversy" was but the first of many to follow over the issue of teaching religion in public schools. Jefferson, as Robert Healey has declared, may have been guilty of some intolerance himself in his zeal to promote the teaching of true morality instead of mistaken dogma.[43] Yet Jefferson was right in his belief that without the restraints of morality and education men cannot live together in modern society.

Man and Social Evils

Jefferson's emphasis upon the goodness of man, his refusal to admit the presence of sin in human life, and his optimistic belief in science and education to cure all ills did not go unchallenged by events in his lifetime but were maintained in the face of severe social problems.

Man and Social Disturbances

The first social problem that challenged Jefferson's belief in the trustworthiness of the common man was the issue of riot and civil disturbance. While Jefferson and Adams were abroad as American representatives to France and England respectively, there came news of Shays's Rebellion in Massachusetts against oppressive taxes. Adam was concerned, but Jefferson was disturbed more by the exaggerations of the British press than the threat to law and order. "A little rebellion, now and then," he wrote to Madison, "is as necessary in the political world as storms in the physical." He continued, "God forbid we should ever be twenty years without such a rebellion." It was better for the people to be restless than apathetic. "The tree of liberty," he concluded, "must be refreshed from time to time, with the blood of patriots and tyrants. It is its natural manure."[44]

Jefferson, then, believed that excesses were deplorable but understandable, that social disturbances brought to light social wrongs which needed attention, and that the participation of the people in the democratic process was a good thing. John Adams was not so sure. He wrote to Jefferson testily that when he was president he had been threatened by mobs in "Markett Street before my door . . . while you was fast asleep in philosophical Tranquility."[45]

A much more serious testing of Jefferson's faith in the common man came with the French Revolution. He was present at its beginnings, and his letters from France contain striking firsthand accounts of bread riots in Paris. He recognized the injustices that caused the Revolution and had high hopes that France would follow America's democratic example. Unfortunately, the "madness" of the later leaders of the French Revolution and the devastations of Napoleon led to a "mournful period in the history of man," he wrote.[46] The excesses of the revolution not only caused miseries in France and Europe, and embarrassment for Jefferson in America but also raised doubts concerning the validity of the very foundations of the Enlightenment. If man was by nature good and without sin, endowed by nature's God with the rights of freedom and with the moral sense of duty to make free government possible, how could one explain the failures of the revolution and the rise of the tyrant Napoleon?

Adams put the question to Jefferson with his usual bluntness: "Where is now the progress of the human Mind? Where is the Amelioration of Society?" Jefferson's answer was to admit the world's sufferings and to acknowledge that social evils were more difficult to solve than the philosophers of the Enlightenment had realized. The ideals of the Enlightenment were still valid, however; progress had been made, and history was on their side, Jefferson concluded.[47]

Man and War

Jefferson estimated that eight to ten million people had been killed in the wars that devastated the world during his lifetime. Even worse than the human sufferings and physical destruction caused by war, he declared, was the loss of belief in moral principles. He marveled that civilized nations such as England and France "threw off suddenly and openly all the restraints of morality," plunging national morality back into the "depravity of the Borgias." Jefferson's conduct in a world gone mad with war was to adhere more firmly to his moral principles and to direct the United States in a course of neutrality.[48]

The fate of the neutral is often not a happy one. As conditions grew worse, Jefferson resorted to economic sanctions and embargo as an alternative to war in order to protect the interests of the United States. But the embargo hurt the United States as much as the nations against which it was directed and eventually had to be abandoned.[49]

Jefferson could only shake his head over times that had forsaken reason and morality. He could not understand individuals or a world that lived by evil and fury when all the laws of reason and morality dictated the opposite conduct. He could only take comfort in the knowledge that he and his country, at least, had been "most exact in its moral conduct towards others."[50]

Man and Slavery

Of all the social evils with which Jefferson and the Enlightenment had to contend, slavery was the ugliest and the one in which progress was the slowest. There was something terribly inconsistent for men of the Enlightenment to argue that the savage in nature was noble while holding other primitive people in slavery, and it smacked of hypocrisy for Americans to proclaim liberty and equality for themselves on the basis of the God-given rights of man while accepting without question that their Negro slaves "were as legitimate subjects of property as their horses and cattle."[51]

What was Jefferson's position? Despite his ringing declarations of the rights of man, he was a southern aristocrat; his wealth was based on the plantation system, and all his life he owned slaves. It has even been argued that he kept a household slave as his concubine after his wife died.[52] Jefferson has been criticized for not working more forthrightly for his ideals of freedom and equality both during his lifetime and by later scholars.[53] Therefore, Jefferson's thoughts and actions on the moral issue of slavery need to be examined with some care.

Arguments against Slavery

In the first place, few men of his time, and certainly none of his class, were such early and persistent foes of the institution of slavery as Jefferson was. In the original draft of the Declaration of Independence he introduced a clause condemning the slave trade as a moral outrage.[54] He helped prevent slavery from being extended to the Northwest Territory. As president, he influenced the Congress to abolish the slave trade and prohibit any further importation of slaves into the United States. On the other hand, he defended slavery in the southern states and protected its continuation in the Louisiana Territory.[55]

He wrote a number of articles and letters attacking slavery during his long lifetime, marshaling his arguments in his usual thoughtful way. Slavery was, to begin with, contrary to the rights of man and basic beliefs of the American Revolution. This was the reason that he regarded it as a great tragedy that his attempt to outlaw slavery in the Declaration of Independence was defeated. He lost only by the vote of one state. It is interesting to speculate how different America's history might have been had Jefferson won. He wrote to a French friend, "The voice of a single individual of one State would have prevented this abominable crime from spreading itself over the new country. . . . Heaven was silent in that awful moment!

But it is to be hoped it will not always be silent and that the friends of human rights will prevail." Writing for French readers who sympathized with the American Revolution, Jefferson was critical of his countrymen who sacrificed so much for their own liberties but condemned some of their "fellow men to bondage and misery." In time, he continued, "their tears and groans will awaken a God of justice to their distress" to deliver them either "by diffusing light among their oppressors or by His exterminating thunder."[56]

The violation of the God-given rights of the black people, Jefferson felt, weakened the American belief that human rights and liberties were a "gift of God" that no human could rightfully take away. Slavery was wrong because it violated God's will. "I tremble for my country," he wrote in 1782, "when I reflect that God is just; that his justice cannot sleep forever. The Almighty cannot take side with us in such [an issue]."[57]

Another reason for condemning slavery, according to Jefferson, was the bad effect it had upon those who were held as slaves. He was thinking not so much of physical cruelty, which was rare in his experience, as of the damage to human character. Living in slavery very often weakened personal ambition and morality. Slaves, he complained, required constant supervision and coercion to make them work. Because as slaves they were denied positions of responsibility, they were "pests in society by their idleness." They were "children incapable of taking care of themselves" whom a "responsible father could not abandon." Jefferson blamed this indolence and dishonesty upon slavery rather than upon the people: "A man's moral sense must be unusually strong if slavery does not make him a thief. He who by law can own no property can hardly conceive that property is founded in anything but force." Slavery also injured the slave's love for this country in which he was abused and destroyed his hope for a better life for his children, who were "entailed with his own miserable condition for endless generations." Slavery, in fact, had so injured the character of the blacks that they could not be "amalgamated" with whites because of the "degradation of human character" that would result, Jefferson believed.[58] Jefferson has, understandably, been attacked by some scholars for his unflattering views of American slaves, even though he owned slaves and knew them well.[59] He, of course, would have seen things differently had he lived in the slave quarters instead of the master's house. However, he did emphasize the "degrading submissions and injustices" of the institution of slavery.[60]

Jefferson was equally scathing in his comments about slave-owners. Slavery not only degraded the slaves. It had a depraving effect upon their masters, who were encouraged to "give a loose to the worst of passions, and were nursed, educated, and daily exercised in tyranny." Living in the master's house tended to "deprave the manners and morals" of the white people, both adults and children. Slavery also tended to destroy the "industry" of the masters, "for in a warm climate, no man will labor for himself who can make another labor for him." Slavery hardened the consciences of the masters. Used to "seeing the degraded condition, both bodily and mental, of those unfortunate beings daily," they came to regard them as property like their "horses and cattle." By legalizing slavery, he wrote, "the statesman, permitting one half the citizens thus to trample on the rights of the other, transforms those into despots, and these into enemies," surely an unwise policy for those who believed in liberty and equality.[61]

The wonder was that the spirit of man endured so nobly the injustices of slavery, Jefferson wrote, and that so many of the slaves displayed "integrity, benevolence, gratitude, and unshaken fidelity, as many as among their better instructed masters!" Jefferson himself enjoyed a good relationship with his slaves, especially capable ones like Isaac Jefferson, who remembered "Old Master's kindness" and being taken to Philadelphia with Jefferson "to larn the tinner's trade." Jefferson freed such capable slaves and established them as artisans with a trade. Slavery itself, however, remained a baffling problem.[62]

Efforts to Overcome Slavery

From his first abortive attempt in the Declaration of Independence until the end of his life, Jefferson was involved in various schemes to end slavery in the United States. As he wrote in his old age, the problem "has been through life one of my greatest anxieties." One solution that occurred to Jefferson while in Europe was to try to establish the slaves on small farms of their own such as European peasants farmed. Nothing came of this plan, but he did succeed in a plan for utilizing slave artisans in a blacksmithing and nail business supervised by Isaac Jefferson and Great George, the Monticello smith.[63]

Another solution to the problem of slavery, which Jefferson first proposed in his draft for a constitution for the new state of Virginia and which he continued to advocate all of his life, was the gradual, compensated emancipation of the slaves and their establishment in a colony elsewhere after suitable training in farming and handicrafts. His plan found few supporters, but he hoped a "new generation trained in free democracy" would favor the end of slavery. Such favorable public opinion did not develop. As a result, Jefferson feared that a bloody slave revolt, such as happened in Santo Domingo, might occur in the United States.[64]

As the slave population grew, Jefferson came to believe it would be too expensive to free all of the slaves. But it would cost very little to buy the freedom of the children when they were young, and the cost of training and outfitting them in a colony could be provided by the sale of the western lands claimed by slave states. After Santo Domingo gained its independence, he thought that would be an ideal place for the freed slaves. Thus the problem of slavery in the United States could be overcome in one generation.[65]

Jefferson also encouraged the settlement of American Negroes in Africa. While president, he encouraged the colonization efforts of American missionary societies who settled freed slaves on the African coast at Sierra Leone and Cape Mesurado and eventually founded the African republic of Liberia. He hoped the whole American slave population could gradually be sent there. He also encouraged others such as Edward Coles and Frances Wright in their experiments to establish slaves in freedom in the American West.[66]

It seems clear that Jefferson might have had more success in his plan of gradual, compensated emancipation of the slaves if he had not combined it with the very difficult proposition of colonization outside of the United States. Why did he add to the problems of emancipation the impractical idea of colonization? It was, he wrote, because he feared that "white prejudices, black hatreds, and the real differences of the races" could not be overcome. He feared the animosities of the races would lead to "the extermination of the one or the other race." His very sensitiveness to the evils of slavery may have made him more fearful of violence than other slave owners who were more inured to the conditions of slavery.[67]

Jefferson had a second, and probably more compelling, reason for wishing to transport the Negroes far away. He disliked intermarriage and the "mingling" of the races. He believed the black slaves were inferior and that racial intermarriage would degrade the whites. He supported this belief with his observations of the black slaves. They were, he thought, "less physically beautiful" than the whites; "inferior in reasoning ability"; talented in music but not in oratory, painting, or sculpture; and were "brave but lacked forethought." He admitted that no scientific study of the racial and cultural differences of man had been made. So he concluded: "I advance it, therefore, as a suspicion only that the blacks, whether because of race or circumstances, are inferior to the whites in the endowments both of body and mind." These opinions explain Jefferson's desire to deport the black slaves at the same time that he emancipated them.[68]

These views were not unusual for Jefferson's time and place, even among men of the Enlightenment. The study of anthropology had scarcely begun, and little was known of other cultures, although there was a lively curiosity. Edward Tyson had studied the orangutan and written of its close similarity to man. His study had raised the question among Enlightenment writers whether the African race might not be an intermediate link in the great chain of creation between the ape and European man. Hence, Jefferson casually accepted the idea that orangutans preferred black women as mates, a view that even the accomplished French naturalist Georges Buffon had accepted as true.[69]

Jefferson was criticized for his writings on white superiority and was quick to retreat from ideas which, he plaintively said, he had voiced only "tentatively and tenderly." After reading an almanac created by Benjamin Banneker, an American Negro of considerable engineering genius, he wrote him, offering to forward the almanac to the French Academy of Science, and commented, "Nobody wishes more than I do to see such proofs as you exhibit, that nature has given to our black brethren, talents equal to those of the other colors of men."[70]

Jefferson's Involvement in Slavery

It has been suggested by some scholars that Jefferson's lifelong concern with slavery, and the strong emotions he felt about it, may have been due to his ownership of slaves. The speculation that he may have had a slave mistress has been periodically revived. It was first publicized in 1800 by James Callender, a disgruntled office-seeker and journalist with a fancied grievance against Jefferson, and by some Federalist newspapers. Later an English writer, Frances Trollope, exaggerated Jefferson's mistress into a harem. The stories were revived again by the Abolitionists and have continued in currency; Virginius Dabney made a thorough review and rebuttal of "the Jefferson scandals" in 1981.[71]

His account and Dumas Malone's biography of Jefferson present an objective summary of the facts as they can be determined after all these years, based upon records of plantation life kept by Jefferson and the recollections of the Monticello slaves, of Edmund Bacon, the overseer at Monticello, and of members of Jefferson's family. From these accounts it is clear that there were at Monticello a group of slaves, some of them very light-skinned, who were the most capable of the household servants and plantation artisans. Most of them were the children and grandchildren of Betty Hemings, who came to Monticello with her ten children in 1774 on settlement of the estate of Jefferson's father-in-law, John Wayles. The oral tradition handed down among the slaves was that Betty Hemings was half white, the daughter of an English sea captain and an African Negress, and that her younger children were fathered by John Wayles in his later years after his third wife died.[72]

Sally Hemings, one of these younger children of Betty Hemings, is the one who is supposed to have been Jefferson's mistress. Isaac Jefferson remembered her as "mighty near white and very handsome with long straight hair down her back. Sally had a son named Madison, who learned to be a great fiddler." It was this son, Madison, resembling Jefferson in appearance, who claimed years later that his mother had told him that Jefferson was his father. According to Madison's account, his mother became Jefferson's mistress while in Paris and agreed to return to America only upon receiving promises of special treatment for herself and her children. She bore

Jefferson five children, four of whom lived, two girls and two boys. The girls, Beverly and Harriet, were freed and went to live in Washington, D.C., where they married white men. The boys, Eston and Madison, learned trades, married "colored" girls, and migrated to Ohio. Madison remembered many details of life at Monticello: "It was my mother's duty, up to the time of father's death, to take care of his chamber and wardrobe, look after us children and do such light work as sewing."[73]

Although the Hemings descendants were not the only slaves freed by Jefferson who claimed him as their ancestor, Madison's testimony has been the basis of most accounts concerning Jefferson's slave mistress, sometimes in twisted versions. His freeing of handsome Harriet and sending her to live with her uncle James Hemings in Washington probably provoked the later Abolitionists' tale that "the daughter of Thomas Jefferson was sold in New Orleans for one thousand dollars." Fawn Brodie, in order to justify her acceptance of Sally Hemings's claim to having been Jefferson's mistress from the time of her stay in Paris, has suggested that Jefferson had a special attraction to "forbidden" women. As a young man before his marriage, he made advances to a friend's wife. While in France he was deeply attracted to Maria Cosway, also married and beyond reach. Sally was forbidden by race, hence attractive to Jefferson, Brodie argued. However, Sally was only a child when she sailed as companion to Jefferson's younger daughter to France in 1787. Moreover, the records show that Sally's oldest child was not born until 1798.[74]

The question remains, could she have been Jefferson's mistress later at Monticello? The oral tradition from the slaves and statements made by Edmund Bacon, the overseer, by Jefferson's grandson Thomas Jefferson Randolph, and his granddaughter Ellen Randolph Coolidge agree that either Peter Carr, a favorite nephew of Jefferson who was treated like a son, or his brother, Sam Carr, was the father of Sally's children. Ellen described her cousin Sam as "the most notorious, good-natured Turk that ever was master of a black seraglio kept at other men's expence." During this period, Jefferson was engrossed with his political life and was not often at Monticello, but the two Carrs were close to Sally Hemings's age and were more of the temperament to be intimate with her than

Jefferson. They came with their mother, Jefferson's sister, to live at Monticello after the death of their father and were brought up there. Such paternity would also account for the family resemblance in Sally's children. It is not likely Jefferson would have approved of such relationships, considering his views on morality and slavery, but he was ever reticent about forcing his ideas on others, and sexual intimacy with slaves was regarded with tolerance by many Southerners then.[75]

Most scholars who have studied Jefferson closely have felt that such an intimacy was out of character for him. It does not seem likely that, with his prejudice against blacks and the mixing of the races, he would have deliberately "stained" his own blood with a slave and "entailed" the terrible condition of slavery upon his own children, to use his own terms. Nor does such an intimacy seem in character for a man who admired the blushing, fair white woman but viewed with distaste the black woman. If these favored slaves were the descendants of his beloved wife's father and of his sister's sons, it would have been entirely like Jefferson to remain silent about their paternity, trusting that those who knew him well would make the proper judgment, while at the same time he made every provision for their care, training, and eventual freedom. "No repugnancies," he wrote Edward Coles, should lead a master "to abdicate his duties" to his slaves.[76] Thomas Jefferson Randolph said that his mother would have liked to send the whole Hemings brood away but knew that his grandfather would not consent. Although his code of responsibility would not allow it, Jefferson might have shared something of this desire and expressed it in his plan for colonization of the slaves far away, beyond any further mixing of the races.[77]

Noting that Jefferson did not remarry, although he was only thirty-nine when his wife died, Brodie deduced that it was because Sally Hemings was his mistress. The southern plantation system, however, with its plentiful supply of domestic servants, relieved Jefferson of much of the pressure to remarry that a widower with two daughters to raise might otherwise feel. Jefferson had married sisters nearby and at Monticello to help with raising the children. While he was in France and later when he was president in Washington, servants could care very well for his modest entertaining and domestic needs. Isaac Jefferson remembered fellow slaves taken to Washington as servants and carriage drivers wearing bright uniforms. Jefferson's older daughter was his hostess upon occasion. After his two surviving daughters were married, he was constantly urging them to make long visits with their families at Monticello. Eventually he persuaded Patsy and her family to make their permanent home with him there so that he could spend his retirement years happily surrounded by his grandchildren.[78]

Had Maria Cosway been free to marry when she enchanted him in France, it is likely that the arguments of "Heart" would have overcome the doubts of cautious "Head," and Jefferson would have sought her as a compatible second wife. Once he survived this romantic encounter in his mid-forties, however, he was increasingly absorbed in the greater affairs of government and politics and·the lesser affairs of his family, friends, and plantation life, and so less susceptible to marriage as middle age wore into old age. Even in his youth he had a certain diffidence in approaching women which became, in his older years, a remote courtesy.

There is, however, besides his natural caution, another and more valid reason for his avoiding entangling alliances with the fair sex. Jefferson's love for his wife was unusually deep. They shared common interests in music and culture. Monticello was begun as their "Honeymoon Lodge," and there they had their six children. Daughter Patsy remembered their close companionship.[79] Jefferson's marriage was made stronger by sorrows shared. One after another, all but two of the children died. Then, after a long illness during which he was constantly at her bedside, Jefferson's wife died. Before she died, Jefferson promised her never to remarry, according to a conversation Sally Hemings said she overheard.[80] Jefferson went nearly insane with grief. He refused to take his place in the Virginia legislature; indeed, he wrote later that he was "absolutely unable to attend to anything like business." Although just a child, Patsy remembered his grief well: "He walked almost incessantly night and day, only lying down occasionally, when nature was completely exhausted. He rode out on horseback, rambling about the mountain, in the least frequented roads. I was his constant companion, a solitary witness to many a violent burst of grief."[81] At last time healed his sorrow, a circumstance which Jefferson ever afterwards was wont to offer as the only real cure for grief to friends with similar

losses. This experience seems to have produced in Jefferson a reluctance to ever again expose himself to the pain of becoming emotionally involved with another woman. Although in his dialogue
on love between "Head" and "Heart" Jefferson concluded that
"friendship is precious" and worth what it cost, he revealed more
truly his deepest feelings when he wrote: "The most effectual means
of being secure against pain, is to retire within ourselves, and to
suffice for our own happiness by intellectual pleasures. Friendship
is an alliance with the follies and misfortunes of others. A friend
dies or leaves us: we feel as if a limb was cut off."[82]

Considering his experiences and temperament, it seems quite
understandable that Jefferson never married again or even had a
serious love affair. In the light of his deepest feelings and convictions, it is equally unlikely that he ever had relations with a slave.
It seems more likely that he followed his own prescription of "time,
silence, and occupation," contenting himself with the satisfactions
of his career, his home at Monticello, the companionship of mas-
culine friends who shared his interest in politics, and the feminine
companionship of his family and grandchildren.

Conclusions

Jefferson's interest in history, sociology, and political science greatly
influenced his ideas about the nature of man. Although he never
formulated a philosophy of man, he adopted and developed many
ideas of the Enlightenment to explain man's thinking, behavior,
and essential nature. It was part of his intellectual creed that God
and his creation were good. Since man was part of God's good
creation, the idea of the complete sinfulness of man emphasized by
so many "hell-fire and damnation" preachers of his time violated
Jefferson's creed. Hence his attacks upon Calvin's theology. The
lifelong conflict between Jefferson's religious liberalism and his
conservative opponents began a confrontation that has continued
in American Protestantism between liberals and conservatives ever
since.

Jefferson was not entirely consistent in his determined optimism
about human nature, however, when he acknowledged another,
"darker" side to human beings, and he never came to grips with
the question of why there were seeds of evil in human society and

why some people lacked the moral sense. He had great faith in the ability of education and social reforms to overcome these defects, save individuals from their evils, and create a new social paradise to replace man's lost Garden of Eden, but he finally had to admit that moral progress had not kept pace with scientific advance. He could only cling to his belief that man's fundamental goodness would eventually triumph.

The most serious problems about Jefferson's doctrine of the goodness of man arose when he attempted to apply it to such social problems as civil disturbances, war, and slavery. He could believe that good triumphed in family life and polite society for he had considerable success in bringing out the best in his family and friends by moral teachings and polite behavior. But reform of society and international affairs did not result so easily from emphasizing the moral law.

Slavery, in particular, was an ethical issue that Jefferson was never able to solve. In spite of his eloquent denunciations of slavery, which later inspired éven the Abolitionists, Jefferson exhibited a certain equivocation about the emancipation of the slaves and a lack of zeal in enacting the reforms that he advocated. John Quincy Adams believed that Jefferson "abhorred slavery from his soul" and wrote "flaming denunciations of slavery" which he then was afraid to have published. He projected great plans for emancipation but, Adams complained, "left slavery precisely where it was. Mr. Jefferson had not the spirit of martyrdom."[83]

Adams' opinion of Jefferson may be somewhat suspect, since they were of different political parties. He may well have been right, however, in judging that Jefferson did not have the violence of a zealot that was necessary in dealing with the entrenched social evil of slavery. Jefferson was willing to endure a certain amount of abuse for causes in which he was sufficiently concerned. He always felt his work for religious freedom and separation of church and state earned him the opposition of many of his southern friends. The price of abuse for emancipation of the slaves was either too high, or the problem too difficult, for the amount of leadership that he was willing to invest. The abuse that he and an admired older friend, Colonel Richard Bland, received for early attempting moderate reforms of slavery in Virginia seems to have discouraged him from further attempts. After his retirement, Jefferson offered encouragement to those who sought his help in freeing the slaves but declined to lead the battle. "This is like bidding old Priam to buckle on the armour of Hector," he said. "This enterprise is for the young who can bear it through to its consummation. It shall have all my prayers, and these are the only weapons of an old man."[84]

In fairness to Jefferson, it should be stated that there were few others who had any more taste for martyrdom for the cause of emancipation than he had. He was never a flaming orator or fiery prophet. By temperament, experience, and practice he was a statesman and politician who accomplished his reforms by persuasion and compromise, which was the course he counseled for ending slavery. William Freeling believes that Jefferson's writings and deeds of opposition to slavery did lead to forces that restricted its spread and weakened it as an institution in the United States, eventually resulting in the Civil War and that sad solution to the problem of slavery.[85] Jefferson himself expressed fears that conflicts over slavery would lead to such "mortal hatred and eternal discord" as to imperil the American achievement of "self-government."[86] That Jefferson failed to overcome the evil of slavery simply illustrates that sometimes there are social issues which only time and history can resolve.

He does deserve credit for maintaining throughout his life that slavery was chiefly a moral issue. It was the destructive moral effects upon both master and slave that most concerned Jefferson. Slavery was one of the few things that aroused his passions because it destroyed the very things for which he cared most deeply: the rights, sense of duty, and moral character of every human being created by God. It was unfortunate for America that Jefferson's program of education, compromise, and moderate reform, which accomplished so much for human rights in the causes of political independence, religious freedom, and republican democracy, proved less successful in dealing with the social evils of civil disturbances, war, and slavery. Yet his faith in the fundamental goodness of people and the power of human reason to overcome social problems never wavered.

Jefferson's beliefs about the nature of man and his efforts to enhance human freedoms—political, religious, and economic—in the New World marked a flowering of the eighteenth-century

Enlightenment. His achievements indicate the values of the Enlightenment, and his failures reveal its weaknesses. Jefferson's unwavering belief in the goodness of human beings, in God's influence on human efforts, and in a future better than the past has given him an influence that still inspires people today.

CHAPTER VII

JEFFERSON'S

RELIGIOUS IDEAS OF GOD

Thomas Jefferson did not write as much about God as he did about man and society. He was a lawyer and statesman, and his main interests were political and social rather than theological. He was, however, interested in religion and had well-considered beliefs about God that he discussed at some length with friends, although he learned to be reticent about disclosing his religion to strangers and critics.

Jefferson Not an Atheist

During his long public career, Jefferson was frequently accused of being an atheist by his enemies. There was a certain plausibility about the charge because he had spent several years in France, spoke and read French fluently, and was a good friend to many of the French reformers who were considered atheists. During the bitter presidential campaign of 1800, Jefferson was widely attacked by the Federalist press as being a "French infidel" who did not observe the Sabbath. The Federalist preachers warned that electing a "deist or infidel" to the presidency would be "no less than rebellion against God" and would end in the destruction of the churches and a reign of infamy. Jefferson defended himself against this charge of atheism as being but one more "calumny" from his political opponents.[1]

Years later, Jefferson wrote to John Adams that he could never be an atheist and asserted that Calvin was the atheist or at least worshiped a demonic God. Calvinistic sects, he continued, gave "a great handle to atheism by their general dogma that proof of God depended on revelation" and not reason. Five-sixths of the present world, Jefferson wrote, had never accepted the Christian revelation of God, and many thinking Christians had been repulsed by the dogmatic sects into believing in atheism. It was those narrow Christians who accused him of atheism who were the real atheists, Jefferson insisted. He was a real Christian in the sense of believing and following the simple teachings of Jesus.[2]

Adams, for his part, had little patience with French atheism. Although he answered Adams mildly, Jefferson never consented to the vilification of the French atheists and did not agree that either their character or their teachings were immoral. He knew them to be honorable men. Those reacting against traditional religion in Protestant countries, he observed, had generally turned to Deism but in Roman Catholic countries to atheism. Jefferson pointed out to Adams that there was not as great a difference between French atheism and Adams's own liberal theism as Adams supposed. Both the atheism of Catholic liberals and the theism of Protestant reformers, he wrote, "agreed in the order of the existing system of Nature, but the one supposed it from eternity, the other as having begun in time by God."[3]

Most modern scholars of the Enlightenment agree with Jefferson that the repressive power of the Roman Catholic church in France helped engender a more virulent opposition and criticism by intellectuals there that resulted in a movement toward atheism; whereas in England, where religious reform had already taken place, a more open and less hostile discussion of religion was possible. In France, the Catholic church was rich and powerful and had little tolerance for other beliefs.

The first French radicals, such as Voltaire, followed English deists in believing in God and natural religion and in advocating a reformation of the established church in France such as had taken place in the Church of England. The flavor of the religious fervor of Voltaire, and proof that he was not an atheist, is shown in an experience quoted by Peter Gay. Voltaire invited an old friend to go up on a hill with him to watch a sunrise. There he knelt and prayed: "I believe in you, Powerful God, I believe! As for monsieur the Son and madame His Mother, that's a different story." As time went on, the conflict over religion in France sharpened. Other French writers, such as Diderot and d'Holbach, went beyond Voltaire, extending their opposition to all of Christianity and any belief in God, which they blamed for the superstitions, exploitations, and sufferings of man.[4]

While Jefferson and the French atheists shared some of the same ideas, study of Jefferson's religious beliefs and their sources supports his contention that he was not an atheist and was relatively little influenced by the French radicals. The influence was rather the other way, for Jefferson was held in high esteem by French reformers. Similar elements in Jefferson's religion and that of the French revolutionaries came, instead, from the common source of the English deists.[5]

Jefferson Was a Deist

To most religious people, including Jefferson's enemies, there was little difference between being atheist, deist, or infidel. All were suspected of being nonbelievers, opponents of Christianity, and dangerous to society. Jefferson vigorously defended himself against the charge of being atheist or deist in this derogatory sense. "The priests," he complained, "have ascribed to me anti-religious sentiments of their own fabric. They wished him to be thought atheist, deist, or devil, who could advocate freedom from their religious dictations."[6]

But in the intellectual sense of being one who believed in the Deity, as opposed to the atheist who did not, Jefferson was a staunch deist.[7] His religious thought is steeped in the ideas of the English deists, Baron Herbert of Cherbury, Charles Blount, Matthew Tindal, John Toland, and Conyers Middleton.[8] His own religious notes and comments indicate a special debt to Lord Bolingbroke and Joseph Priestley, whom he had "read over and over." They formed "the basis of my own faith," he wrote to Adams.[9] From these favorite deist writers Jefferson drew authority for his preference for a religion based on reason rather than supernatural revelation or mystical faith, his fondness for historical study of religion and the Bible, his belief in natural law rather than miracles, and his conviction that medieval mysticism was a corruption of the original teachings of Christ.[10]

Jefferson adopted and adapted these main tenets of English deism in the light of his own experiences and used them as the framework upon which he built his own ideas of God, his nature, and his purpose for man and the world. Jefferson was enthusiastic about the intellectual deist interpretation of God and religion. Such beliefs, he thought, would save from atheism and loss of faith those thinking people who had "too hastily rejected" a belief in God and Christianity because of the bigotry of sectarian dogma. They would be more receptive to "the sublime doctrines of philanthropism and deism taught us by Jesus of Nazareth."[11]

God, Seen in the Creation

Belief in the existence of God was the most important element in the religion of a reasoning man, and Jefferson thought that he could prove this existence from God's creation. As he explained to Adams, "When the atheist descanted on the unceasing motion and circulation of matter through the animal, vegetable and mineral kingdoms, gifted with the power of reproduction; the theist, pointing 'to the heavens above, and to the earth beneath, and to the waters under the earth,' asked, if these did not proclaim a first cause possessing intelligence and power."

Continuing the discussion later with Adams, he pointed out, "The atheists say that it is more simple to believe at once in the eternal preexistence of the world, as it is now going on, and may forever go on by the principle of reproduction which we see and witness, than to believe in the eternal pre-existence of an ulterior cause, or Creator of the world, a Being whom we see not and know not." Jefferson gave this eloquent answer to the atheists: "I hold, on the contrary, that when we take a view of the universe; . . . the movements of the heavenly bodies, so exactly held in their courses by the balance of centrifugal and centripetal forces; the structure of our earth itself, with its distribution of lands, waters, and atmosphere; animal and vegetable bodies, each perfectly organized whether as insect, man or mammoth; it is impossible, I say, for the human mind not to believe, that there is in all this, design, cause and effect, up to an ultimate cause, a Fabricator of all things from matter and motion."[12]

These words of Jefferson extolling the design and order of nature reflect the enthusiasm he had caught from Newton and his Enlightenment heroes for the wonders that science and knowledge were revealing about the natural world. In his study notes, for example, Jefferson copied approvingly from Bolingbroke, "Modern discoveries in astronomy have presented the works of god to us in

a more noble scene." Researching the deists' "first cause" argument
for God, Jefferson copied a long passage from Claude Helvétius
contending that "the order and movement" of the universe in all
its marvelous complexity suggested "an unknown force and cause
of that which is" which men "give the name of God."[13] It is significant that, for Jefferson and the deists, the more they learned by
science of the world of nature, the stronger grew their belief in
God, the Creator of it all. Evidence of Jefferson's belief in God is
seen in his many references to "God," "Deity," "Almighty,"
"Supreme Being," "Creator," "Fabricator," "Intelligent and Powerful Agent," "Common Father," "Giver of Life," "Holy Author of
our Religion," "Infinite Power," "Supreme Ruler," etc. Healey has
counted twenty-six different terms used by Jefferson for God.[14]

Jefferson and the deists believed in God as necessary to explain
the first cause and beginnings of the universe. They also found
evidence of God in the perfect outcome of everything in creation,
what Jefferson termed "final causes"; that is, "that the eye was made
to see and the ear to hear, and not that we see because we have
eyes, and hear because we have ears." For Jefferson, there was so
much intelligence and planning evident in creation that it was
impossible not to believe in God.[15]

God, the Creator of Man

Jefferson saw the handiwork of God not only in the beauties and
perfections of nature but in the highest traits of man, which were
also, he believed, the creation of God and revealed his planning
and forethought. Jefferson and the Enlightenment reformers were
even more interested in the world of human society than they were
in the world of nature, and it was their hope and belief that the
perfection which science was revealing in God's natural creation
was also implicit in his human creation and would, by proper social
and political reforms, be brought to fruition. Their political and
social convictions were thus based upon their religious belief that
God had created man with a particular nature. The Jeffersonian
philosophy of human rights, which was the basis of the American
and French revolutions, depended upon a deist conviction that God
had made man with certain rights, hungers, and worth which were

above and beyond the power of men or governments to bestow or withhold.

"The God who gave us life, gave us liberty at the same time: the hand of force may destroy, but cannot disjoin them," Jefferson wrote. It was the "Creator" who, by "the laws of nature," entitled people to "life, liberty, and the pursuit of happiness." The hunger for freedom and equal rights established by God in creating man appertained not only to his body, and hence his political and social rights, but even more to his mind and soul, and thus his religious rights.[16]

Man's moral conduct was especially important in establishing just and peaceable human society. In the human conscience or moral faculty, Jefferson saw evidence of God's foresight and providence, present in all cultures and societies. Man's reason, which distinguished him from other aspects of creation, was also seen by Jefferson as a gift from the Creator.[17]

Jefferson thus found traces of God and evidences of his foresight and provision for man's best interests in the human characteristics of freedom, sociability, conscience, morality, and reason created in man from the beginning by God.

One God, Not Three

As one might expect from his belief in deism and his emphasis upon reason in religion, Jefferson was opposed to the Christian doctrine of the Trinity. He referred to the belief sarcastically as "an unintelligible proposition of Platonic mysticisms that three are one, and one is three; and yet one is not three, and the three are not one."[18] "I had never sense enough to comprehend the Trinity," he wrote in refusing to be godfather for a friend's child, "and it has always appeared to me that comprehension must precede assent." In the Episcopalian baptismal service he would have been required to profess publicly his belief in the Trinity.[19]

Jefferson was incensed against Trinitarian Christianity because he regarded it as a relapse from the true "religion of Jesus founded in the Unity of God into unintelligible polytheism," he wrote Jared Sparks, a minister friend. To James Smith, Jefferson expressed the belief that it was the emphasis by Christianity upon "the unity of the Supreme Being which gave it triumph over the polytheism of

the ancient" religions and their immoral and all too human divin-
ities. He regretted the subsequent growth of Trinitarian Christianity, which he called "the hocus-pocus phantasm of a God like
another Cerberus, with one body and three heads." Over the centuries, the pure, "primitive deism" of Jesus had been changed and
degraded by the church, Jefferson believed.[20]

Plato was one of the earliest philosophers who was used to corrupt
the pure Unitarianism of Jesus, in Jefferson's disparaging view:
"Plato's foggy visions have furnished a basis for endless systems of
mystical theology."[21] Jefferson was probably led by his reading of
Priestley, who quoted Saint Augustine and Constantine as both
saying that Plato was the source of their knowledge of the Incar-
nation of God in Christ. Priestley explained that early Christian
philosophers had "confounded" Plato's idea of the Logos, or Word,
with that found in the Gospel of John, "making of it a second
person in the Trinity, than which no two things can be more
different."[22]

Jefferson adopted and elaborated on Priestley's explanation of
Logos in a letter to Adams in which he quoted the Greek of the
Logos passage of John, chapter 1, and translated it to mean: "In
the beginning God existed, and reason (or mind) was with God,
and that mind was God. All things were created by it." This text
showed, Jefferson argued, that Jesus taught "that the world was
created by the supreme, intelligent being." Later Christians, in
order to make sense out of their "mistranslation" of Logos to mean
"word or speech" "undertook to make of this articulation a second
pre-existing being, and ascribe to him, and not to God, the creation
of the universe."[23]

Jefferson engaged in considerable research into early Christianity
from his extensive library. He mentioned William Enfield's summary of religion and philosophy as being useful and said that he
had read Priestley's *Corruptions of Christianity* over and over. These
readings strengthened his belief in deism and Unitarianism. He
took approving notes, for example, about the "Sabellians" and
"Socinians" who were regarded as heretics by early Christians
because of their Unitarian beliefs.[24] He read that Priestley spoke of
Justin Martyr as being the first church father who mentioned Jesus
as the Son of God when he wrote to a philosophical Roman emperor
an apology for Christianity in which he compared Christ, the Son

of God, to Mercury, Jupiter's son, "his interpreter, and the instruc-
tor of all men," and called them both the "*Logos* of God." From
his research into early Christian beliefs, Jefferson concluded, "The
Trinity is nowhere expressly declared by any of the earliest fathers,
and was never affirmed or taught by the Church before the Council
of Nice."[25]

As the result of his study of church history, Jefferson picked out
Athanasius, the bishop of Alexandria who vigorously championed
Trinitarianism against other groups of Christians, and who was
responsible for the Trinitarian emphasis of the Nicene and Athanasian creeds, as the chief villain who burdened Christianity with
this "metaphysical insanity." It seems evident that it was the Creed
of Athanasius, which was in the Anglican Book of Common Prayer,
that convinced Jefferson that the doctrine of the Trinity was "incomprehensible, unintelligible, and insane." Three-fourths of the
Athanasian Creed seeks to explain "one God in Trinity, and Trinity
in Unity," using such terms as "confounding the Persons"; "divid-
ing the Substance"; "the Godhead of Father, Son, and Holy Ghost";
"Glory equal, Majesty co-eternal"; "Father, Son and Holy Ghost
uncreate, incomprehensible, and eternal"; "Father made of none,
Son begotten, Holy Ghost preceding"; "in this Trinity none is afore,
or after, or greater, or less." It is not surprising that the Athanasian
Creed was dropped from later prayer books for lack of use.[26]

Jefferson also condemned the teachings of Calvin and his burning
of "poor Servetus" at the stake because he would not subscribe to
Calvin's Trinitarian doctrines. "The Trinitarian idea triumphed in
the church's creeds," he wrote to James Smith, "not by the force
of reason but by the word of the fanatic Athanasius, and grew in
the blood of thousands and thousands of martyrs." Jefferson's
vehemence in his opposition to orthodox Christian Trinitarianism
indicates the strength of religious controversy in his time. It should
be remembered that these views were expressed in his private correspondence with personal friends and were not intended to be
made public. Jefferson never used his public position and influence
to advocate his religious ideas. "I write with freedom," he told
Smith, "because, while I claim a right to believe in one God, I yield
as freely to others that of believing in three. Both religions, I find,
make honest men, and that is the only point society has any right
to look to."[27]

Jefferson Was a Theist

It is a moot question whether Jefferson was a deist or a theist in his belief about God. He has been called both. Part of the confusion comes from the fact that the terms *deist* and *theist* are often used interchangeably, though they had distinct, if varying, meanings.[28]

Early in the Enlightenment, the term *theism* was used to denote the ideas of those who believed in God as the Creative Power behind the universe, in contrast in atheism, which denoted the ideas of those who did not. The term is derived from the Greek word for God, *theos*.[29] Jefferson, accordingly, used *theist* to describe one who believed in a "first cause" behind the creation, in contrast to the atheist who instead believed in the "unceasing motion of matter." Later in the movement, the term *deism* came to describe the ideas of those who believed in a great, unknown Power behind the creation, and the term *theism* was left for the thoughts of the medieval theologians and those who believed in orthodox, revealed religion. Jefferson, thus, employed the term *deism* for the belief in one God, Creator of man and the universe, in contrast to orthodox, Christian, Trinitarian theism. He even went so far as to characterize Jesus' teachings as "pure deism," and the teachings of the Jews as "degraded deism," though both might more properly be termed theistic.[30]

To be theologically accurate, the distinction between *deist* and *theist,* as it finally developed in philosophy, was based on whether man could know the attributes of God, and whether God continued to be active in His creation. The deist believed in a Creator of the universe who had determined the scientific laws by which it operated but did not interfere in the operation of those laws. The deist also held that, although something could be sensed about the greatness, intelligence, and wonder of the Creator from the creation, there was much that was beyond the comprehension of man, particularly about the characteristics and final purposes of the Creator. The theist believed that man could know God and His nature and purposes not only by reasoning from the creation but by faith, devotion, and mysticism as well and that the Creator continued to guide and direct his creation. Immanuel Kant made the distinction, "The deist believes that there is a God; the theist believes that there is a living God."[31]

Pursuing the analogy of the seventeenth-century deists' concept of the "Watchmaker God" may sharpen the distinction. They argued that the universe which Newton revealed was like an intricate, marvelous watch ticking away in space according to the laws of science. From the evidence of the watch, which man could observe, he could deduce a "Watchmaker" who had made the universe. Man could form a few guesses as to the nature of the Watchmaker from the watch, but essentially men knew very little about him who had made the great watch of creation. The atheist argued that man was not justified in deducing a Maker. The watch might always have existed, and it was enough to be absorbed with the watch itself. The theist agreed that there was a Watchmaker behind the universe and further argued that the Watchmaker had not just created the watch and then left it to run by itself but was continually at work, winding up the watch, tinkering with it, and improving it. Furthermore, man was able to communicate with and learn from the Watchmaker himself.

Jefferson's Theism

In the light of these distinctions, how should Jefferson's ideas about God be classified? He called himself a theist in opposition to the atheist. He followed and promulgated the ideas of the English deists, particularly their belief in a Creator of the universe, known by reason, in opposition to orthodox Christian theism based on revelation, theology, and mysticism. He had little sympathy with metaphysical speculation and was more concerned with practical things that he could learn about the "watch" of creation than with speculations about things that no man could know. He tended to dismiss any knowledge except that which came by reason. He frequently reflected his deistic readings and wrote that man could not know God: "He is far above our power." On another occasion he argued that Jesus never "defined God and we have neither words nor ideas adequate to that definition."[32] Jefferson may thus well be called a deist.

He did, however, reflect the philosophical views of the theists, and may be properly called a theist himself, although his library reflects few theist authors.[33] He did not know the German writers and lived too early for the later English theistic philosophers. His theistic views, then, were largely his own.

Often, when Jefferson was arguing that the creation indicated a "first cause, possessing intelligence and power, power in the production, and intelligence in the design," he also went on to argue that the universe indicated power and intelligence in the "constant preservation of the system." In his eloquent statement to John Adams of the evidence that he found in the heavenly bodies and in the earth, with all its intricate forms of life, of "an ultimate cause, a Fabricator of all things," Jefferson went on also to affirm his belief in "their Preserver and Regulator and their regenerator into new and other forms. We see, too, evident proofs of the necessity of a superintending power to maintain the universe in its course and order." He argued from the disappearance of some stars and the extinction of some species that God must "renovate and restore" his creation constantly else "all should be reduced to a shapeless chaos."[34] Jefferson thus clearly indicated that he was a theist.

His theistic views most likely came from his own religious nature. For all his leaning toward an intellectual religion, he also had a deeply devotional side. He loved the Psalms and liturgy of his own Anglican church and practiced private devotions before he slept at night. He believed firmly in a God of providence who was active in his world and was guiding human affairs. His long struggles in the political arena for man's betterment were supported by his belief in a God who guided the affairs of nations. He wrote to a political friend: "We are not in a world ungoverned by the laws and the power of a superior agent. Our efforts are in his hand, and directed by it; and he will give them their effect in his own time."[35]

Jefferson's public addresses are studded with references to "that overruling Providence which governs the destinies of men and nations" and "watches over our country's freedom and welfare." In his second inaugural address, Jefferson expressed his belief in "the Being in whose hands we are, who led our fathers, as Israel of old, from their native land and planted them in a country flowing with all the necessaries and comforts of life." God's Providence, he continued, had "covered our infancy and His wisdom and power" had guided "our riper years." He prayed that God "will enlighten the minds" of America's leaders and "guide their councils." Jefferson, it would seem, chose the best of both deistic and theistic beliefs to make his own.[36]

Attributes of God

One of the characteristics of theism was that it maintained that the attributes of God could be known from evidences seen in the creation and in the spirit of man created by God, as well as from knowing God directly, whereas deism insisted that the Creator was too far beyond man to be fully understood. Deism further distrusted the intuitive and mystical approach to God. While Jefferson, to the end of his days, shared this deistic point of view, he was not willing to accept the idea that God was unknowable, and he believed that he could detect many of the attributes of God from the creation, both natural and human.

Attributes Seen in Creation. Both the theists and deists agreed upon certain attributes that Newton's marvelous universe revealed about the Creator, and no one pointed to these with more conviction and eloquence than Jefferson. He was intrigued with the "design, skill and power" with which the world of nature was "fabricated and regulated," indicating an "intelligent and powerful agent" behind the creation, he said. Jefferson found evidence of his belief in the creative power of God's reason in the Bible when he translated the "Logos" of God creating all things as found in the Gospel of John to mean the "reason or mind of the Supreme, Intelligent Being." Jefferson also found support for his idea of God as the intelligent, all-powerful cause of creation in the theological arguments of the church fathers proving God's omnipotence. It was from the evidence of intelligence and design in nature that Jefferson and the Enlightenment deists gained their great admiration for the human faculty of reason. Since the creation was made and governed by reason and law, it was by the exercise of his God-given faculty of reason that man could learn the secrets of the universe and improve his social and political institutions.[37]

In the world of nature, so marvelously fashioned by its Creator, Jefferson and the deists saw not only reason and intelligence in the earth's plan and design but wonder and power in its tremendous forces and awesome grandeur. It was perhaps because of this aspect of his belief in God that the Psalms appealed to Jefferson so much.

He praised Psalm 148 over the best of classical literature for the "sublimity of its conceptions of the majesty of God" in a discussion with Adams.[38] In his youth, Jefferson was fond of similar poetic descriptions of the wonders of God in nature's beauty which he found in English literature. A friend recalled being entertained at Monticello most of the night reading poetry and imbibing from the punch bowl.[39]

Perhaps influenced by his love of nature, Jefferson often wrote of the evidences of a benevolent, wise, and good God that he found in the works of the Creator. Both in his public and private statements, he frequently referred to the Providence that loves and cares for men. He sometimes varied his words by speaking of "the favor of Heaven" interchangeably with that of God or Providence. In his first inaugural address, Jefferson spoke of God's love and care when he referred to "an overruling providence, which by all its dispensations proves that it delights in the happiness of man here, and his greater happiness hereafter."[40]

At different times, Jefferson enumerated the blessings that he believed came from the good God. He wished his old friends John and Abigail Adams "safe deliverances, life, health, and happiness," as well as God's love and protection. To another old friend he wrote, "God bless you all, and send you a safe deliverance." To a political ally he replied, "The Lord have you and all good men and true in His holy keeping." In his second annual message as president he listed God's blessings to the country, "peace and friendship abroad; law, order, and religion at home; good affection with our Indian neighbors; our burdens lightened, yet our income sufficient, and the produce of the year great."[41]

As a plantation farmer, Jefferson was conscious of the Creator as the source of the bounty of the crops, and as a lawyer he wrote repeatedly of God as the source of man's ownership of the land.[42] In many of Jefferson's statements of God's blessings bestowed upon man are echoes of his great summary of the fundamental rights of "life, liberty, and the pursuit of Happiness" given to man by his Creator. Reflecting his long concern with governmental and world affairs, Jefferson frequently spoke of God leading the nation in peace and protecting it from war.[43]

Far from believing that God was unknowable or unapproachable, Jefferson did not hesitate to seek and acknowledge God's guidance for the nation, for himself, and for his fellow statesman on many occasions. Jefferson, like many Americans, had a consciousness of God guiding and blessing America in a special way, and he drew parallels between God leading Israel through the Red Sea to the Promised Land and God guiding "our forefathers" across the oceans to America.[44]

Jefferson went beyond his deistic teachers in attributing love, care, concern, guidance, providence, protection, and wisdom to God, the Creator of the universe, but he agreed with them in stressing the might and power of God. He frequently referred to the Creator as "Almighty God" or "Almighty Being." He also alluded to "that Infinite Power which rules the destinies of the universe" and to "the Supreme Ruler of the Universe."[45] This belief in God's guidance gave Jefferson a confidence which lesser leaders lacked.

It is instructive to note that, among the references by Jefferson to the different blessings that a "benevolent Being" had bestowed on man, it is difficult to find any reference to evils or sorrows. Just as Jefferson refused to admit the existence of sin in man, so he refused to admit the existence of any evil in God's good creation. For example, in discussing epidemics of deadly yellow fever, Jefferson spoke of the goodness of Providence that "lessened the number of usual victims." Even while depicting a depressing picture of the last years of human life, he found evidence of God's goodness to people in the way old age reconciled them to death. He compared old age to the experience of "the horse in his mill plodding round and round the same path," as people lost more of "their faculties of enjoyment and their sensibilities" until they were glad to abandon the effort of living. He remembered a "very old friend saying he was tired of pulling off his shoes and stockings at night, and putting them on again in the morning."[46]

In his determined conviction that God's creation was the best of all possible worlds, Jefferson was true to the Enlightenment writers who had so greatly influenced him. In his commonplace book, for example, he copied approvingly this passage from his favorite, Bolingbroke: "Since infinite wisdom established it, the system of the universe must be necessarily the best of all possible systems. Questions of evil have been answered in many instances by new discoveries."[47]

The deists, who glorified God in nature, seem always to have viewed nature in the gentleness of the sunset and never in the violence of a storm, although they stressed the power of the universe as indicative of God's attributes. Perhaps the fact that most of them were men of wealth and leisure, protected from the harshness of nature and life, may be part of the explanation, along with a doctrinaire bias against any religion that featured appeasement of an angry god.[48] Jefferson, however, was a man of the country who lived at Monticello in full view of the mountain storms, but it was his father, not himself, who had gone into the frontier to create a new home. Although Jefferson built his own home and worked his own land, it was always by directing the work of others. He also spent much of his life in various cities of the world and was protected by his position, comforts, and culture from a world of want and violence. Whatever the explanation, nature and God were good, and only man's social institutions evil, as Jefferson and the gentlemen of the Enlightenment viewed the world.

It was, therefore, a prominent part of Jefferson's beliefs that there were no evil attributes to be found in God. Religions that saw such attributes in life and in God were mistaken; worse yet, they were reverting to paganism and blaspheming God. This conviction was the real reason for Jefferson's strong aversion to the conservative sects. He believed, based on his readings, that the God of the Old Testament worshiped by the Jews who followed the teachings of Moses was "cruel, vindictive, capricious, and unjust" as well as "bloodthirsty and remorseless."[49]

Unfortunately, Jefferson and the men of the Enlightenment overlooked the high moral and religious peaks in the Old Testament. For example, in praising Jesus' teachings of the love of God and love of neighbor, they overlooked the fact that this idea was part of his Jewish heritage, learned as a child from the Old Testament.[50] Similarly, in praising God's justice, the Enlightenment failed to perceive that the earliest formulation of this attribute is to be found in Old Testament writings of the great prophets of the eighth century B.C. It is unfortunate that Jefferson did not include Hebrew among his many languages and never undertook a personal study of the Old Testament for himself, for he surely would have found an enthusiastic kinship with the prophets' ideal of justice.

Jefferson was one of the Enlightenment's most eloquent spokes-
men who maintained that the Creator of the universe and Ruler of
the destiny of man was a God of justice. During the struggle for
American independence he frequently appealed to the "even-handed
justice" of God. When he was considering the suffering of the slaves,
Jefferson found hope in "a God of justice who will awaken to their
distress and, by his exterminating thunder, right the things of this
world." He sometimes wrote that none but God was just enough
to judge people, especially in matters of faith, and strongly condemned religious bigots who "usurping the judgment-seat of God,
condemn all others to his wrath." One of Jefferson's favorite beliefs
was that the Creator ruled the world of nature by scientific laws
and ruled the world of man by moral laws of justice.[51]

Jefferson thus found many of the most important attributes of
God, from intelligence, might, and power to benevolence, guidance,
and justice, indicated by his creation of the world of nature.

Attributes Seen in Man. Dovetailing with this philosophy of God
and life which Jefferson built upon the qualities that he found in
the creation were similar attributes of God that he saw created in
man. Counterparts of the Creator's wisdom, goodness, perfection,
and foresight could also be found in the human creation, and Jefferson's writings on human qualities reflect his concept of the nature
of the God who gave man these characteristics. Jefferson frequently
referred to God as "the common Creator of man" and "the Father
of all the members of the human family." If God was the Father of
man, it followed that man had a moral inheritance from God, and
that God, the Creator of man, was the source of man's aspirations
and finest qualities. These qualities, in turn, revealed more of the
nature of God.[52]

Man's hunger for freedom of body, mind, and soul was divinely
inspired. "The holy author of our religion, and lord both of body
and mind, chose not to propagate it by coercions on either, but
created the mind free," Jefferson declared.[53] Thus, the multitudi-
nous variety of the species and the precious individuality of humanity meant that the freedom to develop uniquely was a sacred quality
created by God which men must respect and encourage.

Man's reason was highly valued by Jefferson because, like the intelligence evident in the laws of nature, it reflected God's character. Reason was the quality by which man could understand the intelligence of God behind nature's mighty creation and the meaning of human life. It was, Jefferson stated, "the only oracle which God has given us to determine truth."[54] So from man's search for truth and freedom, guided by his reason, Jefferson looked back to a wise, benevolent, purposeful God who was directing man for his own good.

The human conscience was especially regarded by Jefferson as evidence of a wise and good God. "Man was destined for society," he reasoned. "Therefore, he was endowed with a sense of right and wrong, as much a part of his nature as hearing, seeing, feeling." Since man's sense of justice came from God, it revealed the moral nature of God. One of the chief indictments of the Enlightenment against traditional religion was that its teachings of eternal punishment or salvation by faith rather than virtuous deeds belittled a true sense of God's moral justice.[55]

However, it was in the life, character, and teachings of the greatest man of all, Jesus Christ, that Jefferson saw the highest attributes of God. He often praised the "pure, simple" teachings of Jesus of "love for one only God, and He all perfect." He saw the ministry of Jesus as an attempt to reform the Jewish religion of the evil attributes of God taught by Moses and to substitute those of the "perfect Supreme Being," which, Jefferson said, Jesus took from "the best qualities of the human head and heart, wisdom, justice, and goodness, and added to them power and infinite perfection." In the moral teachings of Christ, Jefferson found "the most sublime morality which has ever fallen from the lips of man."[56] These teachings revealed the highest attributes of God, in Jefferson's religion.

Conclusions

It can be seen that Jefferson was both more radical and more conservative in his theology of God than many people have supposed. Far from being an atheist, as many of his opponents declared, he had a strong belief in God and his guidance of the world.

He was greatly influenced by the English deists and developed a wide range of concepts about the nature of God based on the qualities that he saw in God's creation, both natural and human. Beginning with the ideas of the deists about a First Cause and mighty Originator of a universe based on law and order, Jefferson proclaimed a God of skill and design, power and might, wisdom and benevolence. But he soon went beyond deistic qualities of God to the more expanded ones of the theists, such as seeing not only a Creator in the world of nature but also a Sustainer and Director. From there, Jefferson moved on to a firm conviction of the guidance of God over the affairs of man and of the goodness of God in all human experiences. From a belief in the design of creation, Jefferson proceeded to a belief in God's design for the human world, citing such examples as God's providing man with a conscience in order to make society possible and providing old age as a preparation for death. In all things he saw God's goodness and firmly refused to attribute any evil qualities to God or creation.

Jefferson's deistic beliefs have been attacked by modern critics on several grounds. Daniel Boorstin has argued that Jefferson was casting God in his own image when he called Him "Architect and Builder." He states, "The talents which men in eighteenth-century America called Godlike were those which they most wanted for themselves." Their task was to build a new civilization in the wilderness, and their view of nature was limited by a situation of limitless resources. The deists' idea of God as Supreme Designer was no more valid than the Puritan concept of an Omnipotent Sovereign which they attacked.[57] Granted that any idea of God is limited and different occasions teach new duties, the passage of time has not canceled the splendor of Jefferson's vision of the Creator of the universe nor negated the tendency of men in using the natural and human resources of that universe to see the handiwork of God.

Despite his intellectualism, there was a surprising conservativism in Jefferson's beliefs about God. He had an Anglican reverence for God and Jesus Christ and a fondness for worship and private devotions. He believed firmly not only in the existence of God but in the continuing, guiding presence of God in the lives of individuals and the nation. His great-grandson was quite correct in calling Jefferson "a conservative Unitarian."[58] Jefferson was radical, however, in his outspoken attacks upon traditional Christian Trinitarianism. He was sharply impatient with mystical ideas and philosophical speculations. He proclaimed his tolerance for religious differences, but at times his impartiality wore´thin, as when he declared that "the Presbyterian clergy are the loudest, most intolerant, tyrannical and ambitious of all sects," and he expressed the hope that "Unitarianism would become the general religion of the United States."[59]

Jefferson's critical statements about religion came from some of his deepest convictions, the need for a new emphasis upon belief in one God, the Creator of the universe, and upon the simple teachings of Jesus, which, he felt, had been too long obscured by passion and bigotry. He wanted to "do away with the incomprehensible jargon of the Trinitarian arithmetic, that three are one and one is three and knock down the artificial scaffolding reared to mask from view the structure of Jesus' doctrines," but only so that people would be "truly and worthily His disciples." Jefferson was convinced, from much unpleasant personal experience, that orthodox Christianity, with its emphasis on faith and emotion, was dangerous. "Once surrendering his reason," he observed, "man has no remaining guard against monstrous absurdities and, like a ship without a rudder, the mind becomes a wreck." It should also be noted, in considering Jefferson's energetic iconoclasm, that he never used his power as a public figure to foster his own religious ideas and steadfastly refused to publish them.[60] He sought to avoid the argumentation and debate about religion that his intellectual ideas provoked from more orthodox people but did not always succeed. He did, however, become a champion of the right of religious dissent and a hero for later Unitarians.[61]

It is evident that Jefferson's belief in God and his habit of private prayer strengthened his personal life and his belief in a moral purpose for human affairs. Behind his political philosophy were his religious convictions about God and the characteristics that God had given to man and his world. Jefferson believed in freedom and equality, for example, because people had been "endowed by their Creator" with these traits, and he believed that men could govern themselves well in society because such was God's purpose. It was Jefferson's faith in God and the moral purposes underlying human life that gave him courage and purpose as a national and world leader, strengthened him in times of discouragement and attack, and gave his life and the causes he championed enduring meaning.

CHAPTER VIII

JEFFERSON'S RELIGIOUS
IDEAS OF JESUS CHRIST

J efferson was so interested in the teachings of Jesus Christ that while he was president, he made a study of the New Testament. He told friends of relaxing in the evening by studying the Bible after "getting through" necessary state papers and letters. The discovery of this work and Jefferson's later revision some years after his death resulted in publication of what has been called "Jefferson's Bible."[1]

Besides these two studies, Jefferson wrote one extended essay and many shorter accounts to friends about Jesus Christ. It is thus possible to be more certain about Jefferson's Christology than one can, for example, about his belief in immortality, about which he wrote sparingly.

Jefferson's Writings on Christ

Jefferson called the first of his works on Jesus Christ a "Syllabus of an Estimate of the Merit of the Doctrines of Jesus, Compared with Those of Others." In this study, he compared the moral teachings of "the most esteemed of the sects of ancient philosophy, of the Jews, and of Jesus." Jefferson became interested in making such a comparison of the great moral teachers of the ages from reading his friend Priestley's work *Socrates and Jesus Compared,* which concluded that Socrates and Jesus were both great moral teachers and heroic spirits, but that Jesus was greater because he taught people of all ages and classes. Writing to congratulate his friend on this work, Jefferson stated he hoped to see a study comparing the ethics of such ancient philosophers as "Epicurus, Socrates, Cicero, and Seneca with the degraded ethics of the Jews and the benevolent and sublime life, character, and doctrines of Jesus." His "Syllabus" was the result, although he never had time to turn it into the full book he envisioned.[2]

Jefferson also wrote this statement of his ideas about Jesus' teachings in order to defend himself against the attacks made upon his religion in the recent presidential campaign and to prove that he was "a Christian in the only sense in which Christ wished any one to be, sincerely attached to his doctrines in preference to all others." He made copies of the "Syllabus" for Rush, Priestley, and a few other trusted friends, as well as for members of his cabinet and his surviving daughters. He even consented to having it published in a British theological magazine, providing it was done anonymously.[3]

The second of the extended studies of Jesus Christ that he made was headed "The Philosophy of Jesus of Nazareth" and was, according to Jefferson, "an abstract from the Evangelists of whatever has the stamp of the eloquence and fine imagination of Jesus." It was made, he wrote, "by cutting the texts out of the book, and arranging them on the pages of a blank book, in a certain order of time or subject. A more beautiful or precious morsel of ethics I have never seen."[4] This work has been lost to posterity except for the title page and a few sheets which turned up at a book auction in 1934 and the New Testaments cut up by Jefferson which were given to the University of Virginia by his descendants. Fortunately, when Randall was writing his biography of Jefferson, he heard of Jefferson's "Bible" and published a description of it, along with a list of its contents, which was furnished him by Jefferson's grandson George Wythe Randolph. Jefferson briefly considered publishing this work as a simplified New Testament for instructing the Indians in Christianity. He quickly changed his mind, for there was great excitement when the rumor got out that Jefferson the infidel had been converted and would publish a book on religion.[5] He was "unwilling to draw on myself a swarm of insects whose buzz is more disquieting than their bite," he wrote to a friend. "The Philosophy of Jesus" was probably only in English since Jefferson wrote of doing it hastily in "two or three nights only" and that he intended later to "add to my little book the Greek, Latin and French texts, in columns side by side. Later, in his retirement, Jefferson carried out his intention, for that is exactly the format his second version presents.[6]

Although Jefferson wrote to like-minded friends about his New Testament studies, he was so reticent about his religion that even his family did not know of his interest in studying the New Testament until after his death when a more elaborate version, bound

in red morocco with gold lettering, was found in his library by his
grandson. This second edition of the Gospels, which was entitled
"The Life and Morals of Jesus of Nazareth," might also have been
lost to posterity had it not been for the bibliographic detective work
of Cyrus Adler when he was librarian of the Smithsonian Institution. Learning of the existence of a "Jefferson Bible" by finding the
mutilated New Testaments used by Jefferson, he eventually located
the work in the possession of one of Jefferson's great-granddaugh-
ters and arranged for its purchase by the United States National
Museum. A limited edition exactly reproducing the work, red
morocco binding, gold edges, and all, was printed. Several other
editions have since been published.[7]

A study of Jefferson's two versions of the New Testament indicates that he emphasized the moral teachings of Jesus and avoided
the incidents and declarations in the New Testament which suggest
Jesus' divinity, which was his avowed intention in making his
edition.[8] If the contents of "The Philosophy of Jesus" and "The
Morals of Jesus" are compared (see Appendix), it will be found
that they do not differ greatly. The second version is longer, but
much of the extra length was caused by including the texts in four
languages. Jefferson added a few more of the parables and teachings
of Jesus when he redid his editing. Foote believes he improved the
continuity also.[9] In both versions he deftly wove the texts from
different Gospels together into one account, leaving a bewildering
textual path to follow but making a smoothly flowing edition of his
own emphasis. A detailed list of all the verses in the four Gospels
of the New Testament showing which ones Jefferson used in each
version of his New Testament and which ones he omitted is given
in the Appendix. This material supplements and supports the beliefs
about Jesus Christ that are revealed by Jefferson's letters and other
writings.

Jefferson and Biblical Criticism

In his studies of the New Testament, Jefferson's aim was to be a
constructive critic. Part of this task was destructive, as his opponents
were quick to point out. Unlike the fierce iconoclast, Thomas Paine,
however, Jefferson never publicly attacked anyone's religion, and
he carefully protected his own children from the destructiveness of

his own ideas. Privately discussing religion with interested friends, though, he was just as vehement as Paine or Rousseau in separating what he called "the grain from the chaff," "the gold from the dross," and "the diamond from the dunghill" in biblical passages. It was necessary, Jefferson wrote, "to knock down the mysticisms, fancies and falsehoods by which the religion-builders have distorted and deformed the doctrines of Jesus and get back to the pure and simple doctrines He inculcated." Reflecting the influence of his Enlightenment readings, he argued that in order to free men from the oppressive power of the church it was necessary to destroy its false system.[10]

If Jefferson was critical of traditional religion and wanted to tear down the false, it was only so that something better might be erected in its place. He wanted to throw out the "rubbish" in the New Testament of "so much ignorance, absurdity, untruth, charlatanism and imposture" so that the "gold of fine imagination, correct morality and most lovely benevolence" might shine forth. When he rejected "mysticisms incomprehensible to the human mind fathered blasphemously on Him whom the special servants of the church claimed as their Founder, but who would disclaim them with the indignation which their caricatures of His religion so justly excite," it was in order to better behold "the outlines of a system of the most sublime morality which has ever fallen from the lips of man." Jefferson's preference for moral teachings, upon which all religions could agree, over "incomprehensible dogmas and mystifications" about which religions argue not only reflected his Enlightenment studies but his work as a practical statesman endeavoring to reform society.[11]

Jefferson's concept of Jesus as a moralist superior to any other that ever lived, which he stated repeatedly, was a change from his earlier ideas, for as a student he had copied approvingly from Bolingbroke that "a system of ethics collected from antient heathen moralists would be more full, entire and coherent than the ethics scattered about in the whole new-testament."[12] Jefferson's "Syllabus" comparing the ethics of Jesus with classical moralists may well have been his mature answer disproving Bolingbroke, for he used the same material but came to a different conclusion. By way of explanation for the lack of system decried by Bolingbroke, he noted that Jesus never wrote any of his teachings down and had no scribe to do it for him. The writing of his "life and doctrines fell on unlettered and ignorant men long after the events." Moreover, Jesus only had a short time to live and teach. Only "mutilated fragments" of his teachings survived, "still more disfigured by the corruptions of schismatizing followers." Despite these drawbacks, his "system of morals is the most perfect and sublime that has ever been taught by man." Ever after, Jefferson blamed Jesus' "ignorant biographers and corrupting followers" for any defects in his doctrines.[13]

Jefferson believed that people of "ultra-Christian sects raised the hue and cry of infidelity" against him because he was "not able to swallow their impious heresies" and the "absurdities of Athanasius, Calvin and Plato." Nevertheless, he thought that the people who were repelled by the "mysticisms, fancies and falsehoods of these distorted and deformed" interpretations of Jesus' doctrines might be saved from "infidelity" if they discovered Christ's ethics "in all the purity and simplicity in which it came from the lips of Jesus." Therefore, Jefferson sought to pare everything down to the "very words and pure doctrine of Jesus." He wanted to "restore primitive Christianity," that is, the first teachings of Jesus.[14]

Jefferson was seeking not only to rediscover the true teachings of Jesus by means of his biblical criticism but also to reveal the true person of Christ. By stripping away "the rags of imposture" depicting Jesus as a miracle worker and the immaterial divinity put upon him by his "ignorant followers" and revealing Jesus as a "great reformer and sublime moralist," Jefferson believed he might save other men of reason from "rashly revolting against Christianity and pronouncing its Founder an impostor."[15]

Even though his own preferences colored the enthusiasm with which he tossed aside as "rubbish" certain verses of the New Testament and treasured as "diamonds" other verses found beside them, Jefferson was a diligent student and had considerable research to support his choice of the most authentic elements in the New Testament. It was unfortunate that he did not read German and was unaware of much of the early research into biblical criticism by German scholars, but he did possess the works of Enlightenment authors on the Bible and had absorbed their views and techniques of biblical criticism.

Modern scholars of the Enlightenment have noted that it was characterized by a renewed interest in the study of history in order to understand better the existing political and social order and to develop a program of reform.[16] Jefferson enthusiastically shared this interest in history, as the contents of his library prove.[17] He also shared the Enlightenment's admiration for the classical age, particularly Cicero's republican Rome.[18] His study of ancient history and the Greek and Roman classics and his knowledge of Greek equipped Jefferson with the tools for New Testament criticism. His preference for reading the classics in the original Greek and his awareness of the misleading effects of translations has been noted by scholars. He studied philology, compiling vocabularies and grammars for American Indian languages, and was more aware than most people of the importance of textual study. His scholarly interest in the New Testament is shown by the fact that he included in his second version the Greek text as well as Latin, French, and English translations.[19]

From his studies of classical Greece and Rome, Jefferson had an extensive knowledge of ancient history, Roman life, classical literature, and mythology for the period covered by the New Testament. In discussing the New Testament account of the virgin birth of Jesus with John Adams, for example, he cited a similar account from Roman mythology of the miraculous birth of Minerva from the head of Jupiter. He also compared accounts of miraculous events in the book of Joshua with similar stories recounted by Livy and Tacitus. Because he had studied Roman law, he could discuss the legal grounds for the crucifixion of Christ. He thus had a considerable body of knowledge of the Greco-Roman world of the New Testament times upon which to base his estimate of the unique contributions of Christ as opposed to the pagan cultural materials of the first century which he rejected as superstition.[20] In using historical knowledge as a tool for biblical criticism, Jefferson not only followed the guidance of the Enlightenment critics but also used the method that has guided all later biblical research.[21] Jefferson's classical education stood him in good stead in his study of the New Testament. He also made good use of his knowledge of church history and the writings of the early church fathers and Greek philosophers in his library.[22] In a letter to Adams, for example, he mentions "the Platonists and Plotinists, the Stagyrites and Gamalielites, the Eclectics, the Gnostics and Scholastics."[23]

From his own studies and those of his friend Priestley, Jefferson gathered material to support his conviction that the philosophical and theological interpretations of Christianity were later additions to the original, simple teachings of Jesus. In Priestley's work *The Corruptions of Christianity,* which Jefferson "read over and over," he found evidence that "when heathens embraced Christianity, they mixed their former tenets and prejudice with it." Priestley delved into the works of Justin Martyr, Clement of Rome, Tertullian, Origen, and Irenaeus to prove his point. Priestley also pointed to the Logos passages in the New Testament as evidence of the influence of Plato's and Philo's Greek philosophy upon Christian thought.[24] It is not surprising, then, that Jefferson did not include the Logos section of the first chapter of the Gospel of John in either of his New Testament versions (see Appendix, section 1).

It is evident from studying Jefferson's writings and the authors in his library that he was influenced by Enlightenment thought both in his interest in biblical criticism and in the point of view and methods that he employed. Although the history of biblical criticism goes back at least to Origen's work on the corrupt text of the Septuagint version of the Old Testament and Jerome's work on the Vulgate Latin translation of the Bible, the Enlightenment, with its emphasis upon reason and the study of history, resulted in a new and more critical study of the Bible and religion. Descartes, Spinoza, Grotius, Ernesti, and Diderot were all Enlightenment writers studied by Jefferson who called for a critical and historical study of the Bible. By Jefferson's time the Enlightenment had developed the purposes and many of the techniques of modern biblical criticism, although much remained to be done in the way of increasing knowledge through archaeological excavations, textual research, and linguistic studies. Jefferson was familiar with the work of many of the pioneer scholars in the field of biblical criticism. Although he had neither the time nor the interest to become an expert in the field, he did use the techniques of criticism in his own studies of the Bible.[25]

For example, when he advised Peter Carr "to read the Bible as you would Livy or Tacitus" with the critical judgment of reason, and when he wrote to William Short that in reading the biographies of Jesus he "asked only what is granted in reading every other historian, such as Livy and Siculus," Jefferson was practicing the use of reason and the knowledge of history in biblical criticism that he had been taught by his study of Enlightenment authors. When he further maintained that he could separate the "vulgar ignorance, superstitions and fabrications" in the New Testament which came from Jesus' ignorant followers from Jesus' own "sublime ideas of the Supreme Being and precepts of the purest morality" by the "style and spirit which proved them genuine," he was employing a technique long used and later perfected by scholars in evaluating both the text and the meaning of the Bible, that of judging by style.[26]

In one aspect of biblical criticism only did Jefferson make a serious mistake and miss an opportunity to lay a scholarly foundation for his study of the New Testament: that was the method he used for editing the passages from the Gospels that dealt with the same materials when he formulated his two versions of the New Testament. Jefferson was influenced in making his New Testament synopses by similar work done previously by his two friends Charles Thomson and Joseph Priestley, both of whom sent him copies of "Harmonies of the Four Evangelists" which they had compiled. In these early harmonies of the Gospels, Jefferson and his friends took small parts of the life or teachings of Christ from each of the Gospel accounts, weaving them all together into one narrative in such a way as to avoid "long repetitions of the same transaction," as Jefferson explained.[27] The harmonies of later biblical critics consisted instead of arranging the same incidents or sayings of the four Gospels in parallel columns side by side (see harmony format, Appendix). Jefferson used four parallel columns, but in them he reproduced his own mosaic version in four different languages. It was only by minutely comparing the repetitious four Gospel accounts, passage by passage and word for word, in parallel columns in later harmonies that scholars were able to establish which were the earlier and more authentic parts of the New Testament and thus indicate the original figure of Jesus and the true words of Christ, for which Jefferson was seeking, with a greater degree of precision than he could.[28]

The task of untangling the earliest accounts of Christianity and the true words of Jesus proved to be more complicated than Jefferson realized. German biblical criticism might have suggested to him the importance of studying more closely the repetitious, parallel accounts in the Gospels and so have provided him with a more objective basis for his selection of the earliest sayings of Jesus to treasure, although most of the advances of "form criticism" of biblical sources came after his death. Jefferson possessed the pieces of the puzzle necessary to recover the account of early Christianity, but he failed to put the puzzle together in the proper way.

In his use of ancient history and his knowledge of the Greco-Roman world and culture, Jefferson proved to be on firmer ground. Later additional knowledge and research has only elaborated and further proved the modifying, if not "corrupting," influence of Greek philosophy, pagan religions and customs, and Roman law and culture upon early Christianity. Jefferson's goal of properly evaluating their influence in order to separate these elements from the unique contributions of Jesus Christ to mankind's religious insight and moral knowledge, so that the true greatness of the historical person of Jesus might shine through, has been the goal of New Testament criticism ever since.

The Person of Jesus Christ

Jefferson was more interested in the teachings of Jesus than in ideas about the person of Christ. He stated many times that his chief concern was with the moral teachings of Christ rather than with theological theories about the nature of Christ as a divine being. This preference resulted from his aversion to religious argumentation and his practical desire to find an agreed-upon basis for moral and social reform. He explained, "If all Christian sects would rally to the Sermon on the mount and make that the stamp of genuine Christianity, why should we further ask, 'What think ye of Christ?' " Everyone could agree upon the moral teachings of Christ, but all sects differed with each other on dogmas about the person of Christ, Jefferson believed.[29]

In his own writings about Christ, Jefferson deliberately avoided interpretations about the person of Christ as much as possible. As he wrote Priestley, "In my review of the Christian system and the life, character and doctrines of Jesus I would purposely omit the question of his divinity and his inspiration."[30]

Jefferson, however, could not avoid forming opinions about the character of Jesus, as his writings amply prove, despite his caution in publicizing them. In the same letter in which he urged Christian sects to unite around the Sermon on the Mount, Jefferson outlined four possible views of the person of Jesus Christ: "He is a member of the God-head; another, He is a being of eternal pre-existence; a third, He was a man divinely inspired; and fourth, He was the Herald of truths reformatory of the religions of mankind." Jefferson argued for mutual tolerance of all views of Jesus, but it is easy to discern, by the detail with which he presented the argument, that the fourth idea of Jesus as a reformer and teacher was the one he supported. His many written comments document this conclusion. Despite his preoccupation with the teachings of Christ, Jefferson was enthusiastic about his interpretation of the person of Christ. He wanted, he said, to defend Jesus against the "fictitious," exaggerated beliefs about his person written by later Christians and against his being thought "an impostor."[31] It is important, then, to examine Jefferson's writings to determine what he thought about Jesus as a person.

Jesus Was Not a Divinity

The question of Jesus' divinity was being heatedly debated during the Enlightenment, especially in France while Jefferson lived there. Writing to his nephew Peter Carr from France, Jefferson outlined the two arguments: "Some say Jesus was begotten by God, born of a virgin, suspended and reversed the laws of nature at will, and ascended bodily into heaven." Those on the opposite side, he went on, argue that "he was a man of illegitimate birth, of a benevolent heart, enthusiastic mind, who set out without pretensions to divinity, ended in believing them, and was punished capitally for sedition, by being gibbeted, according to Roman law." Jefferson here was summarizing the opposing beliefs of French Catholic scholars and the French atheists during the Enlightenment. Although he carefully refrained from indicating his own conclusions to Carr, it is clear from Jefferson's other writings that he rejected the first argument favoring the divine nature of Christ.[32] In this letter, he seemed to be inclined toward the atheistic view of Jesus as being illegitimate and deluded. Later he repudiated this argument also.

Writing to trusted friends, he explicitly rejected a belief in the virgin birth of Christ. As he stated to Adams in a heated letter opposing the doctrines of Calvin, "The day will come, when the mystical generation of Jesus, by the Supreme Being as His Father, in the womb of a virgin, will be classed with the fable of the generation of Minerva in the brain of Jupiter." To other friends, he indirectly made the same point when he objected to "the demoralizing dogmas of Calvin that there are three Gods." In one of his most critical statements about religion to his confidant William Short, Jefferson rejected all aspects of the divinity of Christ: "E.g. The immaculate conception of Jesus, His deification, the creation of the world by Him, His miraculous powers, His resurrection and visible ascension, His corporeal presence in the Eucharist, the Trinity, original sin, atonement, regeneration, election, orders of Hierarchy, etc."[33] In the two versions of the New Testament which he edited, Jefferson rejected all parts of the New Testament related to the divine and miraculous aspects of Jesus' nature. He included only four miracles performed by Christ, all acts of healing that showed Jesus' compassion for humanity and could be explained by natural causes (see Appendix, sections 5–8, 10, 13, 14, 46, 50, 60, 61.)

In his letter to Short, Jefferson expressed his debt to the "labors and learning" of Priestley for his ideas. The question of the virgin birth occupied a good part of Priestley's book *The Corruptions of Christianity.* Priestley began by pointing out that the Jewish concept of the Messiah was that of a great man descended from the royal family of David who would come to help his people, not that of a god, and that Jesus himself always attributed "his extraordinary power to God, his Father." The first apostles, such as Peter and Paul, Priestley argued, spoke of Christ as one from God, "a man like themselves," not "of the most high God." The account of the miraculous birth of Christ is only found in the first chapters of the Gospels of Matthew and Luke. Priestley suggested that the earliest copies of Matthew and Luke did not have these introductions, citing the writings of Marcion of the second century as evidence. The early Gnostics, he argued, held beliefs that would have benefited from "the doctrine of miraculous conception, but they rejected it as fabulous." And few of those who knew Jesus or wrote about him were familiar with the tradition of the virgin birth. Priestley attributed the growth of the idea of Jesus being a god to second-century Christian leaders "who had been heathen philosophers and were admirers of the doctrine of Plato, favoring a second God." But even these philosophers, Priestley pointed out triumphantly, "acknowledged that their opinion was exceedingly unpopular with the unlearned Christians, as it infringed upon the supremacy of God the Father."[34]

Jefferson adopted Priestley's belief that the growth of the exalted view of a divine Christ came from these philosophers who had been influenced by Plato's writings. In fact, Jefferson was more heated than Priestley in condemning the "Platonic Christianity" of the conservative sects. Plato, he declared sarcastically, was the "saint" of such Christians "because in his foggy conceptions, they found a basis of impenetrable darkness whereon to rear delirious fabrications of their own invention fathered blasphemously on Him whom they claimed as their Founder."[35]

Another reason Jefferson opposed the belief in the divinity of Christ stemmed from his opposition to Trinitarian theology. The Trinitarian theorem that "three are one, and one is three, and yet that one is not three nor the three one," as Jefferson was wont to put it, outraged the reason, science, and logic his Enlightenment studies had taught him to reverence. The metaphysical ideas of "Athanasius, Loyola and Calvin" were "insanities" to Jefferson and represented "relapses into polytheism" and "corruptions of Jesus' doctrine of one only God." He thought they "differed from paganism only in being more unintelligible."[36]

The conflicts Jefferson had with "fanatic" Christians over religious freedom and with "priests" and "religion-builders" who used the church as an "instrument of wealth, power, and preeminence to themselves" over the disestablishment of the church strengthened his opposition to orthodox Christianity. Conservative Christians who emphasized being saved by believing in Christ's divine birth instead of by obeying Jesus' teachings not only "distorted, deformed and abused the holy doctrines of their Master" but, by arguing that only their interpretation was correct, proclaimed themselves Christ's "special followers and favorites and all understandings but theirs" to be "snares." As a result, Jefferson believed, "They made of Christendom a slaughter-house through so many ages, and at this day divide it into castes of inextinguishable hatred to one another." Jefferson supported this conviction by extensive studies in church history.[37]

The passages Jefferson used in his two versions of the New Testament confirm his Unitarian conviction. He omitted the accounts of the virgin birth and the miraculous aspects of the birth of Christ as well as the Logos passage in the Gospel of John, but he included the genealogies of Jesus that trace his ancestry through Joseph from the royal family of David (see Appendix, sections 1–14). In Jefferson's account of the baptism of Jesus, he omitted the verses that tell of the voice from heaven calling Jesus God's "beloved Son" (see Appendix, section 19). He used the Gospel of John for its account of incidents in the life of Christ but generally omitted its elevated discourses that indicate Jesus' divine power and omniscience, as, for example, the discourse during the Last Supper (see Appendix, sections 133–35). Jefferson included a full account of the trial and crucifixion of Christ but ended with the burial and omitted all of the resurrection and ascension accounts (see Appendix, sections 137–51).

Jefferson, in short, believed Jesus to be a man, a great man, but not divine, and he chose his texts accordingly. All of his studies, training, and experience convinced him, as he wrote to Short, "that Jesus did not mean to impose Himself on mankind as the Son of God."[38]

Jesus Was Not a Deluded Impostor

Having rejected the idea that Jesus was divine, Jefferson likewise rejected the opposing idea that Jesus was a deluded impostor of illegitimate birth, as the French atheists argued. By studying carefully Jefferson's statements about the person of Christ, it is possible to trace the development of his thought about the humanity of Jesus.

In his early statement about the "personage called Jesus" to Peter Carr, it is clear that Jefferson was leaning toward the beliefs of the French deists and atheists, for his very phrasing of the arguments for the divinity of Christ as one who "suspended the laws of nature and ascended bodily into heaven" prejudice a rational reader against the argument.[39] Jefferson here was reflecting his Enlightenment-inspired respect for reason and distaste for the miraculous, a conviction which he shared with the French freethinkers. For such men of reason, the virgin birth and the miracles performed by Jesus, far from authenticating the greatness of Christ as they did for others, cast doubt upon the whole matter, for miracles were violations of the laws of God and of his reason and intelligence.[40]

The French atheists, in their struggle against religion, used wit and gossip to attack the "superstitions of the church." Some of these were poems attacking the birth of Jesus and Mary's immaculate conception which were handwritten and unprinted, in fact unprintable and scurrilous. These French writings, some of which were in his library and others of which he must have known from frequenting intellectual circles during his stay in France, were evidently the source for Jefferson to write to Carr, with some sympathy, the thought that Jesus was illegitimate and had pretensions of divinity before he died. Even though Jefferson here seems to have been influenced by French thought, there is no hint of any disrespect for Christ, but rather an admiration for him as a good person.[41] Although he was influenced by the French atheists' view of Jesus and Mary, Jefferson never shared their derogatory feelings. His early Anglican spirit of reverence was too strong.

Later religious studies led him to find a third understanding of Jesus which enabled him to reject both the orthodox belief in Christ's divinity and the atheistic idea of Jesus as an illegitimate, deluded fanatic. His critical study of New Testament sources enabled Jefferson to blame the extremes of both ideas of Christ upon the later followers of Jesus and, instead, to see Jesus as "the most innocent, benevolent, and sublime character that ever has been exhibited to man."[42]

In his own "Bible," Jefferson rejected the passages that showed Jesus as a miracle worker or an exalted divinity in favor of those depicting him as a great and good man who taught the highest ethics known to man (see Appendix). Thus he moved progressively to a higher idea of the person of Jesus. At first he thought of him as a good man who had delusions of divinity near the end of his life; then he thought the delusions were attributable to Jesus' followers, not Christ himself. From thinking of Jesus as a "benevolent man," he moved to regarding him as a "sublime moralist," and finally to thinking of Christ as "a man divinely inspired."

The question of Jesus' inspiration gave Jefferson some problems. In his "Syllabus," he "purposely omitted the question of Christ's divinity and even his inspiration," he wrote to friends. These elements of the New Testament were evidently too controversial and perplexing. Later, Jefferson accepted Jesus' belief in his own inspiration from God as being similar to the idea of Socrates that he was "under the care and admonitions of a guardian Daemon." As a Jew, Jesus had been taught to believe in "divine inspiration and might mistake the coruscations of His own fine genius for inspirations of a higher order," he argued. Both Socrates and Jesus might well have thought that the ideas of their superior minds were "inspirations from the Supreme mind, bestowed, on important occasions, by a special superintending Providence." In fact, "many of our wisest men believe in these inspirations," Jefferson concluded. Jefferson himself distrusted inspiration as too often indicating a "disordered imagination rhapsodizing in allegories, figures, types, and other tricks upon words."[43] He had no sympathy with the allegorical and apocalyptic works of the Bible and left those portions out of his New Testament (see Appendix, section 131).

Near the end of his life, in contrasting the various beliefs about Christ for George Thacher, Jefferson, while still rejecting the view of Christ as being a "pre-existent God," accepted Jesus as a "divinely inspired Herald of truth."[44]

Jesus Was a Great Religious Leader

After rejecting both the idea that Jesus was divine and the opposite argument that he was an impostor, Jefferson developed his own belief that he was a man of exceptional greatness and winsomeness. In developing this insight into the person of Christ, Jefferson was indebted to Priestley and other early Unitarians, but he, in turn, foreshadowed the future development of both Unitarianism and liberal Christianity in general.

Jefferson referred to the man Christ Jesus by a variety of descriptions, such as: the "best preacher of religious truth," one "who needed no explanation and concealed nothing in mystery," the "first of human sages" whose teachings are greater than those of Socrates or other ancient philosophers, a "master workman," and "the most eloquent and sublime character" ever seen by man.[45]

It was Jesus' greatness as a teacher, however, that most impressed Jefferson, particularly the way Jesus' life and example illustrated his instructions. He wrote of the way Jesus' "sublime ideas and precepts were sanctioned by a life of humility, innocence, and simplicity of manners, neglect of riches, absence of worldly ambition and honors, with an eloquence and persuasiveness which have not been surpassed." It was the "beauty of His moral precepts" which Jesus taught by his words and his life that especially impressed Jefferson, as he emphasized in his "Syllabus" comparing different moral teachings. By presenting the genuine words of Jesus instead of the false dogmas of his ignorant followers, Jefferson felt that his editions of the New Testament resulted in the most "precious morsel of ethics ever seen."[46]

For Jefferson, great teachings always involved morality, and the world's important teachers were moralists. It was inconceivable to him that a great philosopher could teach a system that justified evil. This moral view of man and society accounts for the fact that Jefferson's discussion of Jesus and other great teachers of history was always related to morality.

A case in point is Jefferson's concept of Christ as a moral reformer. Jefferson frequently referred to the idea that the Gospels revealed Christ as an earnest reformer, particularly of mistaken ideas of morality. He spoke of Jesus to John Adams, for example, as the "most venerated Reformer of human errors," and to another friend as "the Herald of truths reformatory of the religions of mankind in general, but more immediately that of his own countrymen." He often wrote of Christ as "the great reformer of the depraved Jewish religion," which in Jesus' time, he thought, was narrow, legalistic, and degraded in ethical standards and proclaimed a "vindictive, capricious, and unjust God."[47]

The selections that Jefferson made from the New Testament to form his two versions of the "Philosophy" and "Morals" of Jesus indicate the high regard he had for Jesus as a moral teacher. Of the 151 sections into which William Stevens and Ernest Burton have divided the four Gospels of the New Testament, Jefferson included all or parts of 81 in his two versions (see Appendix). These 81 selections used by Jefferson are evenly divided between sections dealing with incidents in the life of Christ (41) and sections dealing with the teachings of Christ (40). This fact alone indicates how much of Jesus' life was concerned with being a teacher, in Jefferson's estimation.

Of the 40 sections dealing with the teachings of Jesus, four are concerned with teachings about God's judgment of men (see Appendix, sections 55, 95, 108, 131), four deal with Christ's attempt to reform Jewish society (see Appendix, sections 94, 125, 126, 127), and the rest teach the necessity of moral conduct for individuals. Jefferson, for example, selected such obvious teaching passages as the Sermon on the Mount, the parables of Jesus, the story of the good Samaritan, and many of the sections labeled "discourses," "warnings," or "teachings" (see Appendix, sections 49, 57, 102, 103, 88, 69, 81, 93, 95, 100, 101, 124, 134). He also selected incidents from the life of Jesus for their teaching value, such as the incidents of the Samaritan woman at the well and the woman taken in adultery (see Appendix, sections 32, 83).

Reflecting the idea that one of Jesus' chief purposes was to reform the religion of his own people and change the evils of their society, Jefferson's versions of the New Testament emphasized the verbal debates and conflicts of Christ with the Jewish Scribes and Pharisees, such as those occurring at the time of Jesus' cleansing of the temple and during his trial and crucifixion (see Appendix, sections 55, 94, 123, 125, 27, 121, 132–41).

It is no coincidence that Jefferson emphasized Jesus' conflicts with the Jewish priests and authorities in his "Bible" and that he gave over so much space—one tenth of the whole narrative—to the account of Jesus' betrayal, arrest, trial, and tragic death. He saw Jesus as more than just a sage teacher of morals comparable to Socrates or Epicurus. Jesus was also a reformer of society, government, and religious institutions. It was Jesus' work of attempting to reform the moral institutions of his time, Jefferson wrote, that brought about his death. In his "Syllabus," Jefferson summed up the life of Jesus in this way: "According to the ordinary fate of those who attempt to enlighten and reform mankind, he fell an early victim to the jealousy of the altar and the throne, entrenched in power and riches."[48]

It is not surprising that Jefferson saw a similarity between Jesus' struggles against the religious and political authorities in Jerusalem during the first century and his own struggle for religious freedom and political reforms on the American continent in the eighteenth century, especially since he was smarting under abuse from political and religious opponents to his presidency while he was working on his "Bible." He saw little difference between the Jewish priests who plotted the death of Jesus and Christian priests who condemned heretics to death and engaged in religious persecution. It was a tragic irony of history that Christianity, which began with the death of Christ at the hands of "this loathsome combination of Church and State," should be taken over by other priests and nobles and, with the help of theologians, make the people "willing dupes and drudges of emperors, princes, popes, and cardinals." He continued: "I place Him among the greatest reformers of morals and scourges of priest-craft that have ever existed. They never rested until they had silenced Him by death. His teachings prevailed over Judaism in the long run, but the priests have rebuilt upon them the temple which He destroyed, as splendid, as profitable, and as imposing as that of before to make instruments of wealth, power, and pre-eminence to themselves." Jefferson could only "weep over the follies of men."[49]

The belief that Jesus was one of the world's great moral teachers was a contribution of the American deists, for the English deists, such as Bolingbroke, preferred the classic moralists to Christ, and the French atheists were hostile to Christ. Priestley, after coming to America, first developed the argument that Jesus as moral teacher was superior to Socrates, and Jefferson, influenced by his work, elaborated on Jesus' superiority.[50] Thomas Paine, the Englishman who became spokesman for the American Revolution and deism, was more critical of religion than either Jefferson or Priestley but gave credit to Christ as a moral teacher.[51]

Jefferson was original, however, in seeing Christ as a reformer of society and viewing his life as an unsuccessful struggle against church and state, since none of the other Enlightenment writers and reformers stressed this idea. This estimate of Christ may have been one-sided, but it supported the Jeffersonian vision of building a free, democratic, and enlightened country on the new continent where people might develop their own potential and the resources of God's creation free from the exploitation of nobles and priests. Jefferson thus began what was to be a long tradition in liberal American denominations of trying to create in the political and social order the moral and ethical life taught by Jesus of Nazareth.

Jesus Was Not a Sin-Sacrifice or an Apocalyptic Judge

True to his liberal convictions, Jefferson rejected the atonement theory of the New Testament, which saw Jesus as the means of the redemption of sinful man from the wrath of God by the sacrifice of Christ on the cross. He had early followed the clue of John Locke in preferring the Gospels, which contained the accounts of the life and teachings of Jesus, to the Epistles, which contained the theology about Christ's death. Jefferson also had absorbed Bolingbroke's criticisms of Paul's theology as being unnecessary additions to the "perfect system of belief and practice, which Jesus, the finisher as well as the author of our faith, left behind him." It was by design, not accident, that Jefferson excluded the Epistles of Saint Paul from his "Bible," for he was seeking, he said, "the correct morality" and true words of Jesus, rather than the "untruth and charlatanism of Paul, the first corruptor of the doctrine of Jesus."[52]

One of Jefferson's main reasons for rejecting "the Trinity, original sin, and atonement" was because these beliefs offended his concept of God and his justice.[53] He cherished in his notes Bolingbroke's explanation of Pauline theology: "God sent his only begotten son, who had not offended him, to be sacrificed by men, who had offended him, that he might expiate their sins, and satisfy his own anger. Surely our ideas of moral attributes will lead us to think that god would have been more satisfied by the repentance of the offenders, or with any other expiation rather than this." Jefferson explained, "The efficacy of repentance towards forgiveness of sins needs a counterpoise of good works to redeem it." "A god sacrificing his son to appease himself who was himself his own father and his own son" (as Bolingbroke put it) seemed quite pagan to Jefferson and full of "follies, falsehoods, and charlatanisms."[54] It was the Calvinistic emphasis upon original sin and predestination, which disregarded just punishment for offenses committed and fair reward for good deeds, that made Jefferson so opposed to Calvin's teachings. As Jefferson read history, it was such "heresies of bigotry and fanaticism which have so long triumphed over human reason that have so generally and deeply afflicted mankind."[55]

Jefferson, therefore, rejected the theology that saw Jesus Christ as the sacrifice for human sin by which man was saved from the wrath of God. Instead, he saw Jesus as a reformer who tried to teach people a higher way and died in the attempt. Unlike the Calvinistic Puritans of New England or the evangelical Presbyterians of the frontier, Jefferson and his friends of the Enlightenment did not see a divine drama in the Old Testament fall of Adam to sin and the New Testament salvation of man by the atoning death of Christ on the cross. They saw the historic struggle of mankind to rise above its ignorance and superstition, as seen in the Old Testament, to a new creation of reason and goodness which Christ, the moral reformer of the New Testament, taught. The crucifixion, in such a view, was but a temporary setback in the rising consciousness of truth and goodness. Society, not God, killed Christ, and society was learning better. It was Jesus' life of goodness and the influence of his moral teachings that would lead men to the new age of reason, not a superstitious belief in the magic of his bloody death.

Jefferson's "Bible," accordingly, does not have the theological atonement texts of the New Testament, such as John 3:16, "God so loved the world that He gave his only begotten Son," or John 1:29, "Behold the Lamb of God, which taketh away the sin of the world!" Jefferson also omitted from his account the passages where Christ foretells his crucifixion for the salvation of men and the accounts of the resurrection and Jesus' appearances to the disciples to prepare them to go forth and preach salvation (see Appendix, sections 28, 22, 113, 134, 142–51).

Similarly, Jefferson did not select the passages that depict Jesus as a divine judge of men or those that tell of the end of the world and of Christ's coming to earth again. Jefferson's texts must be examined with some care to show these omissions, for he picks his way delicately through the verses. Jefferson did believe in moral judgment; in fact, he regarded Jesus' teaching of a future existence where men are judged for their behavior as a sign of its superiority over the commandments of Moses, which did not include such a teaching.[56] So he included the parables of judgment, especially those that taught the necessity of good deeds, such as the ones about Lazarus the beggar, the wicked steward, the unjust judge, and the judgment of people according to their deeds of compassion (see Appendix, sections 103, 108, 131). Jefferson likewise included Jesus' parables about being ready for the coming of God's Kingdom, such as the parable of the talents and their reward and the parable of the ten bridesmaids waiting for the bridegroom (see Appendix, sections 108, 124, 131). He even kept in his versions "the little Apocalypse" of Matthew 24 and 25 that describes the end of the world and Christ's coming to earth again, but only so that he could use the account of Jesus judging people from his throne and separating the good from the bad as a shepherd separates his sheep from his goats, for he omitted the verses that tell of Christ coming down from heaven with his angels (see Appendix, section 131).

Jefferson's objections to the apocalyptic passages about the end of the world were much the same as his objections to those describing a God of wrath found in the writings of Moses and Calvin. He thought they were based on a low idea of God and the worst of human emotions. He also disliked exalted and mystical beliefs about Christ. He wrote that he could "really see nothing but demonism in the Being worshipped by many who think themselves Christians" and objected to "the metaphysical abstractions of Athanasius, and the maniac ravings of Calvin, tinctured plentifully with the foggy dreams of Plato."[57]

Jefferson impatiently rejected the ecstatic, allegorical, and imaginative parts of the Bible as "vague rhapsodies, the fumes of the most disordered imaginations." He distrusted a religion of emotion that lacked the balance of reason. For these reasons he did not include the book of Revelation in his New Testaments. Near the end of his life, he admitted that he had not read Revelation for "between fifty and sixty years" and affirmed his lifelong opinion of the work as "merely the ravings of a maniac, no more worthy nor capable of explanation than the incoherences of our own nightly dreams."[58]

Jefferson's condemnation of the apocalyptic idea of Christ as a divine judge who would sentence evil people at the end of the age stemmed from the fact that he was not one to condemn people, particularly over dogma. One of his favorite anecdotes concerned a preacher who said there were no Quakers, Presbyterians, or Methodists in heaven, only Christian brethren. Jefferson agreed and added, "I believe, with the Quaker preacher, that he who steadily observes those moral precepts in which all religions concur, will never be questioned at the gates of heaven as to the dogmas in which they all differ."[59] It was the arrogance and divisiveness of those who saw Jesus as an atoning sacrifice for sin and a stern judge of the unbelievers at the end of the age that offended Jefferson.

The Teachings of Jesus Christ

There were many reasons why Jefferson believed the most important aspect of the Christian religion was the teachings of Jesus. In the first place, people could readily agree with the simple teachings of Jesus in contrast to their arguments over the dogmas about Christ. "No doctrines of His lead to schism," he wrote. "It is the speculations of crazy theologists which create differences."[60]

Second, studying the teachings of Christ led to emphasizing moral conduct, which, by inclination of temperament, legal training, and his Enlightenment studies, always seemed the most important aspect of religion to Jefferson. To Dr. George Logan, Jefferson wrote approvingly that Jesus summed up all religion as "fearing God and loving your neighbor." This emphasis upon good works instead of faith and mystery always seemed more important to Jefferson the statesman in his efforts to reform society and improve the life of man. He wrote to the wife of a Washington official, "I have ever judged the religion of others by their lives." The emphasis upon dogma and theology by the priests and the orthodox and their branding of their enemies as infidels had hindered the progress of true religion, Jefferson argued. It was necessary to "knock down their artificial" interpretations of Jesus' life and teachings and to extract "the diamonds in the dunghills of the true, precious morsel in ethics" of Jesus' words, restoring the original, "primitive" teachings of Jesus Christ.[61]

In referring so often to Jesus as a great moralist, Jefferson reflected his belief in the utmost importance of the teaching side of Jesus' life. As he analyzed the most important of Jesus' teachings, Jefferson naturally followed the ways of thought he used in studying Jesus as a person. For example, he wrote most often about Jesus' teachings concerning the moral duties of people, Christ's high ideas of God, his lessons for the reform of society, and his concepts of future rewards and punishments for human conduct. Jefferson downgraded the theological and metaphysical teachings about Christ found in the New Testament.[62]

The Most Sublime Morality

Whenever Jefferson wrote about the teachings of Jesus, he was most apt to mention "the pure morals which Jesus inculcated" or the "sublime doctrines of philanthropism and deism taught us by Jesus of Nazareth." The results of his New Testament study to find the original teachings of Jesus, Jefferson confided repeatedly to his friends, was "the most sublime, beautiful, pure, and benevolent code of morals which has ever been offered to man." As he told a Quaker friend, "Of all the systems of morality, ancient or modern, which have come under my observation, none appear to me so pure as that of Jesus." Indeed, Jefferson saw most of the work and teachings of Jesus as being related to improving ethics and "reforming religion."[63]

Jefferson's belief that Jesus was a greater "human sage and moralist" than Socrates and the other classical moralists whom he admired was a later development of his thought. As he wrote to a critic, "I give them their just due, and yet maintain that the morality of Jesus, as taught by himself, and freed from the corruptions of latter times, is far superior." Jesus did not contradict the other moralists, Jefferson argued in letters to his friends and in his "Syllabus" on Christ's teachings, but went beyond them and supplemented their deficiencies. The ancient philosophers taught individuals to master their feelings and gain "tranquility"; they also taught one's duty to family and country. But they were "short and deficient" in teaching about duties to other people, while Jesus taught us to love "our neighbor and the whole family of mankind." On another occasion Jefferson put it more succinctly, "Epictetus and Epicurus give laws for governing ourselves; Jesus a supplement of the duties and charities we owe to others."[64]

The ethical teachings of Christ were superior to others not only for their inclusiveness of all people but because they dealt more profoundly with human conduct by considering the inner motivations of men. "The precepts of philosophy, and of the Hebrew code laid hold of actions only," Jefferson explained in his "Syllabus." "Jesus pushed his scrutinies into the heart of man; erected his tribunal in the region of his thoughts, and purified the waters at the fountain head." Thus, it was Jesus' emphasis upon the pure, inner "moralities of life" and "the duties of a social being to do good to all men" that enlisted Jefferson's enthusiasm, especially since he felt this teaching had been too long overlooked.[65]

The two editions of the New Testament prepared by Jefferson for his personal study of the teachings of Christ verify his preference for ethical rules over theology. At the outset he had ruled out any consideration of any theological questions about Jesus' divinity or inspiration in favor of studying "the intrinsic merits of his doctrines" only.[66] In his choice of passages, Jefferson omitted those supporting the idea of Christ "being a member of the God-head," such as the accounts of the virgin birth of Jesus, Peter's confession of Christ being "the Son of the living God," the transfiguration of Jesus on the mountaintop, and Christ's walking on the water (see Appendix, sections 9, 75, 77, 67). As might be expected from his praise of Christ as a moralist, Jefferson included full accounts from several Gospel sources of the Sermon on the Mount, emphasizing the inner goodness that goes beyond the law (see Appendix, section 49). He also selected the passages that applied moral conduct to people other than one's own family, race, or nationality, such as the Samaritan woman at the well, the parable of the good Samaritan, and Jesus' kindness to the outcaste Zacchaeus (see Appendix, sections 32, 88, 116).

Jefferson believed Jesus' ethical teachings were important when they illustrated going beyond the law, such as the account of the rich young ruler who kept all the commandments but could not give all his possessions to the poor, the widow who gave all she had, and Christ's new commandment "to love one another" (see Appendix, sections 112, 128, 134). Jefferson likewise emphasized Jesus' teaching in the Sermon on the Mount that his followers must avoid even thinking or feeling evil and must do good to their enemies as well as their friends, culminating in the "golden rule" of "doing unto others as you would they should do unto you" (see Appendix, section 149). He also included the two accounts in the Gospels in which it is stated that loving God and loving one's neighbor as oneself is the meaning of all the law (see Appendix, section 125).

Jefferson believed Jesus' ethical teachings were superior not only to the ethics of the "Ancient philosophers" but also to the law of Moses. Accordingly, he included in his "Bible" many of the passages dealing with Jesus' debates and conflicts with the Jewish authorities (see Appendix, sections 55, 94, 126, 132). One of Jefferson's firmest convictions about the teachings and work of Jesus was that they represented an attempt to reform "the vicious ethics of the Jews and show what a degraded state they were in."[67] He criticized the Jewish religion on four main grounds—narrowness, exclusiveness, ceremonialism, and legalism.

As Jefferson read his Bible, the orthodox Jews displayed a distressing lack of tolerance for different classes and nationalities in the time of Christ. They had no use not only for people of other races and nationalities but also for those of their own people who disobeyed the law. Their standards of ethics were judged wanting by the Enlightenment ideals. So Jefferson admired the reforms of Jesus in "inculcating the love of mankind, instead of the anti-social spirit with which the Jews viewed all other nations." As Jefferson contrasted Moses and Jesus: "The one instilled into his people the most anti-social spirit towards other nations; the other preached philanthropy and universal charity and benevolence." Jesus' moral doctrines were superior, Jefferson wrote, because "they went far beyond others in inculcating universal philanthropy, not only to kindred and friends, to neighbors and countrymen, but to all mankind, gathering all into one family, under the bonds of love, charity, peace, common wants and common aids."[68]

Jefferson also saw in Jesus' teachings an attempt to reform Jewish ceremonialism. Christ emphasized the inner life of devotion and motive rather than the ceremonies of the temple or sacrifices on the altar. "Moses had bound the Jews to many idle ceremonies, mummeries, and observances of no effect toward producing the social utilities which constitute the essence of virtue," Jefferson commented. "Jesus exposed their futility and insignificance."[69]

Although he was a lawyer himself, it is clear that Jefferson the moralist regarded the Jewish religion as excessively legalistic. His choice of texts in the New Testament indicate that he was influenced by the accounts of Jesus' arguments with the Scribes and Pharisees to believe that the Jewish teachings on moral conduct were rigid and lacked human understanding. In a letter to John Adams, he described research he had done of the Jewish religion based on a study of "their Mishna, Gemara, Gabbal, Jezirah, Sorar, Cosri and Talmud." Not knowing Hebrew, Jefferson had used a secondary source, "Enfield's judicious abridgment of Brucker's *History of Philosophy*," which he summarized for Adams: "Their books of Morals chiefly consisted in a minute enumeration of duties. From the law of Moses were deduced 613 precepts. In order to obtain salvation, it was judged sufficient to fulfill any one single law in the hour of death. What a wretched depravity of moral Doctrine." In this study, Jefferson showed his usual scholarly interest and thoroughness. His source, however, reflected the anti-Jewish bias of post-Renaissance

Europe and suggests the source of some of Jefferson's attitudes and beliefs about the defects of Judaism.[70]

Another of Jesus' reforms of the moral code of the Hebrews, in Jefferson's opinion, was "teaching them the doctrine of a future state of rewards and punishments." As Jefferson explained: "Moses had either not believed in a future state of existence, or had not thought it essential to be explicitly taught to his people. Jesus inculcated that doctrine with emphasis and precision." It may seem strange that Jefferson so heartily approved of Jesus' teachings about eternal judgment in the light of the doubts he expressed about life after death. He believed in "materialism rather than spiritualism," he told many friends. Nevertheless, the teachings of Christ describing a final judgment by a master upon his servants' good or bad service, which Jefferson emphasized in his versions of the New Testament (see Appendix, sections 95, 103, 108, 117, 131), appealed to Jefferson's legal training, his moral beliefs about God and human conscience, and his religious feelings. In any case, he wrote approvingly of Jesus' teachings in the "Syllabus": "He taught, emphatically, the doctrines of a future state, which was either doubted, or disbelieved by the Jews; and wielded it with efficacy, as an important incentive, supplementary to the other motives to moral conduct."[71]

To sum it up, Jefferson saw Jesus Christ as something of the ideal Enlightenment man, admonishing, reforming, and awakening his countrymen, and all mankind, from their superstitions and mistaken moral codes to "the most sublime moral code ever taught to men." To like-minded Priestley he wrote: "Jesus, sensible of their incorrectness, endeavored to reform the Jews' ideas of moral doctrines to the standard of reason, justice and philanthropy, and to inculcate the belief of a future state."[72]

"More Worthy Ideas of the Supreme Being"

Jefferson also believed that Jesus taught the highest ideas of God. In his discussion with Adams on the nature of true religion, Jefferson defined it as "the sublime doctrines of philanthropism and deism taught us by Jesus of Nazareth." Writing to George Thacher, Jefferson mentioned "more worthy ideas of the Supreme being" as one of the most important of Jesus' teachings. Jefferson frequently referred to the "deism" of Jesus, by which he meant Jesus' teachings about God, and often in connection with "reforming the deism of the Jews." Deism, to Jefferson, meant belief in one God, and he gave the Jews credit for this belief, but he disapproved of the "injurious ideas they had about God." He explained to Priestley that Jesus' work of teaching about God was primarily an attempt to overcome "the degraded deism and ethics of the Jews and bring them to the principles of a pure deism and juster notions of the attributes of God."[73]

In objecting to the "degraded" ideas of God held by the Jews, Jefferson was thinking of the Jehovah of the Old Testament who thundered his commandments from Mount Sinai and led his people into battle. The God described by Moses, Jefferson complained, was "a Being of terrific character, cruel, vindictive, capricious, and unjust" who "punished the sins of the fathers upon their children, unto the third and fourth generation." The persistence of this theology in his own time dismayed Jefferson. His chief objection to the Calvinists of his day was that they had "copied from the Jews their idea of a Supreme Being" who predestined the innocent to be damned. It was indicative of Jesus' greatness that "he corrected the Deism of the Jews, confirming them in their belief of one only God, and giving them juster notions of his attributes and government."[74]

Jefferson only sketched lightly what he believed the higher ideas of God were that Jesus taught. To Ezra Stiles he explained, "The benevolent and sublime Reformer of religion has told us only that God is good and perfect, but has not defined Him." Jefferson explained to William Short: "Jesus, taking for His type the best qualities of the human head and heart, wisdom, justice, goodness, and adding to them power, ascribed all of these, but in infinite perfection to the Supreme Being, and formed Him really worthy of their adoration." In summing up "the pure doctrines of Jesus" in contrast to the "demoralizing dogmas of Calvin," Jefferson listed what he considered to be the main teachings of Christ:

1. That there is one only God, and He all perfect,
2. That there is a future state of rewards and punishments,

3. That to love God with all thy heart and thy neighbor as thyself, is the sum of religion.[75]

Jefferson was indebted for his ideas about the religion of the Jews to the Enlightenment authors that he studied. He had copied in his notes Bolingbroke's objection to the anthropomorphic ideas of God found in the book of Genesis. The source of his belief that Moses and Paul were to blame for fostering the concept of a cruel and unjust God is also found in passages of Bolingbroke that he copied. He found authority for his idea that the deism of the Jews needed reforming in Locke and Bolingbroke. Bolingbroke also furnished Jefferson with many passages attacking the Old Testament's lack of scientific understanding of God's universe and its primitive belief in miracles.[76]

The quotations of Bolingbroke copied by Jefferson do not indicate, however, that Jesus was the one to reform Jewish moral teachings. Bolingbroke, instead, was critical of New Testament ethical teaching. Since no source of Jefferson's idea of Christ's contribution to ethics is to be found in his reading, it is clear that Jefferson derived this idea of Jesus as the reformer of men's ideas of morality and God from his own studies of Jesus' life and words in the New Testament. It was his own work of searching out the true words of Jesus that suggested this concept to him, as Jefferson stated explicitly to his friends.[77]

Following the lead of his studies, Jefferson came to the belief that the Old Testament contained objectionable views of God, morality, and the world of nature, but that the New Testament contained the admirable ethics of Christ and elevated teachings about God. Hence the New Testament was superior to the Old. This emphasis seems to have been a contribution of the American deists, for there is evidence that Adams and Priestley agreed with Jefferson about it.[78] Jefferson largely confined his studies of the Bible to the Psalms and the New Testament, particularly the Gospels.

Jefferson's choice of materials in editing his own versions of the New Testament is also revealing. He omitted the sections of the New Testament that emphasize Jesus' Jewish heritage, such as the proclamation by John the Baptist that Jesus was a fulfillment of the prophecy of the coming of the Jewish Messiah, and emphasized the passages in which Jesus argued against the "degraded" legalism and parochialism of the Scribes and Pharisees (see Appendix, sections 21, 30, 55, 69, 94, 109). Jefferson also emphasized the teachings and parables of Jesus that taught a more charitable and inward understanding of ethics, such as the Sermon on the Mount, a more universal application of brotherhood to other races and peoples, such as the story of the good Samaritan, and higher concepts of the love and forgiveness of God the Father, such as the story of the prodigal son (see Appendix, sections 49, 88, 102).

Another of the important teachings of Christ about God, according to Jefferson, was the belief in one God. The phrase frequently used by Jefferson was "the deism taught us by Jesus of Nazareth," which he used in contrast to "atheism," meaning belief in no god, and "theism," by which he meant orthodox Trinitarianism. Jefferson argued that the belief of deism in "the unity of the Creator was the pure doctrine of Jesus also."[79]

From his classical studies, Jefferson knew of the many Greek and Roman gods that were worshiped in the ancient world and the low moral attributes they displayed, in contrast to the belief in one exalted, moral God that Jesus taught. "No historical fact is better established," he commented, "than that the doctrine of one God, pure and uncompounded, was that of the early ages of Christianity, and was among the efficacious doctrines which gave it triumph over the polytheism of the ancients, sickened with the absurdities of their own theology." He wrote, "Thinking men of all nations rallied to the doctrine of one only moral God."[80]

Jefferson acknowledged the fact that the Jews had developed the idea of "deism" before Christ did, but he belittled their accomplishment because of the "terrible Being" they worshiped.[81] Jefferson and the English deists he studied did not sufficiently appreciate the religious achievements of Old Testament monotheism. Even the belief in one mighty and jealous God who fiercely punished any deviation from his commandments, so much attacked by Bolingbroke and Jefferson, represented an advance over the religious beliefs of other primitive groups of the time in many gods who demanded human sacrifice and immoral fertility rites of worship.[82] Jefferson and the men of the Enlightenment, moreover, did not recognize that, in teaching His higher concepts of God and man's duties,

Jesus drew upon reform elements already present in Judaism. As early as the eighth century B.C., the great Hebrew prophets were already teaching the same "reforms of the degraded deism and ethics of the Jews" admiringly attributed by Jefferson to Christ.[83]

The teachings of Jesus, Jefferson believed, were superior not only to any of the ancient world or of the Jews but to those of his followers and of the later Christian church. Christian metaphysicians and theologians degraded the simple, universal charity of Christ's ethics and the pure Deism of his teaching of one God, "relapsing into an unintelligible polytheism," Jefferson wrote his correspondents. These retrogressions from Jesus' teachings continued in his own time, Jefferson believed. Commenting on the opposition of conservative groups to his appointment of a Unitarian, Thomas Cooper, as professor to the new University of Virginia, he complained that the "Calvinists" were persecuting Cooper "as a monotheist in opposition to their mystical theogony" and that they wanted "to rekindle the flames" of Calvin's religious persecutions "in this virgin hemisphere."[84]

Jefferson, thus, looked to Jesus of Nazareth as the greatest moral teacher of ideas about God and the ethical behavior of men who ever lived. He looked upon his teachings as a watershed in history that marked the highest level of religious and ethical ideas. Jesus' teachings were far above those of the Jews who preceded him, the classical moralists of his own time, and the teachings of the theologians of the church who followed him. To the Enlightenment admiration of ancient philosophers and attacks upon the ethics of the Jews and the theology of the church, Jefferson added a new dimension of appreciation of the teachings of Christ.

Jesus' Teachings on Reform of Society

An important aspect of the teachings of Jesus noted by Jefferson concerned the reform of society. Because Jefferson absorbed the subject of social reforms into the larger subject of morality, he did not write often about this aspect of Jesus' teachings, but he made many references to Jesus as a great "moral reformer." Jefferson's emphasis was usually on an individual person's code of conduct, but he always saw the individual in a social context. His favorite Bible passage, Psalm 15, is concerned with the individual good man, but it illustrates his virtue by his social conduct, refusing to slander and disdaining bribes.[85]

It was Jesus' teachings about man's duties to his fellow men that most intrigued Jefferson. In his New Testament he placed great emphasis on the Sermon on the Mount and on love of neighbor (see Appendix, sections 49, 88, 112). In his writings, Jefferson frequently referred to the greatness of Christ in teaching "that to love God with all thy heart and thy neighbor as thyself, is the sum of religion." The moral reforms seen by Jefferson as the most important of those taught by Christ were reforms of the attitudes of men toward their fellows. Jesus "inculcated the love of mankind instead of the anti-social spirit with which the Jews viewed all other nations" and reformed their "repulsive and anti-social laws as they respect intercourse with those around us." Jesus' great superiority over the classical moralists, likewise, was in the field of social relationships. Jefferson wrote, "Jesus went far beyond others in gathering all mankind into one family."[86]

Although Jefferson emphasized morality as a code of individual behavior, he placed the individual in a social setting and was more concerned with the morality that affected social conduct than with that encouraging peace of mind. The moral code also must be applied to the conduct of nations, he believed. Thus the social implications of Jesus' moral reforms were of the utmost importance. It was the fact that Jesus' moral teachings demanded social reforms of the Jewish and Roman religious and political institutions that was the reason "he fell an early victim" to those who were exploiting the status quo, Jefferson believed.[87]

Jefferson quite naturally saw the teaching work of Christ in terms of enlightening the minds of men and reforming their social practices. Jesus, he believed, presented an example to follow in the eighteenth-century Enlightenment struggle for human progress, especially since, as he read history, the priests whom Jesus died opposing had succeeded in taking over Christianity and "enslaving mankind." Jefferson's studies of the New Testament and the teachings of Christ thus provided him with weapons in his fight for religious freedom, spiritual enlightenment, and social reforms, all of which, he believed, would result if the pure ethics and simple religion taught by Jesus of Nazareth could be restored.[88]

Jefferson's writings make it plain that he held to two main religious convictions that guided his work of social reform. One conviction was his belief that there was a God of justice, goodness, and morality who had created both man and the world and was directing the affairs of both. The other belief was that the moral code taught by Jesus was the best one by which a person could guide his personal life and that its teachings should be applied to the life of the community. These two basic religious convictions can be seen in many of Jefferson's political writings.

In his first political challenge as a young man, that of American independence and the right of men to be free, Jefferson quickly turned to his ideas of God and the way he had created men "free and equal" for justification for his position.[89] In working for religious freedom, reform of the church establishment, and overcoming ignorance and superstition, Jefferson was guided by his beliefs about what constituted good religion and true Christianity. His belief in a God of justice ruling humanity through the moral law and in the importance of following the ethical teachings of Christ in the larger affairs of the nations was at the root of his concern over the evils of war and the excesses of the French Revolution. Commenting on the devastations of Bonaparte, he wrote, "Such is the moral construction of the world, that no national crime passes unpunished in the long run." Nowhere is Jefferson's belief in a God of justice and the righteousness of Christ's ethical teaching more strongly expressed than in his writings about slavery, an institution whose evils deeply troubled him all of his life. On the whole, however, Jefferson was optimistic about human progress and the possibility of overcoming moral problems through the earnest efforts of good men, guided by the Almighty God of justice, following the teachings of Jesus Christ.[90]

Jesus' Teachings on Eternity

Although most of his interest in the words of Jesus of Nazareth centered around his teachings of better moral conduct and a better understanding of God, Jefferson did have concern for Jesus' teachings on other subjects. One of these interests was in Jesus' teachings about life after death. Both in his letters and in his outlines of the main teachings of Christ, Jefferson emphasized, as one evidence of the superiority of Jesus' teachings, the fact that he taught "the doctrine of a future state of rewards and punishments." Jefferson plainly approved of this doctrine as part of a worthy moral code.[91]

He was less certain about the details of Jesus' teachings on the nature of eternal life. On some occasions he indicated his disagreement with Jesus' teachings of "spiritualism." On other occasions he thought Jesus had believed in "materialism" and argued that immaterial, spiritual ideas of eternal life were the results of later "Platonists and corrupters." In these discussions, he dealt at some length with spiritual interpretations of God, the universe, Christ, and the meaning of the term *Logos*.[92]

Conclusions

In many ways, Jefferson's ideas about the person and teachings of Jesus Christ provide the key to understanding his religion. Jefferson was more interested in Jesus and his teachings than in any other aspect of religion. He wrote more about Christ and his words than any other part of Christianity and studied the New Testament more than any other part of the Bible.

His interest in discovering who Jesus really was and what he really taught led Jefferson to become an early biblical critic, using his knowledge of history, the Greek New Testament, and Greco-Roman culture to good advantage. Jefferson's varied interests and abilities in many fields have been noted by scholars, but his role as a biblical scholar and his indirect influence on American religion has long been overlooked.

Studying his statements about Jesus Christ also sheds light on why Jefferson's religion has been so controversial, for he wrote some very sharp attacks on the orthodox idea of Christ as a divine being and on the doctrine of the Trinity. It is evident that orthodox Christianity angered Jefferson and that his attacks on beliefs which many Christians held sacred angered conservative Christians. Scholars have known Jefferson was Unitarian in his beliefs, but they have failed to appreciate how sharp the Unitarian controversy was in Jefferson's time. They have also failed to realize the extent of Jefferson's interest in liberal Christianity and the importance of his championing of it.

Furthermore, Jefferson's researches about Jesus the man and his teachings provided him with some of the most important of his own religious beliefs. He was one of the first and most prominent of religious liberal thinkers to find a middle ground between the orthodox belief in Christ as a divinity and the atheistic conviction that he was a deluded imposter. Jefferson found great inspiration in his New Testament discovery of Jesus as a great teacher, reformer, moralist, and heroic person, a view that has been prominent in American liberal Christianity ever since.

In Jesus' teachings concerning the high moral attributes of the Supreme Being, Jefferson found evidence for his convictions that there was a God of justice behind the creation of man and society who ruled by his moral law. In the ethical teachings of Christ about man's duties to his fellow men, Jefferson found the "best moral code" ever devised both for individual behavior and for governing society. In the life of Christ, he found an example and inspiration for his own work of social reform and enhancing human rights. In the teachings of Christ, he found guidance for his work of reform and for his own personal life and conduct. The idea that theological beliefs and faith were more important than following the example and commandments of Jesus was the antithesis of Jefferson's religion and aroused his strong condemnation. It is surprising that the importance of the teachings of Jesus Christ upon the life, thought, and work of Thomas Jefferson has been so much overlooked.

Jefferson's view of Christ as an ethical teacher and social reformer has been criticized as one-sided and limited by some scholars.[93] While Jefferson did seek to apply the teachings of Jesus to his own problems and saw important parallels between the social problems faced by Christ and those faced by the Enlightenment, such an application of the teachings of Christ to personal ethical living and social reforms was certainly valid. His interpretation of Christ, although by no means the only one that could be made or has been made, has stood the test of biblical research and usefulness to individuals and society better than most.

A more valid criticism of Jefferson's understanding of the Bible was his lack of appreciation of Judaism and the Old Testament. While criticisms of excessive legalism in Judaism and of unworthy concepts of God found in the Old Testament, made by Jefferson and the studies he quoted, are valid, Jefferson was mistaken in believing these elements fairly represented all of Judaism or even the Old Testament. At the beginning of his outline of a comparison of the ethical systems of classical philosophers, of the Jews, and of Jesus, Jefferson set as a guiding principle that he would evaluate each religion by its highest expression, not the "corruptions" of each.[94] In other words, he wanted to compare the best of each system of ethics. He admired Epicureanism, for example, but not the later hedonistic excesses of it. It was manifestly unfair, then, to compare the best expression of classical ethics and the teachings of Jesus Christ with the lowest and most primitive elements of Judaism, which is what Jefferson did, probably without realizing it.

It was unfortunate that he was not more critical of his Enlighten-ment sources, such as Enfield and Bolingbroke, for he had read widely in the Bible and, on other occasions, revealed an extensive knowledge and appreciation of the Old Testament. His public addresses make occasional references to Providence and God, and in his second inaugural address he spoke of "the Being who led our forefathers, as Israel of old, to a country flowing with all the necessaries and comforts of life." Another time, in writing to a British correspondent, Jefferson referred to Genesis when he "blessed the Almighty for gathering together the waters under the heavens into one place" between Europe and America and said "at least be there peace." He showed his knowledge of the Old Testament when he compared arousing the public from political apathy to Samson awaking "from his sleep and carrying away the gates and posts of the city." Commenting on the dangers of the American Revolution, he wrote of "hanging on a gallows as high as Haman's," revealing knowledge of an obscure detail of the Old Testament book of Esther. He used his extensive knowledge of the Scriptures also in a graceful reference to the missionary journeys of Christ's followers when writing to Abigail Adams of the journey of friends through life to heaven: "For this journey we shall need neither gold nor silver in our purse, nor scrip, nor coats, nor staves."[95]

Jefferson's preference for the New Testament over the Old did not prevent him from displaying a deep appreciation of the Psalms. Struck by their beauty and their insight about God and man, he often made the Psalms a part of his devotional reading. This knowl-edge is shown most clearly in his dialogues with Adams in which the old friends discussed their favorite Bible readings. Jefferson assessed various translations of the Psalms, such as "leaden Stern-hold who kindles with the sublimity of his original, and expresses the majesty of God descending on the earth, in terms not unworthy of the subject." He recommended Brady and Tate's version of Psalm 148, which described "the angels, heaven, sun and moon, fire, hail, and snow, mountains, deeps, old men and children all praising God." He also recommended to Adams Psalm 15. This Psalm, which describes the virtues of a good man who has learned of God to be worthy to dwell in his tabernacle, was always his favorite. On two occasions he sent copies of his favorite Brady and Tate version, once to his young namesake Thomas Jefferson Smith as "the por-trait of a good man by the most sublime of poets, for your imitation," and once in answer to a request from an editor for an article on morals, since, he wrote, "I know nothing more moral, more sublime, more worthy of your preservation than David's description of the good man, in his 15th Psalm."[96]

These quotations amply prove that Jefferson, when he was not being unduly influenced by his Enlightenment authors, recognized that worthy ideas of the Supreme Being were to be found in the Old Testament, particularly in the Psalms, as well as high ethical standards. It was unfortunate that he did not follow this lead further to make more of a study of the higher concepts of God and morality found in Judaism.

Jefferson also made the mistake of failing to realize sufficiently the Jewish influence upon Jesus' life and teachings. Jesus may have criticized excessive Jewish legalism and taught a more inward morality, but he was a practicing Jew all his life. He observed the Passover with his disciples, made pilgrimages to the Jerusalem temple to worship, and attended synagogue services on the Sabbath (see Appendix, sections 27, 39, 62, 82, 119, 121, 133, 134 for such incidents from the New Testament included by Jefferson). It was failing to observe the true spirit of the law that Jesus objected to, not the law itself.

Jefferson also failed to recognize that much of what he considered the most original and important part of Jesus' "sublime morality" was rooted in his heritage. Jesus may have been unique in the emphasis and interpretation he gave to life and morality, but every-thing he taught came from his Jewish studies. When Christ summed up religion as love of God and love for one's fellow man (see verses emphasized by Jefferson, Appendix, sections 88, 112), he was really quoting the "Shema" from the Old Testament taught every Jewish child. Similarly, in the Beatitudes, which Jefferson admired (see Appendix, section 49), Jesus was quoting from the Old Testament concerning the meek, those that mourn, and the pure in heart. Even the Golden Rule, which Jefferson included in his "Bible" as the high point of Jesus' formulation of an ethic that applied to all people (see Matthew 7:14 in Appendix, section 49), has similarities to the Old Testament and the Apocrypha.[97]

There was in Judaism the legalistic, narrow, harsh view of religion that Jefferson and Bolingbroke deplored. But there was also the prophetic strain of high moral concepts and exalted ideas of God as a God of love for all mankind requiring mercy and justice from people instead of temple sacrifice. It was this stream of Jewish thought, recognized by Jefferson in the Psalms but not elsewhere in the Bible, that Jesus developed and emphasized.

Jefferson's work for political democracy, religious freedom, and social reform is well known, but too little study has been given to the inner religious sources for Jefferson's beliefs and actions. Those scholars who have studied his political philosophy have dwelt on the intellectual sources of his ideas but have generally dismissed his religious beliefs as of minor or mistaken importance. The general dismissal of Enlightenment philosophy and religion as being simplistic moralizing may be partly at fault, since Jefferson depended so heavily upon Enlightenment sources. Jefferson's reticence about his religion and his tendency to clothe his religious convictions in intellectual and involved language may also be a factor. Even Henry Wilder Foote, the Unitarian scholar who has stressed the work of Jefferson in religious and social reform, emphasizes Jefferson's accomplishments and devotes little attention to his inner beliefs and motives concerning religious and social reform.[98]

Yet Jefferson, in emphasizing works over faith, stressed a tension that has always been characteristic of American religion and theology. In his emphasis upon moral acts as being of more importance than religious mysticism, Jefferson also struck an activist note that has been predominant in American religion ever since, and in his insistence upon applying the ethical teachings of Jesus to America's social problems, Jefferson began an emphasis that has persisted throughout American religious history. The task of Christian reformation, which was difficult enough in the simple society of early national times dealing with the problems of revolution, political organization, and the Napoleonic wars, was to prove even more complex and difficult in the industrial development of the age of the "robber barons" that followed, to say nothing of present global involvements. It is significant, however, that, just as there arose later generations of politicians and statesmen who followed Jeffersonian ideals for society and created social changes, there also arose later religious and ethical writers who tried to apply the ethical reforms of Jesus Christ to American society as Jefferson had done. Jefferson thought in terms of the Enlightenment; Walter Rauschenbush in the early 1900s talked of the Social Gospel; Protestant church leaders today write of Christian Social Action for social justice, racial integration, and a world free from hunger; and Catholic theologians write about liberation theology. While there are interesting differences, as well as similarities, among the later liberal religious movements in America, their goals, emphases, and point of view are essentially Jeffersonian, according to Arthur Schlesinger, Jr.[99]

Jefferson's stress on the importance of the life and teachings of Jesus Christ, particularly the Sermon on the Mount, the parables about the coming of God's Kingdom among men, and the Golden Rule, has been central in the thinking of many American liberal theologians ever since. This emphasis has had enduring influence on the religious thought and life of America, although the fact that it was so much a part of Jefferson's philosophy has been largely overlooked. Nevertheless, the same forces of the Enlightenment and the American political and social situation that influenced Jefferson in his religious views have influenced later religious liberals. The remarkable thing is that Jefferson adopted so early many of the same ideas about religion and social reform that later religious liberals and activists have espoused. As Schlesinger notes, Jeffersonian liberalism can be traced in American religion as well as in political reform.

Although Jefferson was criticized for his liberal ideas about Christ during his own lifetime and later, the account of Jesus that inspired him—as a great and good man of the highest ideals and simple, yet profound, teachings, who died bravely for his beliefs and thereby caused their continuation—has had a strong appeal to Americans through the years. Jefferson, furthermore, was unique among history's great men in that he not only studied and wrote about the meaning of the words and examples of Jesus Christ for the human condition but used his beliefs about Christ as a guide in accomplishing needed social reforms. He was both a thinker and a doer.

CHAPTER IX

JEFFERSON'S RELIGIOUS
IDEAS OF LIFE AFTER DEATH

O f all Jefferson's writings on religious subjects, his comments on life after death have presented the most difficulties to scholars, possibly because the subject itself perplexed Jefferson more than any other. Some scholars have discovered Jefferson's youthful collection of poems on the subject. Others have noted his skeptical and materialistic attitude. A few writers have commented on his positive statements about life after death, but most have concluded that his writings on immortality are so contradictory that they will always be a subject of controversy.[1]

It is necessary then, considering the importance in religious thought of the idea of immortality, to examine Jefferson's sometimes contradictory statements on the subject with some care. He held different ideas about immortality at different periods in his life, and like all people, he reacted to the changing experiences of his long life and career.

Jefferson's Classical Ideas of Immortality

Although the emotional intensity of Jefferson's youthful crisis over religion has at times been exaggerated by his biographers, it is true that, under the influence of his college studies, he early came to question the articles of faith of his Anglican church upbringing concerning life after death. His early letters show signs of this faith, especially when compared with his later letters attacking traditional Christianity. In one such letter to his college friend John Page, for example, Jefferson wrote that the goal of people should be to live with "pious resignation to the Divine will" until they receive their just "reward" from God at their "journey's end."[2]

As Jefferson studied more of the classical writers and great poets, he became less satisfied with simple declarations of belief in immortality and more intrigued with the mystery of death and the romance of life. Years later he wrote of his unsuccessful search for answers to the riddle of life after death during his college years: "The laws of nature have withheld from us knowledge of the country of spirits, and left us in the dark as we were."[3] He was impressed with the skepticism, wonder, and bravery in the face of extinction displayed by the Greek and Roman writers he was studying and copied long passages from Anacreon, Horace, Euripides, and Herodotus in his notebook. In particular, he was influenced by the skeptical writings of Cicero about the immortality of the soul. He carefully noted Cicero's more hopeful speculations about immortality, which he later used in his own writings, as being "a change of abode only from this darkness for that light," or "in the midst of the fatigues of life to sleep to eternity." He was influenced by the Roman Stoics to view suicide with sympathy and helped abolish the legal penalties against suicide in Virginia, arguing that few men would "calmly determine to renounce life and make experiment of what is beyond the grave." He thus did not find in his admired classical writers any firm belief in the afterlife, but he did find a Stoical spirit of courage and virtue in the face of death that he much admired and always practiced.[4] In English literature he also found many passages to stir his imagination and emotions concerning the mystery and finality of death which he copied in his notebook.[5]

These studies indicate that Jefferson was influenced while in college to become more skeptical of his early Anglican teachings about heaven and the bodily resurrection of Christ. This skepticism persisted with him all of his life. On the other hand, he found in the great passages of literature and the classics many statements of hope for the possibility of life after death which strongly appealed to him. These passages convinced him to keep an open mind on the subject.

With the passing of time, Jefferson's youthful interest in the romance of life and death faded. As he wryly quoted from the poet Edward Young, "All men think all men mortal, but themselves."[6] Interesting as speculation about life after death might be, no one could really know the truth, and the business of the living was with life, not death. Jefferson was a leader who was unusually busy with living.

He did not reject a belief in life after death, despite his questions on the subject, but he refused to be told that there was only one orthodox "way which according to the sacred geography leads to Jerusalem straight." He adopted a practical point of view and reacted against futile speculation in favor of studying scientific and historical matters and living a life devoted to improving the conditions of mankind. As he wrote to Adams, "I am satisfied and sufficiently occupied with the things which are without tormenting or troubling myself about those which may indeed be, but of which I have no evidence." As a means of attaining immortality, Jefferson increasingly came to believe in the importance of moral works over religious faith in order, he wrote, "to merit an inheritance in a state of being of which I can know so little." As a result of his studies and his own experiences of life, Jefferson came to hope, if not firmly to believe, that there was a life after death and to think that an intelligent person should live a good life that would deserve a place in God's eternity, trusting to the Creator for the future.[7]

Jefferson's Opposition to Orthodox Christian Teachings on Immortality

It is not surprising that Jeffersonian scholars have been tentative in discussing Jefferson's beliefs about immortality since he emphatically rejected orthodox Christian teaching of the way to attain life after death. It is clear that, under the influence of his college teachers, Jefferson came to reject the orthodox Christianity of revelation based on faith in a divine Savior in favor of the deistic religion of reason advocated by the Enlightenment. The Enlightenment, however, was so much concerned with breaking the bonds of religious superstition and improving man's life here and now that it had little to say about life after death. Accordingly, many of Jefferson's writings on religion oppose orthodox Christian ideas of being saved by faith in order to obtain eternal life.

For example, in a letter to Peter Carr, Jefferson discussed the orthodox Christian theology of his day that believed Jesus was the begotten Son of God who ascended bodily into heaven and the liberal idea that he was a man to be followed. He admitted that belief in Christ as a God and "the hope of a happy existence in a future state" were comforting and inducements to good living but argued that there were "incitements to virtue in the comfort and pleasantness" of the opposite belief as well. Writing to men of his own age with similar ideas, Jefferson was less guarded in his attacks upon traditional Christian ideas of eternal salvation.[8]

The objection that Jefferson and the Enlightenment authors who influenced him in his mature thinking had to the traditional concept of Christian salvation was that it was based on a degraded idea of God's justice and mercy. They contended that orthodox Christianity taught that men were rewarded or punished in the afterlife arbitrarily by a vengeful God and that the fate of the saved was determined by their "election" without regard for their merit.[9] This was the reason for Jefferson's vehement attacks on the theology of Saint Paul and Calvin.[10] Jefferson also objected to the traditional Christian teaching that man was a lost sinner who was saved only by the atoning death of Christ on the cross, and he rejected the picture of life after death given by the book of Revelation as a golden city brought down from heaven for the saints judged worthy by Christ, the mighty Judge, at the end of the world.[11]

Jefferson, therefore, could not accept the supports to a belief in the afterlife that many Christians found in the conviction that Christ was the Son of God who had demonstrated the reality of life after death by the resurrection experiences of the disciples. It was a prime article of Jefferson's deistic religion that Jesus was not a deity, although he tactfully avoided the question of Christ's divinity as much as possible. To his friends, however, he wrote scathing denunciations of the logically incomprehensible idea of one God who was three and three gods who were one. By insisting on a purely rational religion and by rejecting the mystical and divine elements in Christianity, however, Jefferson made it difficult to believe in human immortality.[12]

Jefferson's Belief in an Eternal Judgment

One idea about life after death that persisted throughout all of Jefferson's writings on the subject was a belief that people were judged for the quality of their lives. It appeared not only in the writings of his mature years, as in a passage to the Reverend Isaac Story relating his hope of meriting an inheritance in the future state of being, but also in his earliest writings. In his youthful letter to John Page, Jefferson wrote of receiving from God when we died "such reward as to him shall seem proportioned to our merit." Even in his more skeptical letter to Peter Carr in which he argued that the satisfactions of a virtuous life were rewards enough in themselves, Jefferson declared that "the hope of a happy existence in a future state increases the appetite to deserve it."[13]

It is significant that Jefferson included the "prospects of a future state" among the ingredients he thought necessary for inculcating moral behavior among people. In a well-considered letter to Thomas Law, he listed moral education and "the prospects of a future state of retribution for the evil as well as the good done while here" among the moral forces necessary to motivate individuals to live good lives in society.[14]

Such a belief in a future judgment by God was in opposition to his disbelief in the existence of the traditional Christian heaven and hell, but Jefferson stubbornly clung to both convictions all of his life. A partial explanation lies in the fact that, after his graduation from the College of William and Mary, he studied law with George Wythe, who taught him to "regard law as a branch of the history of mankind."[15] These continuing legal and social studies gave Jefferson a belief in the importance of the sanctions of law and social approval to encourage moral behavior in order to improve society. As a student of law and history and a practicing lawyer and statesman, he saw the importance of a belief in eternal judgment for encouraging a moral life of service to society. In his moral advice to others, he constantly stressed the importance of the expectation of an eternal reward. In letters to two young people who were named after him, for example, he included the thought of eternal reward of "ineffable bliss." In a much earlier letter to his young daughter Patsy, Jefferson gave similar advice to always "obey your conscience in order to be prepared for death."[16]

Jefferson did not accept a literal interpretation of the Bible concerning a last judgment at the end of the world. He believed in progress and "the diffusion of knowledge among the people" to make for a better world rather than in the last judgment of God and the creation of a new heaven and a new earth for the saved. He was influenced in his opposition to the apocalyptic idea of God's judgment and the atonement theory of God's forgiveness by his Enlightenment studies.[17]

Jefferson hedged his belief in a future judgment with several conditions. It was God, not religious people, who was the judge.

"Our particular principles of religion are a subject of accountability to our God alone," he stated. Christ had taught men "to judge of the tree by its fruit," he answered a critic of his religion. "I must ever believe that religion substantially good which produces honest life," he concluded. The only way the world could judge men's religion was by their lives, not their words, he wrote a Washington friend. To his old friend Charles Thomson, Jefferson even more frankly criticized the religious people who presumed to condemn in the name of God those who differed from themselves. "Faith and works," he stated, "will show their worth by their weight in the scales of eternal justice before God's tribunal." A person's religion must be judged by whether it produced "an honest and dutiful life to society." What really aroused Jefferson's ire was the suggestion that God judged people in the afterlife by their correct belief rather than by their behavior. This emphasis upon faith over works was behind his aversion to Pauline theology, which, he argued, departed from the "happy" doctrines of Jesus that taught one "to love God with all thy heart and thy neighbor as thyself, and that there is a future state of rewards and punishments" for man's earthly actions.[18]

So strong was Jefferson's belief that any future judgment of man by God was based upon man's moral deeds that at times he even thought Jesus did not stress this idea sufficiently. On the whole, however, Jefferson greatly admired the moral teachings of Jesus. He called them "the most beautiful morsel of morality which has been given to us by man." And one of his chief reasons for his admiration was that Jesus taught the reality of a future moral judgment "supplementary to the other motives to moral conduct." He frequently argued that Jesus' teachings were superior to those of Moses because "Jesus preached the doctrine of a future state" and Moses did not. In his notes, he concluded, "The advantages accruing to mankind from our Saviour's mission are an inducement to a pious life, by revealing clearly a future existence in bliss, and that it was to be the reward of the virtuous."[19]

The choice of texts that Jefferson made when he compiled his personal versions of the New Testament also indicate that he thought belief in a future state of moral judgment but not an apocalyptic ending of the world was what was valuable in Jesus' teachings. He included in his selection of the teachings of Jesus that he considered authentic the parables of judgment and the coming of the Kingdom of God (see Appendix, sections 103, 108, 112, 117, 124, 131), but he omitted the more extreme prophecies of the destruction of the world (see Appendix, sections 112, 131).

Clearly, then, Jefferson approved of the belief in a future life in which men were judged for their behavior in this life. His early religious convictions and his classical studies inclined him to be receptive to the idea. His long legal training and experience with the sanctions of the law influenced him to see the importance of the afterlife as a moral sanction for the moral law of God. Jefferson's studies in moral philosophy and religion also led him to prefer a future judgment as a reinforcement for the moral beliefs and behavior he was striving to develop as an educator and a statesman for the improvement of society. His occasional statements about the inevitability of God's judgment upon such wicked men as Bonaparte are evidence of this strain in Jefferson's thinking.[20]

It has been argued by some Jeffersonian scholars that, while he approved of the idea of a judgment in an afterlife, Jefferson did not actually believe in it himself.[21] In his letter on religion to Peter Carr, for example, it might be assumed from the skeptical tone that Jefferson did not believe in the existence of God, the divinity of Christ, or the reality of life after death. However, his other writings show that he did believe in the existence of God, did not believe in the divinity of Christ, and nowhere denied the existence of life after death. In his letter to his daughter on the last judgment, he did not mention life after death, an omission which may indicate he was hesitant about accepting the idea at this period of his life, but it is extremely dangerous to argue from omission, especially when dealing with Jefferson's writings. He was always cautious about influencing his family with his own ideas on religion.[22]

Jefferson's Opposition to Soul and Spirit

Jefferson occasionally sounded a doubting and skeptical note on the subject of human immortality, usually in connection with his scientific thought. He was, he often boasted, a determined materialist.[23] Jefferson did not accept the mystical and metaphysical elements in Christianity, which he attributed to Plato's fuzzy thinking. Moreover, he did not believe that Plato's ideas were particularly convincing proofs of human immortality; they were too vague and inexact, "semblances . . . half seen through a mist," he wrote.[24] Along with metaphysical ideas, he also rejected the concepts of soul and spirit, making it more difficult for him to believe in the afterlife.

An example of the difference between Jefferson's scientific deism and traditional Christian theology is the use made of the concept of God's "Word," the Logos, to explain the creation of the universe. The early philosopher Philo of Alexandria, using the theories of Plato, had developed the idea of the Logos as an intermediate reality by means of which the immaterial, immortal, perfect God could have contact with the material, mortal, crass universe. The author of the Gospel of John personified this concept of the "Word" of God and applied it to the divine Christ. Such a deification of the "Word" of God, Jefferson maintained, was based on a "mistranslation of the word *logos* and a perversion of the doctrine of Jesus." It was not Jesus but God's "reason" that created the world, he argued.[25]

Jefferson's most provocative and illuminating discussion of matter, spirit, and soul occurred in a dialogue with John Adams in their later letters. Adams first raised the question of what did people mean by "matter and spirit?" He thought neither "saint," who believed in spirit, nor scientist, who thought everything was matter, knew what either spirit or matter really were. "Your puzzling letter on matter and spirit, with its crowd of scepticisms, kept me from sleep," Jefferson replied. "I read it, laid it down, and read it again." He was forced back to the basic elements of philosophy, he said, according to which he could only know what he sensed. He could sense matter, which he defined as "bodies not myself." He could also feel "motion" or bodies moving. In between bodies was "void, or nothing, or immaterial space." With these concepts, Jefferson argued, "we may erect the fabric of all the certainties we can have or need." "To talk of immaterial existences," Jefferson concluded, "is to talk of nothings. To say that the human soul, angels, god are immaterial is to say they are nothings, or that there is no god, no angels, no soul."[26]

In coming down so strongly on the side of materialism, Jefferson here seems to deny the existence of God and of human immortality. But he was not willing to go that far; instead, he decided that both

God and the human soul were, in some sense, material. The argument over matter and spirit was a favorite battleground during the eighteenth century between the champions of medieval mysticism and the Enlightenment supporters of the new science, similar to the later conflicts between science and religion. Joseph Priestley, who greatly influenced Jefferson, succinctly summarized the medieval view of spirit and matter: "It has been generally supposed that there are two distinct kinds of substance in human nature, matter and spirit. Matter is that kind of substance of which our bodies are composed; perception and thought is said to reside in a spirit, or immaterial principle, intimately united to the body." He concluded, "The higher orders of intelligent beings, and especially the Divine Being, are said to be purely immaterial." This medieval idea of man and the universe was under siege during the Enlightenment. Early scientific studies, such as those of the physics of light and the anatomy of the brain, had shown that matter was not as material and thinking not as immaterial as had been supposed. Such studies led Priestley to conclude that when a person's brain and body ceased to exist, both thinking and life ended.[27]

Jefferson accepted Priestley's thoughts and often called himself a "materialist," but he argued that "the attraction of the Sun which reins the planets in their orbits" and the way man's material brain could exercise the amazing process of thought were both wondrous. He was also influenced to believe in the material and scientific viewpoint by his Enlightenment studies of Locke, Destutt de Tracy, Stewart, Cabanis, and Helvétius.[28]

While Jefferson's belief in materialism had many advantages in explaining the physical world, it had one serious disadvantage. It left little room for the idea of the human soul and made believing in the immortality of the individual more difficult. In discussing with Adams the power of the human brain to think, which he compared to the magnetism of the needle of a compass, Jefferson argued that both magnetism and thought ceased "on dissolution of the material organ."[29]

The problem all along for Jefferson in believing in immortality, as for many modern people, was the question, "What is the soul?" Jefferson was a man of reason and was more dedicated to scientific thinking than many men of his time. He used scientific farming and household inventions at Monticello and was active in scientific studies and societies.[30] Intellectually, he could not accept the idea of an immaterial, immortal soul for human beings different from the rest of the material creation that science was revealing.

There was another side to Jefferson, however, besides his cool rationalism. Despite his reserve, he was a warm and emotional person. His intellect might tell him that the soul was a nothing, but his emotions would not let him believe that the friends and family he loved and grieved for were only bodies dissolving in the grave, never to be known again. The tension between Jefferson's scientific skepticism of the existence of the soul and his grief-impelled belief that somehow loved ones would meet again explains the divergent views held by Jeffersonian scholars about Jefferson's ideas on immortality. Jefferson would not give up his belief in materialism or in the afterlife. In his writings he expounded first one idea and then the other, depending on his subject and mood. The problem is to note how he attempted to reconcile these opposing ideas.

Although he was indebted to Priestley for many of his ideas on religion, Jefferson was unable to accept Priestley's solution to the problem of immortality. Priestley, both an able scientist and a minister, solved the problem of body and soul by rejecting a belief in a separate, immaterial soul in favor of a belief in the later resurrection and "reanimation" of the physical body and personality by the "Being who first composed it."[31] Jefferson's writings indicate he did not adopt Priestley's belief in the bodily resurrection but instead followed the Enlightenment thought of Voltaire, Thomas Woolston, Matthew Tindal, and Gotthold Lessing, who rejected the biblical accounts of the resurrection as "allegories, fables, and unhistoric extravagant stories."[32] Jefferson made a point of excluding the accounts of Jesus' resurrection from his versions of the life of Christ (see Appendix, sections 142–51).

While not accepting Priestley's belief in the resurrection of the body, Jefferson used some of Priestley's arguments to support his own theory that the human soul was material. His reasoning was that matter had clearly been endowed by the Creator in some instances with mysterious properties. He pointed to the magnetism of the lodestone, the gravity of the sun, and the power of the brain to think. Similarly, he reasoned, the property of immortality was to be found in the human spirit, but spirit was also matter. He credited Locke with suggesting this idea to him, saying, "Mr. Locke openly maintained the materialism of the soul, and charged with blasphemy those who deny that Omnipotence could give the faculty of thinking to certain combinations of matter." Jefferson admitted there were difficulties in believing that human thought and spirit were material, but he argued that the medieval idea of thought and life as a separate and different entity from matter called spirit was even more unbelievable, writing, "I should with Mr. Locke, prefer swallowing one incomprehensibility rather than two."[33]

At first his belief in materialism troubled Jefferson's religious feelings, for he felt it conflicted with Jesus' teachings. Later he came to believe that both Jesus and such early church writers as Origen and Justin Martyr shared his idea of unique matter. "The ancient fathers," he wrote Adams, "held spirit to be matter: light and thin indeed, an etherial gas: but still matter."[34] Materialism, he argued, was the original doctrine of Christianity, and the "immaterial spiritualism" of the medieval church was a later "heresy" introduced by the Creed of Athanasius at the Council of Nicaea. Although he found in Jesus' teachings more of spiritualism than he liked, under John Adams's influence he came to believe that Jesus' words could be understood as teaching Jefferson's type of materialism. "Jesus told us," he often wrote to friends, "that 'God is a Spirit,' but He has not defined what a spirit is, nor said that it is not matter." Jefferson went on, "Indeed, Jesus Himself, the Founder of our religion, was unquestionably a Materialist as to man. In all His doctrines of the resurrection, He teaches expressly that the body is to rise in substance. In the Apostle's Creed, we all declare that we believe in the 'resurrection of the body.' "[35] The early church fathers, Jefferson believed, also taught that God and the soul are matter. In his commonplace book, he copied Latin quotations from Tertullian proving that "God is material and that the soul is also material," which he took from d'Holbach's book *Tableau des Saints.*[36]

It may appear that Jefferson was arguing in circles and that it does not really matter whether man has a material soul which has the wondrous and inexplicable attributes of thinking, personality, and immortality or has a material body and an immaterial and immortal soul which in some inexplicable manner inhabits and affects his body for a time. John Adams said as much in reply to his friend's arguments: "The question between spirit and matter appears to me nugatory because we have neither evidence nor idea of either." He concluded, "The faculties of our understanding are not adequate to penetrate the Universe."[37]

These letters between Jefferson and Adams after their retirement indicate that both men found pleasure and mental stimulation in the exchange of ideas. Adams turned to the greater reading knowledge of Jefferson for clarification of authors and ideas and seemed to find comfort in Jefferson's greater optimism about human nature and the future of society. Jefferson, for his part, seemed to be influenced by Adams's stronger religious belief coming from his New England heritage. Jefferson was too strong-minded to alter his belief in science and materialism, but there is evidence that he was influenced by Adams's arguments about spirit to find room for a belief in immortality among the wondrous attributes of certain modes of matter.

Such a belief was not as radical a step for Jefferson's materialism as it might seem, for his idea of Creation was more an organic one than a mechanistic one.[38] Jefferson had begun with the conviction that God had created in man a hunger for the rights of equality, freedom, and life and a desire to follow God's moral law. It was only a small step further to believe that God had also created man with an immortal soul. If Jefferson's scientific rationalism refused to let him call the soul a separate spiritual entity, under Adams's prodding he could believe that, in a universe of matter created by God with many mysterious and inexplicable attributes, immortality for certain modes of human matter was possible.

The Uses of Grief

The subject of immortality presents more than intellectual problems. It also has emotional problems. The conflict between the answers that Jefferson's heart found to the question of life after death and those that satisfied his head account for many of the discrepancies in his writings on the subject. Intellectually he might reject orthodox religious teachings, and scientifically he might believe that the human body died as all other forms of life did. But emotionally he could not accept the idea that the many friends and loved ones he had lost were dead and gone forever.

His early experiences of loss probably account for the classical quotations on the mystery of death and the many sentimental poems from English literature dedicated to lost loved ones that he copied in his commonplace book.[39] His father died when he was only fourteen, and the family record which Jefferson methodically kept in his father's prayer book shows that four of his eight brothers and sisters died in their youth, a not uncommon occurrence in colonial days. He particularly missed his oldest sister, Jane, who used to sing to him the solemn music of the Church of England. This experience gave him a lifelong appreciation of the Psalms. When his close boyhood friend and brother-in-law Dabney Carr died, Jefferson nailed an engraved copperplate on the tree at the foot of his grave containing a poetic tribute from the poet David Mallet.[40]

As the years went by, Jefferson had more sorrows to bear. Only two of his own six children lived to grow up, and only one survived him. Reflecting on the pain that love brings, he wrote to Maria Cosway: "Deeply practised in the school of affliction, the human heart knows no joy which I have not lost, no sorrow of which I have not drunk! Fortune can present no grief of unknown form to me!" He was doubtlessly recalling the loss of his wife, who died after a lingering illness from the aftereffects of childbirth. He was too reticent to ever write about this experience. In his account book under the date September 6, 1782, he wrote, "My dear wife died this day at 11:45 a.m.," and made the necessary entry of her death in his prayer book. In his "Autobiography," Jefferson wrote, "In the autumn of 1782 I lost the cherished companion of my life, in whose affections, unabated on both sides, I had lived the last ten years in unchequered happiness." His daughter Martha later told Henry Randall that her father had been at the bedside of her mother constantly during her four months' illness and, at her death, had been led into the adjoining library where he fell into a deep and prolonged faint. The daughter, nine years old at the time, recalled being frightened by the violence of her father's grief in the weeks that followed as he paced restlessly about his room or rode his horse forlornly through the surrounding woods. Jefferson was unable to attend to any work or any of his duties. He was, he wrote to a friend, in a "stupor of mind which had rendered me as dead to the world as she was whose loss occasioned it. In this state of mind an appointment from Congress found me, requiring me to cross the

Atlantic."[41] So fate resulted in Virginia's losing a retired planter and in America's gaining a statesman.

Jefferson's experiences made him sympathetic to the grief of others. Writing to a friend who had also lost his wife, Jefferson reminded his friend of the consolations remaining to him, the companionship of a son and service to his state as governor of Virginia. He continued, "Long tried in the same school of affliction, no loss which can rend the human heart is unknown to mine. My experience has proved that time, silence and occupation are its only medicines." Jefferson wrote with even more feeling to his old friends, John and Abigail Adams, after learning of the death of their only daughter: "I know the depth of your affliction and can sympathize with it. I have ever found time and silence the only medicine, and these but assuage, they never can suppress the deep-drawn sigh which recollection forever brings up, until recollection and life are extinguished together. Ever affectionately yours." After Jefferson's death, his family found small envelopes with locks of hair from his wife and each of his lost children in a secret drawer of his private cabinet with words of endearment written in his own hand. They showed signs of frequent handling.[42]

Of Jefferson's family, only his two daughters lived to maturity. In 1804 one of them, Maria, died. Jefferson grieved, not only for his lost daughter but for fear he would lose all his family. He wrote to John Page: "I, of my want, have lost even the half of all I had. My evening prospects [of a happy retirement] now hang on the slender thread of a single life." Fortunately, he was spared and did retire to live out his days with his daughter Martha and her children at Monticello.[43]

It is important to notice that in his personal involvement with sorrow and death, Jefferson found no easy solutions to the question of the persistence of the lives of those he loved after death, and he was too honest a man to offer any conventional expression of sympathy or easy assurances to friends in their own losses. He instead wrote what he had found to be true, that love persisted, time healed, and family and memory were one form of immortality.

In his writings, it is possible to catch glimpses of Jefferson desperately seeking honest reassurances of immortality under the impelling circumstances of a long life acquainted with grief and, only slowly, with some hesitation, coming to some firm beliefs about the nature of the afterlife. One of his most illuminating discussions is contained in an exchange with Adams on the reason for grief and suffering in life, a question that had clearly troubled Jefferson for a long time.

The question came up almost by accident. Adams had propounded one of his provocative questions calculated to stir up an interesting discussion by asking his younger friend if he would be willing to live his seventy-odd years over again, knowing all the joys and sorrows it would mean. Jefferson replied that he would, for he thought life was predominantly good. He had always steered his life by hope, not fear, he declared, but added, "I acknowledge, even in the happiest life, there are some terrible convulsions, heavy set-offs against the opposite page of the account." Then Jefferson raised the problem of grief: "I have often wondered for what good end the sensations of grief could be intended. All our other passions, within proper bounds, have an useful object, but what is the use of grief in the economy [of life]?"[44]

The question came from the deistic faith, which Jefferson and Adams shared, that everything in nature and human experience had a good purpose, since everything came from the good design of the perfect Creator, God. Writing to his doctor friend Benjamin Rush, for example, Jefferson had found some good even in yellow fever epidemics in American cities, since it discouraged the growth of cities with their attendant problems. He added, "When great evils happen, I am in the habit of looking out for what good may arise from them as consolations to us, and Providence has in fact so established the order of things, as that most evils are the means of producing some good." But in the case of grief, which Jefferson had experienced so often and so deeply, he was at a loss for its good purpose. Even "Stoical apathy," which he had admired as a young man, Jefferson ruled out as a cure for grief because he found it was impossible to practice.[45]

Adams picked up the challenge with typical zest. He too would like to live his life over, he replied, even though life was but "a Vapour, a Fog, a Dew, a Rose, a blade of Grass, a glass Bubble, a Tale told by an Idiot." He would like to sail along with Jefferson, he said, "Hope with her gay Ensigns displayed at the Prow; fear with her Hobgoblins behind the Stern." In his next letter, Adams considered the reasons for grief and trouble in a good world. He suggested that a merchant who was bankrupted by the loss of his ship at sea might learn prudence; a grief-stricken lover might learn resignation and greater kindness toward remaining family and friends. Men could not become truly understanding and great, Adams argued, who had not "been tossed and buffeted in the Vicissitudes of Life, forced upon profound Reflection by Grief and disappointments and taught to command their Passions and Prejudices." He agreed that "Stoical Apathy" was impossible but thought grief taught "Patience and Resignation and tranquility."[46]

Jefferson was intrigued with Adams's ready answers to the reasons for grief, for he dryly replied: "To the question on the utility of Grief, no answer remains to be given. You have exhausted the subject. I see that, with the other evils of life, it is destined to temper the cup we are to drink," and he included a favorite quotation from Homer about Jove distributing both good and evil to mortals down on earth from the two urns by his throne. In his student days he had copied and preserved this same passage, and its message stayed with him through the years. In his discussion of human sin, Jefferson sided with the Enlightenment thinkers who believed that there was no evil in the Creator's good universe, but his repeated use of this passage shows that when pressed far enough, Jefferson sided with the Greek thinkers in admitting the occasional presence of evil which men must be strong enough to face.[47]

Although Jefferson acknowledged Adams's facile arguments, he remained unconvinced about the useful purposes of grief. "Those afflictions cloud too great a portion of life to find a counterpoise in any benefits," he wrote back. "All the latter years of aged men are overshadowed with its gloom. Whither, for instance, can you and I look without seeing the graves of those we have known? And whom can we call up, of our early companions, who has not left us to regret his loss?" Finally, a reconciliation to one's own death because of loneliness for lost family and friends was the only use Jefferson could find for grief. He continued, "This, indeed, may be one of the salutary effects of grief; inasmuch as it prepares us to loose ourselves also without repugnance." Thus, Jefferson came to see death as a release from the burdens of old age. Although Stoic philosophy was not enough to answer the questions of life after death, its pessimistic courage strengthened him in the end.[48]

"We Shall Meet Again"

If the experiences of grief did not in themselves convince Jefferson's intellect of any certain answers to the reasons for suffering or to the riddle of life after death, they did predispose him emotionally to believe that there was a life after death for friends and loved ones. One of the statements about immortality he most frequently wrote to friends during all periods of his life was, "We shall meet again."

In his letter to John Page while they were in college, Jefferson wrote of their someday arriving together at the end of the journey of life to make a final accounting to their Creator. Some forty years later he wrote again to Page: "When you and I look back on the country over which we have passed, where are all the friends who entered it with us, under all the inspiring energies of health and hope? As if pursued by the havoc of war, scarce a few stragglers remain to count the fallen." He continued, "We have, however, the consolation that 'we sorrow not then as others who have no hope,' but look forward to the day which 'joins us to the great majority,' and to rise in the midst of the friends we have lost."[49]

Among Jefferson's early letters is an exchange with a family friend, Eliza Trist, who had been complaining of certain "crosses and disappointments" in her life, including the illness of her husband and the hardships of traveling without him. Jefferson expressed sympathy but added, "in the meantime you are supported by a certainty that you are again to meet," reminding her that there were "many wretched ones from whom that consolation is cut off." He was thinking of his own loss of his wife. He did not here mention the idea of loved ones seeing each other again in heaven, although it would have been natural for him to have done so; he apparently had not yet reached a firm conviction on the subject. On later occasions, he expressed the hope, "May we meet there again." Still later, he wrote positively to John Adams of "when we meet again in another place, and at no distant period." A year and half later, they were both dead.[50] Jefferson's comments about meeting again in heaven thus show an increasing certainty with the passing years.

As he grew older, Jefferson sometimes combined the two ideas of judgment and reunion in an afterlife. To Charles Thomson,

Jefferson expressed the conviction that religiously intolerant persons who judged others for their lack of faith and those who lived by moral works, such as Thomson and himself, would all meet at God's tribunal to be judged by the "scales of eternal justice." To John Adams, Jefferson wrote of awaiting God's time of judgment "with more readiness than reluctance" and concluded with the hope that he and Adams would one day reconvene with their dead colleagues of the Continental Congress who had accomplished so much for the freedom of men to receive God's approbation. On another occasion he wrote to Adams: "We have willingly done injury to no man; and have done for our country the good which has fallen in our way. I look therefore to that crisis, as I am sure you also do as one 'who neither fears the final day nor hopes for it.'" In a letter to William Canby in which he related a favorite story of the followers of different sects finding no sects in heaven, only Christian brethren, Jefferson wrote that those who practiced good morals would not be turned back from heaven's gates but would "find themselves united in concert with the reason of the supreme mind." To Miles King, Jefferson repeated the anecdote about there being no denominations in heaven and suggested that, though people might differ about "the shortest . . . road to our last abode, . . . let us be happy in the hope that . . . we shall all meet in the end . . . and embrace."[51]

Jefferson frequently referred to the reunion of friends in heaven in his personal correspondence. Reminiscing with Abigail Adams about their families, he wrote, "Those twenty years! Alas! Where are they? With those beyond the flood! Our next meeting must then be in the country to which they have flown—a country for us not now very distant." With a hint of much the same idea of old friends gladly going to heaven to meet again, he commented to John Adams five years later, "When the friends of our youth are all gone, and a generation is risen around us whom we know not, is death an evil?" It is evident that Jefferson's belief in the reunion of friends in the afterlife was strengthened by his discussions with Adams, for the two men agreed on the idea frequently. Adams, for example, concluded one discussion by writing: "We shall meet hereafter and laugh at our present botherations. So believes your old Friend, John Adams." Jefferson agreed that one advantage of the afterlife was the answers and new wisdom it would provide. "All this you and I shall know," he wrote, "when we meet again in another place, and at no distant period."[52]

Jefferson at times expressed the idea of those in heaven looking down on those left behind. To the two young boys who were named after him, Jefferson wrote: "And if to the dead it is permitted to care for the things of this world, every action of your life will be under my regard. Farewell!" In a letter to Adams concerning the eventual triumph of the Spanish people over the oppressions of Bonaparte, Jefferson suggested: "You and I shall look down from another world on these glorious achievements to man, which will add to the joys even of heaven." On another occasion, he predicted: "We shall only be lookers on, from the clouds above, as now we look down on the labors, hurry, and bustle of the ants and bees. . . . We may be amused with seeing the fallacy of our own guesses." To Abigail Adams, he wrote of "the wish of returning once in a while to see how things have gone on."[53]

Among Jefferson's more interesting letters is one written to Maria Cosway over thirty years after they had been romantically involved in Paris. Jefferson brought her up to date about his own grown family among whom he was living in happy retirement and concluded with the wish for a heavenly reunion: "The religion you so sincerely profess tells us we shall meet again; and we have all so lived as to be assured it will be in happiness." Writing to Lafayette in his old age, Jefferson expressed the desire he had long held of visiting France again and "seeing all my friends of Paris once more, a thing impossible now." However, Jefferson continued, he looked forward to a better reunion in the afterlife.[54]

Another time Jefferson gave a different reason for looking forward to reunion with his family after death, the fact that the heavenly life was more attractive than a feeble old age: "I have ever dreaded a doting old age. The rapid decline of my strength during the last winter has made me hope sometimes that I see land." In a farewell poem written for his daughter two days before his death, Jefferson wrote of "going to my fathers" and "welcoming the shore" at the end of life's voyage where "two seraphs await me." He was referring to the wife and daughter whom he had lost and grieved for these many years.[55]

The most eloquent expression of Jefferson's feelings about grief and death were the words he wrote to John Adams upon the death of the one whom Adams called "the dear Partner and Lover of my life for fifty-four years." Jefferson's tactful reply wasted not a word but revealed his sincere sharing of his friend's grief: "I know well and feel what you have lost, what you have suffered, are suffering, and have yet to endure. The same trials have taught me that, for ills so immeasurable, time and silence are the only medicines." Then Jefferson expressed his firm conviction of human immortality: "I will not therefore, by useless condolences, open afresh the sluices of your grief, nor, altho' mingling sincerely my tears with yours, will I say a word more, where words are vain, but that it is of some comfort to us both that the term is not very distant at which we are to deposit, in the same cerement, our sorrows and suffering bodies, and to ascend in essence to an ecstatic meeting with the friends we have loved and lost and whom we shall still love and never lose again. God bless you and support you under your heavy affliction."[56] These words express Jefferson's deepest conviction about human immortality and suggest the solution that he had finally reached to the conflict of the heart with the mind over a belief in the life hereafter—that human personality lives on "in essence."

What Is Immortality?

Besides facing the intellectual questions of what is the soul, what is matter, and what is spirit and the emotional questions of the purposes of grief and suffering and the desire to meet loved ones again in the hereafter, Jefferson considered the other answers that people have given when faced with the mystery of death. He found comfort and satisfaction in many of the answers that thinking people have given to the question of what is immortality.

The Immortality of Posterity

Jefferson, with his strong sense of family bonds, not only found comfort for his griefs in his daily activities at Monticello but also took comfort in the continuity he felt in the lives of his children and grandchildren as he faced his own death. Randall recorded many instances as recalled by Jefferson's family of his thoughtful concern and interest in the lives of even the youngest grandchildren during his retirement years at home.[57]

Jefferson's feeling that one important form of immortality was the survival of his family can be seen behind the words he wrote to his young daughter Martha, after the deaths of his wife and other children: "To your sister and yourself I look to render the evening of my life serene and contented. Its morning has been clouded by loss after loss, till I have nothing left but you." Some years later when his second daughter, Maria, died, Jefferson echoed this thought with even more concern, fearing that he might lose all his family and "see even the last cord of parental affection broken."[58]

In the passages on immortality that he copied from the Greek and Latin classics, Jefferson preserved statements not only about the uncertainties of life and the inevitability of death but also about the immortality that comes from children. In a letter to Adams about improving the race and society, Jefferson quoted a passage from the Greek poet Theognis stressing the physical immortality men find in their children, having been denied the gift of personal immortality by the jealous gods.[59]

In his last decade Jefferson wrote Maria Cosway: "My daughter Randolph, whom you knew in Paris as a young girl, is now the mother of eleven living children and the grandmother of about half a dozen others. Among these, I live like a patriarch of old."[60] His words reflect both his sense of immortality through children and his satisfaction that death in his family had finally been overcome.

The Immortality of Achievement and Fame

Another form of immortality which Jefferson desired was to deserve a place in history for his service to the country. In his first and second inaugural addresses Jefferson indicated a consciousness of being called to lead the nation in an important period of history and showed a desire to deserve the "approbation" and "good opinion" of the people. He sought God's enlightenment in leading the nation properly. To his friend Page, Jefferson wrote of feeling led by "destiny as well as duty." To a leader of the Baptist church, Jefferson wrote of his satisfaction in the part he had played in the cause of human rights, and to the Vermont legislature he expressed his thanks for their congratulations for his forty years of public service.[61]

Jefferson placed a high value on duty and service to country, as is reflected in his study of the classics and his devotion to the Roman ideals of service.[62] There are many references in his letters and studies to the importance of duty and the immortality resulting from being part of a great work.[63] While under political or religious attack for his ideas and policies, Jefferson frequently expressed the feeling that his fame and immortality would be secured by the future judgment of history. In a rare letter defending himself from attack by religious zealots, he wrote to a sympathetic correspondent: "The world must judge me by my life. I am consoled in this course that, notwithstanding the slanders of the saints, my fellow citizens have thought me worthy of trusts."[64]

In letters to Adams, Jefferson frequently wrote of his belief that they and the other members of the Continental Congress would be remembered by posterity. He noted that he and Adams were part of the small group that was left alive from the original Congress that had signed the Declaration of Independence, and he looked forward to their all meeting again in a heavenly Congress to receive God's praise for their part in that historic event. Jefferson had a keen sense of history and frequently expressed his conviction that those who had upheld the rights of man and overseen the achievement of American democracy were part of something that would live on. He called the period of history that he and Adams had helped shape a "Heroic age" and called Adams and himself, and the other founding fathers they had known, "Argonauts" who had piloted America and the world through "the labors and perils of the storm to Halcyon calms" of peace and joy.[65] History has proved Jefferson right in this judgment and awarded him the immortality he strove to earn.

Jefferson's concern for the immortality of fame is evident in his cryptic instructions to his friend James Madison a few months before his death. He wrote: "If I remove . . . beyond the bourne of life itself, as I soon must, it is a comfort to leave . . . [my concerns] under your care. . . . Take care of me when dead, and be assured that I shall leave with you my last affections." Because Jefferson discussed his financial problems and his efforts to settle his debts and save Monticello for his family in this letter, it might be assumed that the care he requested of Madison was concerned with his will and estate. This interpretation is not correct, for Jefferson named his grandson Thomas Jefferson Randolph as the executor to settle the estate, not Madison.[66]

By this time a number of histories of the early days of the American Independence had been written hostile to Jefferson and his party. It was widely believed that Madison, who had kept detailed records, would write an account of the period from Jefferson's point of view. In his letter to Madison, Jefferson wrote: "It has been a great solace to me to believe that you are engaged in vindicating to posterity the course we have pursued for preserving to them, in their purity, the blessings of self-government, which we had assisted too in acquiring for them. . . . It is that to which our lives have been devoted. To myself you have been a pillar of support through life."[67] Accordingly, Jefferson's request to Madison "to take care of me when dead" is best understood as being a desire for a vindication of his reputation and cause.

Both Madison and James Monroe were not only close friends and neighbors but political colleagues. They had fought side by side with Jefferson to win many of his important struggles for religious freedom and political democracy.[68] They succeeded Jefferson in the presidency, carrying on the liberal cause of the rights of man and his democratic dreams for America. With "the hand of time pressing heavily on me in mind as well as body," Jefferson wrote after he had retired, he felt he was right to have "withdrawn my attention from public affairs and resigned them to those who are to care for us all," believing that "approbation for my public services would be reward enough." Like the Roman veterans he admired, Jefferson, the old warrior, felt he could hang up his shield, leaving the battle to the younger and stronger men he had advised.[69]

Jefferson believed that the future belonged to the young. He never wanted to cling to power after his health or competence began to fade. He wrote to his friend Rush, "There is a fullness of time when men should go, and not occupy too long the ground to which others have a right to advance," speaking not only of political careers but of life itself. It was to Madison, upon seeing the social evils of too much hereditary wealth and power in France, that Jefferson earlier had written, "The earth belongs to the living and the dead have neither powers nor rights over it." Jefferson went on to develop the idea that not only wealth and estates must pass on to the next generation but the rights of society and the powers of leadership and decision. He contrasted the immortality of history with the dreadful mortality of the individual in a later letter on the same subject: "The Creator has made the earth for the living, not the dead. Rights and power can only belong to persons, not to things." With brutal truth he declared: "The dead are not even things. The particles of matter which composed their bodies, make part now of the bodies of other animals, vegetables, or minerals of a thousand forms. Nothing is unchangeable but the inherent and unalienable rights of man."[70] Jefferson thus accepted the grim scientific idea which sees immortality in the persistence of energy and matter but not in the individual. Perhaps this was the reason he sought comfort in the realization that his causes and reputation would live on in history.

Despite his occasional protestations to the contrary, all the evidence indicates that Randall was right in his judgment that Jefferson had a strong desire for "the approbation, esteem, and love of his countrymen and neighbors." When his firm pursuit of what he believed to be the right resulted in attacks by his political opponents, Jefferson comforted himself with the thought that posterity would vindicate him. The remark he made at the dinner table to his friend and family doctor Robley Dunglison that "he had no desire for posthumous reputation, nor could he well understand how any one could be anxious for it," is probably best understood as a modest disclaimer of conceit and an assertion of the high cost of public service rather than any real belief in the unimportance of the verdict of history.[71]

In his last public address, written shortly before his death to be read for the celebration of the fiftieth anniversary of the Declaration of Independence at Washington, Jefferson wrote that the Declaration had encouraged "the spread of the light of science" and was still "arousing men to burst the chains under which monkish ignorance and superstition had persuaded them to bind themselves, and to assume the blessings and security of self-government." Jefferson thus died championing the causes of liberty and Enlightenment for which he had lived, trusting in the verdict of history for immortality through his achievements.[72]

The "Pillow of Ignorance"

Another answer to the question of what is immortality which Jefferson frequently used in discussions with his friends was that man could not really know if there was a life after death or what it was like. In a letter to a clergyman who believed in the transmigration of souls, Jefferson expressed his skepticism about human immortality, declaring, "I have for many years reposed my head on that pillow of ignorance which a benevolent Creator has made so soft for us, knowing how much we should be forced to use it." Even in this skeptical letter, Jefferson did not deny that there was an afterlife; he only asserted that people could not really know. Indeed, in this same letter, he expressed his conviction that there was a "future state of being" for those who deserved it.[73]

The expression of resting his tired head on a "pillow of ignorance" was often used by Jefferson. As he explained to Adams, he had a practical viewpoint: "When I meet with a proposition beyond finite comprehension, I abandon it as I do a weight which human strength can not lift, and I think ignorance, in these cases, is truly the softest pillow on which I can lay my head." Adams was delighted with the phrase and agreed that there were "limits to which human understanding may hope to go in this Inferior World" and that there was a need for an "abundance of your pillows of Ignorance—an expression that I very much admire—on which to repose our puzzeld heads." Indeed, one of the attractions of dying for the two old men was the opportunity to satisfy their curiosity about life and death. They assured each other that they would soon find out the desired answers and laugh at their perplexities when they met again in the hereafter.[74]

Death Requires Stoical Courage and Resignation

Another belief of Jefferson concerning death, in the face of the impossibility of being certain about the existence of a life after death, was the necessity for Stoical courage and resignation. Jefferson was constantly pulled between his intellectual doubts about personal immortality and his emotional hopes and desires. He was honest about both his doubts and hopes and found help for this difficult task in his Stoic philosophy. Especially in his later years as he came closer to "the last great step" of death, he turned to his Stoic ideals for help in case "dissolution" proved to be the reality of death. In his retirement, Jefferson wrote to his friend and former secretary William Short, "With one foot in the grave, I beguile the wearisomeness of declining life by the consolations of classical philosophy, equally indifferent to hope and fear."[75]

While admitting that it was impossible to attain the Stoic indifference to life and death that he admired, Jefferson still urged the Stoic attitude upon himself and his friends. He wrote to Adams of being resigned to "the final day." To Page he wrote, "Whatever is to be our final destiny, wisdom, as well as duty, dictates that we should acquiesce in the will of Him who gives and takes away." The passages copied by Jefferson in his commonplace books reveals how much he was indebted to his classical and literary studies for his Stoic leanings.[76]

Reinforcing Jefferson's Stoical inclinations was his conviction that the old must make way for the young. He was too proud to become an enfeebled object of ridicule or pity. When a political friend urged him to become active in politics again after he had retired, Jefferson refused, saying the burden was too heavy and he was resigned to younger men taking over. Not only leadership and power must be given over to the young, but in the fullness of time the old must be resigned to die to make room for the young. "There is a ripeness of time for death," he continued, "regarding others as well as ourselves, when it is reasonable we should drop off, and make room for another growth. I am happy in what is around me. Yet I assure you I am ripe for leaving all, this year, this day, this hour."[77]

Jefferson was generally optimistic about the future. When Adams and other contemporaries despaired for the progress of freedom and Enlightenment during the Napoleonic wars, Jefferson reaffirmed his "belief in the future result of our labors, even though I shall not live to see it. My theory has always been, that if we are to dream, the flatteries of hope are as cheap, and pleasanter than the gloom of despair." He also was optimistic in facing death, believing that, most likely, there was a new adventure of eternal life to move on to as the challenge and flavor of this life palled with old age. He concluded his letter to John Adams: "I like the dreams of the future better than the history of the past. So good night. I will dream on, always fancying that Mrs. Adams and yourself are by my side marking our progress."[78]

Jefferson thus looked forward to death and the next life with a certain anticipation, but even if his worst doubts should turn out to be true and the grave proved to be the end of individual life, he could see an advantage in death that reinforced his stoical attitudes. Death at least brought an end to the loneliness and pains of old age. A few years before he died, he wrote to Maria Cosway: "Our former coterie are dead, diseased, and dispersed. Mine is the next turn, and I shall meet it with good will, for after one's friends are all gone before them, and our faculties are leaving us, too, one by one, why wish to linger in mere vegetation—as a solitary trunk in a desolate field, from which all its former companions have disappeared?" To "my dear Page," he wrote that he had no desire "to witness the death of all our companions and merely be the last victim." To another old friend, he explained: "Man like the fruit he eats, has his period of ripeness. Like that, too, if he continues longer hanging to the stem, it is but an useless and unsightly appendage." Jefferson always feared a doting old age and senility. He was dismayed to find his older friend and fellow signer of the Declaration of Independence, Charles Thomson, "slender as a grasshopper and much without memory." He complained to Adams, "Bodily decay is gloomy in prospect, but of all human contemplations the most abhorrent is body without mind."[79]

Old age would be desirable only if one could remain vigorous and healthy. Jefferson took satisfaction in the health he retained as he passed into his seventies and eighties. Even when he could no longer walk any distance, he boasted of riding around his land. His family remembered his horse Eagle, who had grown old with his master, being led prancing to the terrace, then standing "immovable as a statue" while the old man mounted, before moving off with "careful gravity." The trouble was that Jefferson's body was wearing out. He wrote Adams: "I learned with great regret the serious illness mentioned in your letter. But our machines have now been running for seventy or eighty years, and we must expect that, worn as they are, here a pivot, there a wheel, now a pinion, next a spring, will be giving way: and however we may tinker them up for a while, all will at length surcease motion. Our watches, with works of brass and steel, wear out within that period." On another occasion, he complained that he was experiencing "the hoary winter of age, when we can think of nothing but how to keep ourselves warm, and how to get rid of our heavy hours until the friendly hand of death shall rid us of all at once."[80]

In much of Jefferson's writings on the subject of death and old age, there is a striking kinship with the wisdom literature of the Old Testament, although he did not directly quote it. Compare, for example, Jefferson's writings about the weariness of old age with the words of Ecclesiastes concerning "the evil years when you will say, 'I have no pleasure in them.'" Also compare Jefferson's idea of the place of death in nature's plan with Ecclesiastes' famous poem: "For everything there is a season, a time to be born, and a time to die, a time to plant, and a time to pluck up what is planted."[81] Both life and death, Jefferson believed, required earnest effort, moral conviction, hope and determination, and Stoic courage and serenity.

Death Brings Peace and Rest

Jefferson in his later years frequently pointed out that death at least brought rest from weariness and peace from pain. He exclaimed, "When all our faculties have left one by one, and debility and malaise left in their places, is death an evil?" Then he quoted a favorite poem to the effect that "when man is left alone to mourn, and trembling limbs refuse their weight, 'tis nature's kindest boon to die!" He concluded: "I really think so, I have ever dreaded a doting old age; and I dread it still." The peace, rest, and equality of the grave appealed to Jefferson.[82]

Jefferson complained to Adams about the weariness he felt from long hours at his desk answering letters from publicity-seeking strangers. Randall recorded the burden of work and expense caused by the hospitality Jefferson extended to strangers who came visiting at Monticello. He wrote bitterly: "Is this life? At best it is but the life of a millhorse, who sees no end to his circle but in death." He felt both he and Adams deserved a better retirement after their long campaigns of service to the state.[83]

As life become more burdensome and painful, Jefferson came increasingly to feel, with the classical authors he had studied and noted in his commonplace books in his youth, that death, even without the certainty of immortality, would be welcome. Adams answered his despondent friend more practically, from the point of view of his greater Christian faith, that death was "a blessing not an evil, to the individual and to the world; yet we ought not to wish for it till life becomes insupportable."[84]

Yet, Jefferson was courageous and hopeful enough to find a good purpose even in the grave. Death was a normal end to life, necessary in the plan of life for future generations. It was also a welcome release and brought peace for the aged. He wrote to Abigail Adams: "Nothing proves more than this that the Being who presides over the world is essentially benevolent, stealing from us, one by one, the faculties of enjoyment, searing our sensibilities, leading us, like the horse in his mill, round and round the same beaten circle." Then he quoted the same poem he had many years earlier copied into his commonplace book:

> For what live ever here? with lab'ring step
> To tread our former footsteps? To see what we have seen?
> Hear, till unhear'd the same old slabber'd tale?
> To taste the tasted, and at each return, less tasteful?

Jefferson concluded his letter: "Satiated and fatigued with this leaden iteration, we ask our own Congé. The wish to stay here is thus gradually extinguished."[85] Jefferson's deistic studies and classical readings thus helped him find a beneficial purpose in the "economy of life" for even death itself.

Conclusions

Upon close examination, Jefferson's writings about immortality are more comprehensive than most scholars have realized. It is necessary, however, to follow Jefferson's thought processes during his long and eventful life in order to understand the differing and sometimes conflicting ideas he held.

In his early youth, he reflected his Anglican upbringing and wrote of God suitably rewarding people for doing their duty at the end of the journey of life. His college teachers and Enlightenment studies gave him a lifelong opposition to the traditional Christian concept of heaven and hell and to the orthodox Christian theology connected with "being saved." His emphasis on rational religion and his continuing interest in science gave Jefferson a skeptical attitude toward the existence of the spirit and the soul, and the Enlightenment influenced him to oppose the mystical and spiritual emphasis of the church. On the other hand, his studies of literature and the early experiences of death of family and friends common in colonial times made him interested in the mystery of immortality. They also convinced him of the necessity for ethical behavior and Stoical attitudes in the face of death, resulting in a belief that moral living was of supreme importance for happiness in this life and in the next. His experience as a lawyer and statesman reinforced his belief in the importance of law and a system of sanctions and rewards for governing human life not only by the courts but by God.

Jefferson had a keen interest in nature and the laws of science which gave him a materialistic point of view. His philosophy of materialism was basic to all of his understanding of the universe, God, man, and society and suited his practical nature and legal background. His understanding of matter and motion enabled him to explain the world of nature by scientific law and to apply his knowledge of architecture and agriculture in useful ways to his work at Monticello. A material universe created by his deistic God gave him a rational religion which could be extended and applied to the world of man and his social institutions. The development of man could be studied rationally under the subjects of history and law.[86] The moral law could be considered a corollary to the laws of science by which God ruled the human world as he ruled the world of nature. This materialism, however, made grave difficulties for Jefferson in believing in the human soul and life after death.

Jefferson's materialism conflicted with his inclination to believe that a moral God would recompense each human being suitably in an afterlife. The conflicts of his head, which doubted the existence of an immaterial, immortal soul, and of his heart, which felt there must be an afterlife where friends and loved ones were reunited, increasingly troubled Jefferson as the years brought their weight of disappointments and sorrows. All his life Jefferson sought to reconcile the conflicting convictions about life after death raised by his readings and his experiences. In the wisdom of old age he finally reconciled his questions by discarding a mechanistic materialism in favor of a biological one that left room for mysteries and wonders in the world of nature and a belief in another form of human life besides this mortal one. Once the mind was satisfied for Jefferson, the heart could have its way and Jefferson could firmly assure Adams, in his time of grief, that in death the true, immortal "essence" of the human individual would "ascend to an ecstatic meeting with the friends we have loved and lost, and whom we shall still love and never lose again."[87]

A study of Jefferson's ideas about life after death is rewarding for many reasons. Jefferson was probably the most able American exponent of the Enlightenment and liberal religious thought of his time and was more influential with his contemporaries than has been generally recognized. He not only was remarkably well read on religious subjects but was also highly intellectual and genuinely religious.

He dealt in some depth with a great variety of ideas about immortality and honestly expressed all of the hopes and fears and doubts and beliefs about life after death to which men of reason have always been subject. His handling of complex ideas in literary and clear language is still masterful. His treatment of spirit and matter for those concerned with the skepticism of a scientific age is still helpful, and his dealing with the emotional aspects of grief, old age, and the comforts of immortality through posterity and achievement, as well as the individual's natural hopes for future reunion with loved ones, show great understanding and feeling. Jefferson dealt honestly, out of his own extensive study and varied experiences of life, with the deep issues of life, death, and immortality. He found ways to answer human questions about life after death that were helpful and different from those of orthodox religious faith and that sustained himself and like-minded friends, which are still valid and useful today.

Death of an Enlightened Statesman

It was in the year 1826, at the age of eighty-three, that increasing illness and feebleness made Jefferson feel that the hand of death was upon him and "the end of the journey" near. The preparations he made for his own death verify the beliefs about immortality that he expounded in his writings. Found among his papers after his death were plans that he prepared for his monument. He requested that these words be carved on an obelisk:

HERE WAS BURIED
THOMAS JEFFERSON
AUTHOR OF THE DECLARATION OF AMERICAN
INDEPENDENCE,
OF THE STATUTE OF VIRGINIA FOR RELIGIOUS FREEDOM
AND FATHER OF THE UNIVERSITY OF VIRGINIA

The reason, he said, was "because by these, as testimonials that I have lived, I wish most to be remembered."[88] It should be noted that Jefferson did not request that he be remembered for the public offices he had held, even that of the presidency. It was for his part in establishing in the world the rights of man, freedom from religious tyranny, and an ongoing institution for perpetuating enlightened education that Jefferson thought he deserved enduring fame.

As Jefferson grew progressively weaker during his last illness, he made his farewell to his family, who were gathered by his bedside, not overlooking the youngest great-grandchildren. He gave them each affectionate words of encouragement and practical advice. Then he was heard to murmur, "Lord, now lettest thou thy servant depart in peace," quoting the familiar Nunc Dimittis response of the Anglican service for evening prayer. Two days before his death, Jefferson had handed to his daughter a little casket which contained some favorite verses about death from his reading and a verse he had composed himself. Characteristically, he expressed his hopes of finding rest and reunion with his beloved wife and younger daughter.[89]

By conscious effort Jefferson clung to life throughout the night and into the day of July 4, 1826, so that he might die on the fiftieth anniversary of the adoption of his Declaration of Independence. In his home in New England John Adams also lay dying. He too clung to life until the Fourth came and then died.[90] One is left to imagine the possible surprise and gladness with which the two old friends and "Argonauts of history" joined together to make "the last, great journey to ecstatic meeting" with loved ones lost and regained, and to assemble again with their "ancient colleagues in Congress" to reminisce about the progress of freedom and Enlightenment for which they had worked so long and faithfully, as they had so often speculated would happen.

CHAPTER 10

CONCLUSIONS

What conclusions concerning Jefferson's religious beliefs are indicated by examining his religious writings and studies? One thing is plain: his reputation for being uninterested or opposed to religion is undeserved; he did read and write extensively on religious subjects. It is unfortunate that his strong religious convictions have been so imperfectly understood and so frequently misrepresented. Few Americans have been subjected to as much political admiration and as much religious attack as Thomas Jefferson.[1] This misunderstanding and opposition seems to have been due partly to Jefferson's prominence as a social reformer, partly to his reticence about his religion, and partly to his outspoken attacks on religion written to private parties that were published without his permission.

Conclusions about Jefferson's Religion

Was Jefferson really as radical in his religion as his opponents declared or as some modern scholars indicate?[2] In answer to the charge that he was an "atheist, deist, or devil," he was not an atheist, he was a deist, and personal morality and honor were important elements in his character. He was strongly influenced by the liberal religious ideas of the eighteenth-century Enlightenment, particularly the deism of Scottish philosophers, beginning with the stimulation he received from his favorite college professor, William Small, and continuing through a lifetime of study of the books he acquired for his library.[3]

An evaluation of Jefferson's deism indicates that his beliefs about God were not as radical as those of many of his contemporaries. Jefferson defended his French philosopher friends who were atheists as being honorable men, but he did not share their views that the universe could have always existed without a Creator. Jefferson believed in God as the planner, architect, first cause, and master builder of the universe. He went further and believed that God continued to guide, modify, and sustain his creation. Jefferson's writings and speeches are studded with references to God's providence and guidance over the affairs of men and nations. He stressed as the most important attributes of God his goodness, justice, wisdom, moral perfection, and wise provision for all the needs of people and society. Jefferson thus went beyond the deistic belief that there was a God to the theistic belief that there were attributes of God which people could come to know.

It is probable that it was Jefferson's Christology which earned him his reputation as a religious radical more than his ideas about God, which were quite orthodox in an intellectual way. But when he equated the Christian doctrine of the virgin birth of Christ with the Roman fable of the generation of Minerva in the brain of Jupiter, rejected the miracles of the Bible and the divinity of Christ, and declared the doctrines of original sin, the blood atonement, and the Trinity to be "metaphysical insanities," he undercut the foundation of orthodox Christianity and antagonized many Christians.[4]

The fact that Jefferson wanted to replace what he considered a superstitious Christology with a reasoned view of Christ as a great and good man, inspired of God, and the "greatest teacher of moral truths that ever lived," is usually overlooked. That Jefferson rejected the idea of the French atheists that Jesus was a deluded fanatic of illegitimate birth and formed a high estimate of the character of Jesus from his own extensive New Testament studies is not widely known.[5] Jefferson's knowledge of Greek and of biblical texts and his extensive studies of Roman life and mythology and early church history made him a good biblical scholar. His work of creating his own accounts of the life of Jesus in harmony form in his "Bible" was further refined and developed by later New Testament research.

When considered in the light of the broad spectrum of American religious movements, Jefferson's religion does not seem more radical than the ideas held by many other Americans. The abuse he received does not seem deserved. He was intellectual in his approach to religion and distrusted emotion, mysticism, and a religion based on faith, but so have many other intellectual persons. After due consideration, the judgment of Jefferson's great-grandson that he was a "conservative Unitarian" seems accurate.[6]

Jefferson's beliefs about the nature of man and his relationship to God, likewise, cannot be classified as radical. Although he prided himself on being a "materialist" and rejected the teaching of medieval theologians that man possessed an immaterial soul inhabiting a material body,[7] Jefferson believed along with many eighteenth-century thinkers that man was part of the "great chain of creation." True, man was part of nature, but all nature exhibited wondrous attributes given it by God during creation.

Jefferson's political and social theories about the "rights of man" and the ability of men to govern themselves freely in a democratic society were rooted in his theology—in his religious conviction that man was a creature of God "endowed by his Creator" with these rights. Jefferson also emphasized the duties that responsible people owed to society even more than he stressed the rights that society owed to them. He wrote extensively about "the moral law" by which God governs human affairs even as he governs the world of nature by physical laws. Even when Jefferson wondered about the possibility of individual immortality, he was sure that God would judge all persons and nations for their moral behavior. He also believed all people possessed a "moral sense" which led them to desire to follow a moral life, a sense which was created in them by God in order to make social living possible.[8]

Although Jefferson rejected orthodox Christianity's theology about the sinful nature of humans and their need for atonement and salvation, he replaced this theology with an optimistic view of the moral nature of mankind and the possibility for improvement by education and social reform. Jefferson's religious convictions were thus fundamentally important to his theories of man, politics, and society.

Jefferson's fervent belief in religious freedom likewise was strongly rooted in his religious beliefs about God and man. Granted that his opposition to the official establishment or sanction of any one religion was a politically astute stand, all of his writings indicate that it was on ideological grounds rather than political ones that Jefferson argued for religious freedom. It is true that he wanted to avoid the bad example of Europe with its religious wars and of the American colonies with their witchhunts and persecutions, in which Christians, he said, had over the centuries been "burning and torturing one another for abstractions which no one of them understand."[9] The reason for his opposition to religious persecution was not just political or humanitarian, however. It was that the attempt to enforce religious conformity was contrary to God's purposes when he created people with individual rights and individual differences.

People's ideas and beliefs varied just as their appearances varied. To say that either their appearances or their religious beliefs must be the same was ridiculous. All that coercion in religion had been able to do, he bitterly wrote, was to make those who used it tyrannical fools and those who were forced to conform hypocrites, since force could never convince the inner mind. Truth had no need of police power; it was error that had benefited by force. Attempts at religious dictation were doomed to failure because God had "created the mind free and willed that free it shall remain," Jefferson declared in his Act for Establishing Religious Freedom. In this work, second in importance for human rights only to his Declaration of Independence, he further argued for religious freedom on theological grounds when he proclaimed that it was "sinful and tyrannical" to force a person to support a religion which he "disbelieves and abhors." Man was responsible for his religious beliefs and his ultimate destiny to the God who made him, not to priest, magistrate, church, creed, or public opinion, Jefferson maintained all of his life.[10]

It was because of his religious convictions about God and the impulse he had implanted in people for religious diversity that Jefferson believed America must embark upon the radical experiment of establishing a new government with "a wall of separation" between state and church. It was not that he was opposed to religion. He hoped and believed the churches would prosper with greater variety and enthusiasm under voluntary support than under government subsidy, and he set a good example by his own support of many churches.[11]

Jefferson never advocated freedom from religion. He believed moral teaching and restraint of evil were necessary for social living, and he stressed the importance of the inner morality gained from religion. He feared the dangers of urbanization and industrialization for America and strongly emphasized moral teaching, while insisting upon religious freedom. He also resisted pressure upon individuals from the press and public opinion, declaring, "I have sworn eternal hostility against every form of tyranny over the mind of man."[12]

Jefferson's program of social reform was also based upon his religious beliefs. When he worked for broader education and the end of inheritance laws that encouraged the development of the rich upper class, for example, it was as much to develop new opportunities for all people as it was for the widening of political democracy, for behind his advocacy of democracy was the conviction that it was God's purpose for all individuals to develop their God-given abilities to the highest potential.[13] Jefferson's emphasis upon the reform of social ills such as war and slavery was based upon his view of Christianity as a system of ethical teachings rather than a body of mysticisms. Since Jefferson also saw Jesus as a moral teacher and social reformer rather than a God, his stressing of the social and moral aspect of Christ's life and teachings began an emphasis on "Christian Social Action" which has been characteristic of American theology ever since. Upon close study, Jefferson is seen to be influential not only in shaping the direction of American political liberalism but also in beginning the liberal, Unitarian, and Social Gospel emphasis of much of the American church.[14]

Even in dealing with the question of human immortality, Jefferson's thought reveals more of a religious emphasis than most Jeffersonian scholars have realized. Jefferson's scientific point of view and his idea that man and all life were only matter made it difficult for him to believe in the human soul or in individual immortality.[15] Yet his early studies in classical literature, his emotional nature, and his reaction to his own experiences of grief led him to declare from the beginning, "We shall meet again." By enlarging his ideas of the marvelous attributes created by God in matter to include personal immortality, he was able to become more certain of his belief in the afterlife in his later years.[16]

Jefferson and Modern Religious Beliefs

Jefferson's thought is both a fruition of Enlightenment humanitarianism and a forerunner of modern liberalism, both social and religious. As Merrill Peterson has noted, not only was Jefferson in the midst of yesterday's important intellectual struggles, but his battles forecast the conflicts and problems of the modern world.[17]

His championing of religious freedom and the complete separation of church and state is the most familiar example of his involvement in a continuing social issue, and he is often cited by both opponents and proponents of government aid to parochial schools, prayer in the public schools, or civil observances of religion.[18] The question of individual versus society's rights, of the right to demonstration and revolution versus the need for law and order, and of human rights over against property rights are other modern problems that concerned Jefferson.

In the field of religion, Jefferson was deeply involved in questions that the passing years have made more important. Beyond such obvious issues as war and peace, social justice, and racism, he was concerned with religious and theological problems that have increasingly concerned later religious thinkers. He wrote about the conflict of science with religion and offered solutions to the problem in his deistic proofs for God and his revisions of outmoded biblical concepts of nature long before the issue gained popular religious attention.

Similarly, Jefferson explored the conflict over the use of reason instead of faith in religion and developed a model of a believable religion for a person of intellect and education before increasing education made this an issue for the modern church. He also emphasized the relative importance of faith versus works in theology and the religious life. His bitter arguments over the Calvinist doctrines of religious conservatives of his day and his conflicts with biblical literalists foreshadowed a debate between religious liberals and ultraconservatives that continues to this day in the American church. He also stressed the primary importance of the moral teachings of Jesus Christ and the duty of every responsible person to apply this teaching to his own life and that of his society, the cardinal principles of all Christian activists.

Jefferson wears well, for he dealt honestly and thoughtfully with so many of the deep issues of human life and experience and with so many of the continuing problems of human society.

Jefferson's Immortality

When America was celebrating the fiftieth anniversary of the signing of the Declaration of Independence on July 4, 1826, Thomas Jefferson was invited to take part in the ceremonies in Washington,

D.C., since, as he put it, he was one of "the remnant of that small band who joined in the bold and doubtful election between submission or the sword" and signed the Declaration. He was pleased, he wrote, "that our fellow citizens, after half a century of experience and prosperity, continue to approve the choice we made." Unable to attend the ceremonies because of his failing health, Jefferson sent a speech to be read in which he declared that the American doctrine of "the rights of man" and the light of knowledge were spreading throughout the world. "For ourselves," he concluded, "let the annual return of this day forever refresh our recollections of these rights, and an undiminished devotion to them." Jefferson died still proclaiming the ideals of education, enlightened religion, freedom, self-government, science, and human rights.[19]

For the anniversary, patriotic ceremonies, picnics, and speeches were planned. The festive mood turned solemn and introspective, however, when the news spread that, by the inscrutable workings of Providence, John Adams and Thomas Jefferson had both died on July 4, 1826, as if "Heaven directed a new seal" upon the beliefs of America, President John Quincy Adams, son of John Adams, proclaimed. Sometime before he died, John Adams inquired after his old friend Thomas Jefferson. Being informed that Jefferson was still alive, he murmured contentedly, "Thomas Jefferson still survives," implying that the goals and ideals of the American Declaration of Independence were safe as long as Jefferson lived.[20] Time has proved this belief correct, for the ideals and faith of Thomas Jefferson have survived beyond his own age and spread to nations unknown in the eighteenth century.

Appendix: Jefferson's Bible

Jefferson's "Bible" consists of two different compilations, made at different times in his life, of his favorite verses from the first four books of the New Testament, the Gospels of Matthew, Mark, Luke, and John. The first and simpler version he called "The Philosophy of Jesus of Nazareth" and the second, "The Life and Morals of Jesus of Nazareth." This Appendix gives a summary of every passage in the four Gospels and shows in which Gospel or Gospels the passage is to be found, as charted by William Arnold Stevens and Ernest DeWitt Burton, *A Harmony of the Gospels*, rev. ed. (New York: Charles Scribner's Sons, 1932), pp. 9–14. The passages that Jefferson used and the version of his "Bible" in which they are shown are indicated by the title "Philosophy" or "Morals" under the passages that he selected, as given in Henry Stephens Randall, *The Life of Thomas Jefferson*, 3 vols. (New York, 1858), 3:654–58. (*Port.*) indicates Jefferson used only a portion of the passage.

Sec. no.	Summary	Found in Matthew	Found in Mark	Found in Luke	Found in John
1	Prologue of John's gospel				Jo. 1:1–18
2	Preface of Luke's gospel			Lu. 1:1–14	
3	The two genealogies	Mt. 1:1–17		Lu. 2:23–38 "Philosophy"	

181

Sec. no.	Summary	Found in Matthew	Found in Mark	Found in Luke	Found in John
4	Birth of John the Baptist promised			Lu. 1:15–25	
5	The annunciation to Mary			Lu. 1:26–38	
6	The annunciation to Joseph	Mt. 1:18–25			
7	Mary's visit to Elisabeth			Lu. 1:39–56	
8	Birth of John the Baptist			Lu. 1:57–80	
9	Birth of Jesus the Christ	Mt. 1:18–25		Lu. 2:1–17 "Philosophy" "Morals"	
10	The angels and the shepherds			Lu. 2:8–10	
11	The circumcision			Lu. 2:21 "Philosophy" "Morals"	
12	Presentation in temple			Lu. 2:22–39 "Philosophy" (port.) "Morals" (port.) (Jefferson omitted all but transitional verses.)	

Sec. no.	Summary	Found in Matthew	Found in Mark	Found in Luke	Found in John
13	The Wise-men from the East	Mt. 2:1–12			
14	The flight into Egypt and return to Nazareth	Mt. 2:13–23			
15	Childhood at Nazareth	Mt. 2:23		Lu. 2:39–40 "Philosophy" "Morals"	
16	Visit to Jerusalem when 12 years old			Lu. 2:41–50 "Morals"	
17	18 years at Nazareth			Lu. 2:51–52 "Philosophy" "Morals"	
18	The ministry of John the Baptist	Mt. 3:1–12 "Morals" (port.) (Jefferson pieced the 3 accounts together.)	Mk. 1:1–8 "Morals" (port.)	Lu. 3:1–20 "Morals" (port.)	
19	The baptism of Jesus	Mt. 3:13–17 "Morals" (port.) (Jefferson omitted the descent of the dove and the voice of God.)	Mk. 1:9–11	Lu. 3:21–23 "Morals" (port.)	
20	The temptation in the wilderness	Mt. 4:1–11	Mk. 1:12–13	Lu. 4:1–13	

Sec. no.	Summary	Found in Matthew	Found in Mark	Found in Luke	Found in John
21	John's testimony before priests and Levites				Jo. 1:19–28
22	Jesus the Lamb of God				Jo. 1:29–34
23	Calling 3 disciples				Jo. 1:35–42
24	Philip and Nathanael				Jo. 1:43–51
25	The first miracle: water made wine				Jo. 2:1–11
26	Sojourn in Capernaum				Jo. 2:12 "Morals"
27	First cleansing of temple				Jo. 2:13–22 "Morals" (port.)
				(Jefferson omitted foretelling Jesus' resurrection.)	
28	Discourse with Nicodemus				Jo. 2:23–3:21
29	Christ baptizing in Judea				Jo. 3:22–24
30	John's testimony to Christ at Aenon				Jo. 3:25–36
31	Departure from Judea	Mt. 4:12 "Morals"	Mk. 1:14		Jo. 4:1–3

Sec. no.	Summary	Found in Matthew	Found in Mark	Found in Luke	Found in John
32	Discourse with woman of Samaria				Jo. 4:4–26 "Philosophy" (port.) (Jefferson omitted all but "God is a spirit and we must worship Him in spirit and in truth.")
33	The gospel in Sychar				Jo. 4:27–42
34	Beginning of Christ's Galilean ministry	Mt. 4:12–17	Mk. 1:14–15	Lu. 4:14–15	Jo. 4:43–45
35	The nobleman's son				Jo. 4:46–54
36	The first rejection at Nazareth	Mt. 4:13–16		Lu. 4:16–30	
37	Removal to Capernaum			Lu. 4:31	
38	Call of 4 disciples	Mt. 4:18–22	Mk. 1:16–20	Lu. 5:1–11	
39	Teaching in the synagogue & miracles in Capernaum	Mt. 8:14–17	Mk. 1:21–34 "Morals" (port.) (Jefferson omitted the miracles.)	Lu. 4:31–41	
40	First Preaching tour in Galilee	Mt. 4:23, 8:1–4	Mk. 1:35–45	Lu. 4:42–44, 5:12–16	

Sec. no.	Summary	Found in Matthew	Found in Mark	Found in Luke	Found in John
41	The paralytic bourne by 4 friends to Jesus	Mt. 9:1–8	Mk. 2:1–12	Lu. 5:17–26	
42	Call of Matthew	Mt. 9:9–13	Mk. 2:13–17 "Philosophy" "Morals" (port.)	Lu. 5:27–32 "Morals" (port.) (In "Morals" Jefferson combined the two accounts.)	
43	Fasting for the bridegroom & parables of new patches & wineskins	Mt. 9:14–17 "Philosophy"	Mk. 2:18–22	Lu. 5:33–39 "Morals" (port.) (In "Morals" Jefferson included only the parables.)	
44	The infirm man at the pool of Bethesda				Jo. 5:1–47
45	The disciples pluck grain & Jesus explains Sabboth	Mt. 2:1–8 "Philosophy" (port.) "Morals" (port.) (In "Morals" Jefferson combined the two accounts.)	Mk. 2:23–38 "Morals" (port.)	Lu. 6:15	
46	The man with the withered hand	Mt. 12:9–14 "Philosophy" (port.) "Morals"	Mk. 3:1–6	Lu. 6:6–11	

Sec. no.	Summary	Found in Matthew	Found in Mark	Found in Luke	Found in John
47	The wide-spread fame of Christ	Mt. 4:23–25, 12:15–21 "Morals" (port.) (Jefferson omitted that Christ was fulfillment of Isaiah's prophecy.)	Mk. 3:7–12	Lu. 6:17–19	
48	The choosing of the Twelve Disciples	Mt. 10:2–4	Mk. 3:12–19	Lu. 6:12–19 "Morals"	
49	Sermon on the Mount	Mt. 5:1–8:1 "Philosophy" "Morals"		Lu. 6:20–49 "Morals" (port. that supplements Matthew.)	
50	The centurion's servant healed	Mt. 8:5–13 "Philosophy" (port.) (Jefferson included the lesson but omitted the healing.)		Lu. 7:1–10	
51	The raising of the widow's son at Nain from death			Lu. 7:11–17	
52	John the Baptist's last message: a greater one has come	Mt. 11:2–30 "Morals" (port.) (Jefferson omitted all but "Come unto me ye weary.")		Lu. 7:18–35	

Sec. no.	Summary	Found in Matthew	Found in Mark	Found in Luke	Found in John
53	Annointing Jesus' feet in house of Simon the Pharisee			Lu. 7:36–50 "Philosophy" "Morals"	
54	Christ's companions on his second preaching tour			Lu. 8:1–3	
55	Warning to scribes and Pharisees on "eternal sin"	Mt. 12:22–45 "Philosophy" (port.) "Morals" (port.) (Jefferson omitted the miracle of healing but kept the teaching of judgment.)	Mk. 3:19–30		
56	The true kindred of Christ, those who do the will of God	Mt. 12:46–50 "Philosophy"	Mk. 3:31–35 "Morals"	Lu. 8:19–21	
57	Parables by the sea	Mt. 13:1–53 "Philosophy" "Morals" (port.)	Mk. 4:1–34 "Morals" (port. to supplement)	Lu. 8:4–18	
58	Stilling of the tempest	Mt. 8:18, 23–27	Mk. 4:35–41	Lu. 8:22–25	

Sec. no.	Summary	Found in Matthew	Found in Mark	Found in Luke	Found in John
59	The Gadarene demoniacs	Mt. 8:28–34	Mk. 5:1–20	Lu. 8:26–39	
60	Raising Jairus' daughter & healing the bleeding woman	Mt. 9:1, 18–26 "Philosophy"	Mk. 5:21–43	Lu. 8:40–56	
61	Two blind men and dumb demoniac healed	Mt. 9:27–34 "Philosophy" (port.) (Jefferson omitted healing the demoniac.)			
62	Second rejection at Nazareth	Mt. 13:54–58 "Morals"	Mk. 6:1–6		
63	Third preaching tour continued	Mt. 9:35	Mk. 6:6 "Morals"		
64	Mission of the Twelve	Mt. 9:36–11:1 "Philosophy" (port.) "Morals" (port.) (Jefferson omitted that Christ set families against each other.)	Mk. 6:7–13 "Morals" (port. to supplement)	Lu. 9:1–6	
65	Death of John the Baptist	Mt. 14:1–12 (Jefferson omitted that Christ is John come back to life.)	Mk. 6:14–29 "Morals" (port.)	Lu. 9:7–9	

Sec. no.	Summary	Found in Matthew	Found in Mark	Found in Luke	Found in John
66	Feeding of the five thousand	Mt. 14:13–23	Mk. 6:30–46	Lu. 9:10–17	Jo. 6:1–15
67	Jesus walks on water	Mt. 14:24–36	Mk. 6:47–56		Jo. 6:16–21
68	Discourse on the Bread of Life				Jo. 6:22–71
69	Discourse on eating with unwashed hands: deeds, not ceremonies, important	Mt. 15:1–20 "Philosophy"	Mk. 7:1–23 "Morals" (port.)		
		(Jefferson omitted Jesus' quoting Moses and Isaiah.)			
70	Journey to Tyre and Sidon; the Syrophoenician woman's daughter	Mt. 15:21–28	Mk. 7:24–30		
71	Return through Decapolis; many miracles of healing	Mt. 15:29–31	Mk. 7:31–37		
72	Feeding of the four thousand	Mt. 15:32–38	Mk. 8:1–9		
73	Pharisees and Sadducees demand a sign from heaven	Mt. 15:39–16:12	Mk. 8:10–21		
74	The blind man near Bethsaida		Mk. 8:22–26		
75	Peter's confession	Mt. 16:13–20	Mk. 8:27–30	Lu. 9:18–21	

Sec. no.	Summary	Found in Matthew	Found in Mark	Found in Luke	Found in John
76	Christ foretells his death and resurrection	Mt. 16:21–28	Mk. 8:31–9:1	Lu. 9:22–27	
77	The transfiguration	Mt. 17:1–13	Mk. 9:2–13	Lu. 9:28–36	
78	The demoniac boy	Mt. 17:14–20	Mk. 9:14–29	Lu. 9:37–43	
79	Christ again foretells his death and resurrection	Mt. 17:22–23	Mk. 9:30–32	Lu. 9:43–45	
80	The shekel in the fish's mouth	Mt. 17:24–27	Mk. 9:33		
81	Discourse on humility & parables of forgiveness	Mt. 18:1–35 "Philosophy" (port.) "Morals"	Mk. 9:33–50	Lu. 9:46–50	
82	Christ at the feast of tabernacles				Jo. 7:1–52 "Morals" (port.)
	(Jefferson omitted Jesus' words, "He sent me and I am the living water.")				
83	Woman taken in adultery				Jo. 7:53–8:11 "Philosophy" "Morals"
84	Discourse on Light of the World				Jo. 8:12–30

Sec. no.	Summary	Found in Matthew	Found in Mark	Found in Luke	Found in John
85	Discourse on spiritual freedom				Jo. 8:31–59
86	Final departure from Galilee, "Leave all & follow me."	Mt. 19:1–2, 8:18–22 "Morals" (port.) (Jefferson omitted calling down destruction on unfriendly village.)	Mk. 10:1	Lu. 9:51–62 "Morals" (port.)	
87	Mission of the Seventy			Lu. 10:1–24 "Morals" (port.)	
88	The good Samaritan			Lu. 10:25–37 "Philosophy" "Morals"	
89	Visit to Martha & Mary			Lu. 10:38–42 "Morals"	
90	Healing of man born blind			(Jefferson omitted all except statement that sin was not the cause of the man's blindness.)	Jo. 9:1–41 "Morals" (port.)
91	The good Shepherd				Jo. 10:1–21 "Philosophy" "Morals" (port.) (Jefferson kept, "I am the good Shepherd"; omitted, "Others are thieves.")

Sec. no.	Summary	Found in Matthew	Found in Mark	Found in Luke	Found in John
92	Christ at the feast of dedication				Jo. 10:22–42
93	Discourse on prayer: Lord's prayer, parable of persistent asking			Lu. 11:1–13 "Morals"	
94	Discourses against Pharisees and lawyers			Lu. 11:14–54 "Philosophy" (port.) "Morals" (port.) (Jefferson omitted that Jesus cast out demons by the power of the devil.)	
95	Teachings about the coming judgment, trust in God			Lu. 12:1–59 "Philosophy" (port.) "Morals" (port.) (Jefferson omitted that Christ divided families.)	
96	The Galileans slain by Pilate, a teaching of forgiveness			Lu. 13:1–9 "Philosophy"	
97	The woman healed on a sabbath			Lu. 13:10–21	
98	The question of whether few are saved			Lu. 13:22–30	
99	Reply to the warning against Herod			Lu. 13:31–35	

Sec. no.	Summary	Found in Matthew	Found in Mark	Found in Luke	Found in John
100	Discourse at a banquet. Parable of unwilling guests			Lu. 14:1–24 "Philosophy" (port.) "Morals"	
101	Discourse on counting the cost: parable of unfinished tower			Lu. 14:25–35 "Philosophy" "Morals" (port.)	
	(Jefferson omitted that Jesus' disciples must hate their own families.)				
102	Three parables of grace: lost sheep, lost coin, prodigal son			Lu. 15:1–32 "Philosophy" "Morals"	
103	Parables of warning: the wicked steward, and the rich man and Lazarus			Lu. 16:1–31 "Philosophy" "Morals"	
104	Teachings concerning forgiveness and faith			Lu. 17:1–10 "Philosophy" (port.) "Morals" (port.)	
	(Jefferson omitted that faith could command a tree to move.)				
105	Raising Lazarus from the dead				Jo. 11:1–46

Sec. no.	Summary	Found in Matthew	Found in Mark	Found in Luke	Found in John
106	Withdrawal to Ephraim				Jo. 11:47–54
107	The ten lepers			Lu. 17:11–19	
108	Coming of the kingdom and parable of the unjust judge			Lu. 17:20—18:8 "Philosophy" (port.) "Morals" (port.)	
	(In "Philosophy" Jefferson kept only the parable. In "Morals," he omitted the coming of the Son of Man in the last days.)				
109	The Pharisee and the publican			Lu. 18:1–14 "Philosophy"	
110	Concerning divorce: it should be stricter than Moses' law	Mt. 19:3–12 "Philosophy" "Morals"	Mk. 10:2–12		
111	Christ blessing little children	Mt. 19:13–15 "Morals"	Mk. 10:13–16	Lu. 18:15–17	
112	The rich young ruler and the late laborers	Mt. 19:16—20:16 "Philosophy" (port.) "Morals" (port.)	Mk. 10:17–31	Lu. 18:18–30	

Sec. no.	Summary	Found in Matthew	Found in Mark	Found in Luke	Found in John
		(In "Philosophy," Jefferson omitted rich young ruler. In "Morals," Jefferson omitted Jesus' promise to put the disciples on thrones.)			
113	Christ foretells his crucifixion	Mt. 20:17–19	Mk. 10:32–34	Lu. 18:31–34	
114	Ambition of James and John for chief places	Mt. 20:20–28	Mk. 10:35–45		
115	Blind men near Jericho	Mt. 20:29–34	Mk. 10:46–52	Lu. 18:35–43	
116	Visit to Zacchaeus			Lu. 19:1–10 "Morals"	
117	Parable of the talents			Lu. 19:11–28 "Morals"	
118	Anointing of Jesus by Mary of Bethany	Mt. 26:6–13	Mk. 14:3–9 "Morals"		Jo. 11:55–12:11
119	Triumphal entry into Jerusalem	Mt. 21:1–11 "Morals" (port.) (Jefferson omitted the fulfillment of Old Testament prophecy.)	Mk. 11:1–11	Lu. 19:29–44	Jo. 12:12–19
120	Cursing the fig tree	Mt. 21:18–22	Mk. 11:12–14 "Morals" (port.) (Jefferson kept "Jesus hungered," omitted cursing.)		

Sec. no.	Summary	Found in Matthew	Found in Mark	Found in Luke	Found in John
121	Second cleansing the temple	Mt. 21:12–17 "Morals" (port.)	Mk. 11:15–19 "Morals" (port.) (Jefferson pieced the two accounts together.)	Lu. 19:45–48	
122	Fig tree withered away	Mt. 21:20–22	Mk. 11:20–25		
123	Christ's authority challenged in the temple	Mt. 21:23–27 (Jefferson kept only that Jesus visited temple.)	Mk. 11:27–33 "Morals" (port.)	Lu. 20:1–8	
124	Parables of warning: defiant sons, defiant husbandmen, unwilling guests	Mt. 21:28–22:14 "Philosophy" "Morals" (port.)	Mk. 12:1–12 "Morals" (port. to supplement)	Lu. 20:9–19	
125	Question of tribute to Caesar, marriage in heaven, great commandment	Mt. 22:15–40 "Philosophy" "Morals" (port.)	Mk. 12:13–34 "Morals" (port. to supplement)	Lu. 20:20–40	
126	Christ's unanswerable question, "Who is Son of David?"	Mt. 22:41–46	Mk. 12:35–37 "Morals"	Lu. 20:41–44	
127	Woes upon the scribes and Pharisees who pray but kill the prophets	Mt. 23:1–39 "Philosophy" "Morals"	Mk. 12:38–40	Lu. 20:45–47	

Sec. no.	Summary	Found in Matthew	Found in Mark	Found in Luke	Found in John
128	The widow's two mites		Mk. 12:41–44 "Philosophy" "Morals"	Lu. 21:1–4	
129	Gentiles seeking Jesus				Jo. 12:20–36 "Philosophy" (port.) "Morals" (port.) (Jefferson omitted Christ dying for mankind.)
130	Jews' rejection of Christ				Jo. 12:37–50
131	Discourse on end of the world and parables of judgment	Mt. 24:1–26:2 "Philosophy" (port.) "Morals" (In "Philosophy," Jefferson included only the parables. In "Morals," he omitted Son of Man would come again on clouds of glory.)	Mk. 13:1–37	Lu. 21:5–38 "Morals" (port. to supplement)	
132	Conspiracy between the chief priest and Judas	Mt. 26:1–5, 14–16 "Morals" (port.)	Mk. 14:1–2, 10–11 "Morals" (port.)	Lu. 22:1–6	

Sec. no.	Summary	Found in Matthew	Found in Mark	Found in Luke	Found in John
133	The Last Supper	Mt. 26:17–30 "Morals" (port.) (Jefferson combined the accounts.)	Mk. 14:12–26	Lu. 22:7–30 "Philosophy" "Morals" (port.)	Jo. 13:1–30 "Philosophy" (port.) "Morals" (port.)
134	Christ's farewell discourses	Mt. 26:31–35 "Morals" (port.) (Jefferson omitted John's long discourse and combined accounts in "Morals.")	Mk. 14:27–31	Lu. 22:31–38 "Morals" (port.)	Jo. 13:31–16:33 "Philosophy" (port.) "Morals" (port.)
135	The intercessory prayer				Jo. 17:1–26
136	The agony in Gethsemane	Mt. 26:30, 36–46 "Morals"	Mk. 14:26, 32–42	Lu. 22:39–46	Jo. 18:1
137	The betrayal and arrest	Mt. 26:47–56 "Morals" (port.)	Mk. 14:43–53 "Morals" (port.)	Lu. 22:47–53	Jo. 18:1–12 "Morals" (port.)
138	Trial before Jewish authorities	Mt. 26:57–27:10 "Philosophy" (port.) "Morals" (port.) (Jefferson pieced together these accounts.)	Mk. 14:53–15:1 "Philosophy" (port.)	Lu. 22:54–71 "Philosophy" (port.) "Morals" (port.)	Jo. 18:12–27 "Philosophy" (port.) "Morals" (port.)

Sec. no.	Summary	Found in Matthew	Found in Mark	Found in Luke	Found in John
139	Trial before Pilate	Mt. 27:2, 11–31 "Philosophy" (port.) "Morals" (port.) (Jefferson combined accounts.)	Mk. 15:1–20	Lu. 23:1–25 "Philosophy" (port.) "Morals" (port.)	Jo. 18:28–19:16 "Philosophy" (port.) "Morals" (port.)
140	The crucifixion	Mt. 27:32–56 "Philosophy" (port.) "Morals" (port.) (Jefferson combined accounts.)	Mk. 15:21–41	Lu. 23:26–49 "Philosophy" (port.) "Morals" (port.)	Jo. 19:16–37 "Philosophy" (port.) "Morals" (port.)
141	The burial	Mt. 27:57–61 "Morals" (port.)	Mk. 15:42–47 (Jefferson combined accounts.)	Lu. 23:50–56	Jo. 19:38–42 "Morals" (port.)
142	The watch at the sepulchre	Mt. 27:62–66			
143	The resurrection morning	Mt. 28:1–10	Mk. 16:1–11	Lu. 23:56–24:12	Jo. 20:1–18
144	Report of the watch	Mt. 28:11–15			
145	Walk to Emmaus		Mk. 16:12–13	Lu. 24:13–35	
146	The appearance to the disciples in Jerusalem, Thomas being absent		Mk. 16:14	Lu. 24:36–43	Jo. 20:19–25

Sec. no.	Summary	Found in Matthew	Found in Mark	Found in Luke	Found in John
147	The appearance to Thomas with the other disciples				Jo. 20:26–29
148	The appearance to the seven disciples by Sea of Galilee				Jo. 21:1–24
149	The appearance to the eleven disciples on a mountain in Galilee	Mt. 28:16–20	Mk. 16:15—18		
150	Christ's final appearance and his ascension		Mk. 16:19–20	Lu. 24:44–53	
151	The conclusion of John's gospel				Jo. 20:30–31, 21:25

Notes

Preface

1. Charles B. Sanford, *Thomas Jefferson and His Library: A Study of His Literary Interests and of the Religious Attitudes Revealed by Relevant Titles in His Library* (Hamden, Conn., 1977).

2. See published lectures of Henry Wilder Foote, *Thomas Jefferson: Champion of Religious Freedom, Advocate of Christian Morals* (Boston, 1947) and William D. Gould, "The Religious Opinions of Thomas Jefferson," *Mississippi Valley Historical Review,* 20 (1933): 191–208.

3. See J. Leslie Hall, "The Religious Opinions of Thomas Jefferson," *Sewanee Review,* 21 (1913): 163–76.

4. Robert M. Healey, *Jefferson on Religion in Public Education* (1962; rept. Hamden, Conn., 1970), was interested in the problem of teaching religion in public schools; Sister M. Rosaleen Trainer, "Thomas Jefferson on Freedom of Conscience" (Ph.D. diss., St. John's University, 1966), considered Jefferson's attitudes toward inner conscience and individual religious freedom; Kenneth Raynor Williams, "The Ethics of Thomas Jefferson" (Ph.D. diss., Boston University, 1962), studied the ethical implications of Jefferson's policies on social issues; Constance Bartlett Schulz was absorbed with what she considered the radical influences of American deism in her study, "The Radical Religious Ideas of Thomas Jefferson and John Adams: A Comparison" (Ph.D. diss., University of Cincinnati, 1973).

5. This should be remedied upon the completion of the definitive edition, *The Papers of Thomas Jefferson*, ed. Julian P. Boyd et al., 20 vols. to date (Princeton, N.J., 1950—).

Chapter I

1. See Adrienne Koch, *The Philosophy of Thomas Jefferson* (1943; rept. Gloucester, Mass., 1957), pp. xi–xiv; Karl Lehmann, *Thomas Jefferson, American Humanist* (1947; rept. Chicago, 1965); Merrill D. Peterson, *Thomas Jefferson and the New Nation* (New York, 1970), p. 158; Dumas Malone, *Jefferson and His Time,* 6 vols. (Boston, 1948–81). None of these writers give much thought to Jefferson's religion.

2. Norman Cousins, *In God We Trust: The Religious Beliefs and Ideas of the American Founding Fathers* (New York, 1958), pp. 10, 13–14; Elbert D. Thomas, *This Nation under God* (New York, 1950).

3. Henry Wilder Foote, *Thomas Jefferson: Social Reformer* (Boston, 1947), p. 1; Claude Gernade Bowers, *Civil and Religious Liberty: Jefferson, O'Connell* (Worcester, Mass., 1930), pp. 13, 17; Frank Swancara, *Thomas Jefferson versus Religious Oppression* (New York, 1969), p. 132.

4. Malone, 4:479; Hamilton to John Jay, 7 May 1800, *The Works of Alexander Hamilton,* ed. Henry C. Lodge (New York, 1904), 10:372–73.

5. Henry Stephens Randall, *The Life of Thomas Jefferson,* 3 vols. (New York, 1858), 1:495, 2:567-68, 3:620–22; and Malone, 4:481.

6. Randall, 1:491; Gould, p. 191.

7. According to an experience in 1932 of James Truslow Adams, *Jefferson Principles and Hamiltonian Principles* (Boston, 1932), pp. xv-xvi.

8. TJ to Dr. Benjamin Rush, 23 Sept. 1800, Thomas Jefferson, *The Writings of Thomas Jefferson,* Definitive Edition, ed. Albert Ellery Bergh, 20 vols. (Washington, D.C., 1907), 10:174–75.

9. Malone, 5:192.

10. Merrill D. Peterson, *The Jefferson Image in the American Mind* (New York, 1960), pp. 93–94, 470.

11. Healey, pp. 1–16, 246–73.

12. TJ to Rush, 23 Sept. 1800, Bergh, 10:174–75; Malone, 4:483.

13. Malone, 5:190; Peterson, *New Nation,* p. 143.

14. Hall, p. 173; Foote, *The Life and Morals of Jesus of Nazareth* (n.p., 1951), p. 13, cited by Malone, 5:205.

15. Randall, 1:17, 41–42, 383, 3:349.

16. TJ to Dr. Vine Utley, 21 March 1819, Thomas Jefferson, *The Writings of Thomas Jefferson,* ed. Paul Leicester Ford, 10 vols. (New York, 1892–99), 10:126.

17. Randall, 3:451, 102, 543–47, 559, 554.

18. Bowers, p. 14–15.

19. Hall, p. 165; Adams to TJ, 19 April 1817, TJ to Adams, 5 May 1817, Lester J. Cappon, ed., *The Adams-Jefferson Letters,* 2 vols. (Chapel Hill, N.C., 1959), 2:509, 512.

20. Randall, 3:555; TJ to Justin Pierre Plumard Derieux, 25 July 1788, Boyd, 14:418; *The Book of Common Prayer* (London, 1867), sect. 16.

21. Randall, 1:17, 42, 383; Jefferson, "Autobiography," Ford, 1:3; Foote, *Champion,* pp. 5–6.

22. Malone, 1:52.

23. Foote, *Champion,* pp. 6, 7, 8; TJ, "Subscription to Support a Clergyman in Charlottesville," Boyd, 2:6; Randall, 3:55.

24. Malone, 4:199; Foote, *Champion,* p. 7; TJ to Cooper, 2 Nov. 1822, Bergh, 15:404.

25. Thomas Jefferson Coolidge, "Jefferson in His Family," Bergh, 15:iv.

26. Peterson, *New Nation,* p. 960.

27. TJ to Dr. Benjamin Waterhouse, 8 Jan. 1825, 19 July 1822, Ford, 10:336, 220–21.

28. TJ to Mrs. Samuel Harrison Smith, 6 Aug. 1816, TJ to John Page, 25 June 1804, Bergh, 15:60, 11:32.

29. According to the recollection of Jefferson's oldest grandson, Thomas Jefferson Randolph (Randall, 3:544).

30. Peterson, *Jefferson Image,* pp. 130, 302–3.

Chapter II

1. Shulz, p. 279. Shulz organizes her study according to Jefferson's career and tries to show development but admits, "By 1792, Jefferson had adopted his main religious principles" (p. 193).

2. See Jefferson's account of studying comparative religion, TJ to John Adams, 22 Aug. 1813, Cappon, 2:368–69.

3. Randall, 1:17, 41.

4. Peterson, *New Nation,* p. 50; Malone, 1:109, 106. Jefferson was never emotional about religion, according to Randall (3:451, 555).

5. Thomas Jefferson, *The Literary Bible of Thomas Jefferson: His Commonplace Book of Philosophers and Poets,* ed. Gilbert Chinard (1928; rept. New York, 1969), pp. 31–34.

6. TJ to Carr, 10 Aug. 1787, Ford, 4:430–32.

7. TJ to Thomas Jefferson Randolph, 24 Nov. 1808, Bergh, 12:201, 197–98; Stuart Gerry Brown, *Thomas Jefferson* (1963; rept. New York, 1966), pp. 199–200.

8. TJ to Story, 5 Dec. 1801, Ford, 8:107; Chinard, *Literary Bible,* pp. 31–32.

9. TJ to Peter Carr, 10 Aug. 1787, Ford, 4:429–32; TJ to Miles King, 26 Sept. 1814, Bergh, 14:197; TJ to William Carver, 4 Dec. 1823, Ford, 10:284; TJ to John F. Watson, 17 May 1814, Bergh, 14:136; TJ to Francis Hopkinson, 13 March 1789, Ford, 5:76.

10. Brown, p. 198; TJ to Dr. Benjamin Rush, 16 Jan. 1811, Ford, 9:295–96. Jefferson had many works by Bacon, Locke, and Newton in his library, according to E. Millicent Sowerby, comp., *Catalogue of the Library of Thomas Jefferson,* 5 vols. (Washington, D.C., 1952–59), 5:246, 348, 368. He also copied excerpts from Locke in his notebook (Thomas Jefferson, *The Commonplace Book of Thomas Jefferson: A Repertory of His Ideas on Government,* ed. Gilbert Chinard [Baltimore, 1926], pp. 378, 382).

11. Brown, pp. 188–90; Peterson, *New Nation,* pp. 30, 532; Koch, *Philosophy,* pp. 93–94; Sanford, pp. 79–93.

12. Brown, pp. 198–99.

13. Peterson, *New Nation,* p. 47; Koch, *Philosophy,* p. 90.

14. TJ, *Notes on the State of Virginia,* Ford, 3:264, 263; TJ to Rev. Samuel Knox, 12 Feb. 1810, Bergh, 12:360–62; TJ to William Carver, 4 Dec. 1823, Ford, 10:284.

15. TJ to King, 26 Sept. 1814, Bergh, 14:196; TJ to Carver, 4 Dec. 1823, Ford, 10:284–85.

16. TJ, "Notes on Religion," Ford, 2:101.

17. TJ to John Adams, 15 Aug. 1820, TJ to Miles King, 26 Sept. 1814, Bergh, 15:275–76, 14:196; TJ to Peter Carr, 10 Aug. 1787, TJ to William Carver, 4 Dec. 1823, Ford, 4:430–32, 10:285.

18. TJ to William Short, 4 Aug. 1820, TJ to John Adams, 5 July 1814, Bergh, 15:258, 14:149.

19. According to Peter Gay, *The Enlightenment: An Interpretation* (New York, 1967), pp. 151–53.

20. See passages copied approvingly by Jefferson from Bolingbroke (Chinard, *Literary Bible,* pp. 45, 48–50, 54–55). He had ten works of Bolingbroke in his library (Sowerby, 5:407).

21. TJ to Rev. Charles Clay, 29 Jan. 1815, TJ to James Fishback, 27 Sept. 1809, TJ to Dr. Benjamin Waterhouse, 26 June 1826, Bergh, 14:232, 12:315, 15:385. Peterson discusses this "broad common faith, a *consensus gentium,* uniting all men of reason," in *New Nation,* p. 958.

22. TJ to Stiles, 25 June 1819, Bergh, 15:203.

23. TJ to Rev. Charles Clay, 29 Jan. 1815, Bergh, 14:233; Randall, 3:672.

24. TJ to Richard Rush, 31 May 1813, Ford, 9:385; TJ to Mrs. Samuel Harrison Smith, 6 Aug. 1816, TJ to Samuel Greenhow, 31 Jan. 1814, Bergh, 15:60, 14:81.

25. Peterson, *New Nation,* pp. 140–44, 360–61; TJ to Edward Dowse, 19 April 1803, Bergh, 10:378.

26. TJ to Dr. Benjamin Rush, 21 April 1803; TJ to Edward Dowse, 19 April 1803, TJ to Nathaniel Macon, 23 Nov. 1821, Bergh, 10:380–81, 377–78, 15:341; TJ to Dr. George Logan, 19 May 1816, Ford, 10:26–27.

27. TJ to Mrs. Samuel Harrison Smith, 6 Aug. 1816; TJ to Dr. Benjamin Rush, 21 April 1803, Bergh, 15:60–61, 10:380.

28. Peterson, *New Nation,* p. 958.

29. TJ to Francis Adrian van der Kemp, 25 April 1816, Bergh, 15:2; TJ to van der Kemp, 16 March and 1 May 1817, Ford, 10:77–78. Van der Kemp was a Uniterian preacher (Peterson, *New Nation,* p. 959).

30. TJ to Thomson, 9 Jan. 1816, Bergh, 14:385.

31. TJ to Matthew Carey, 11 Nov. 1816, TJ to Dr. George Logan, 12 Nov. 1816, TJ to John Adams, 11 Jan. 1817, TJ to Charles Thomson, 29 Jan. 1817, Ford, 10:67–68, 73, 75–76.

32. TJ to Francis Hopkinson, 13 March 1789, Ford, 5:76.

33. Sowerby lists 552 works on religious subjects in Jefferson's extensive library (1:286–96, 2:1–191; 210–356, 376–83). For a discussion of the influence of these religious works on Jefferson, see Sanford, pp. 116–43.

34. Koch, *Philosophy,* p. 90; Hall, p. 173.

Chapter III

1. See discussion by Chinard, *Commonplace Book* and *Literary Bible.*

2. TJ, *A Summary View of the Rights of British America,* Boyd, 1:121–22, 133.

3. See Chinard, *Commonplace Book,* pp. 55–56.

4. See Adrienne Koch, *Adams and Jefferson: Posterity Must Judge* (Chicago, 1963), p. 7.

5. Ford, 1:25–26, n. 3, citing Adams to Timothy Pickering, 22 Aug. 1822, source not given.

6. Peterson, *New Nation,* pp. 88, 93–96.

7. Ford, 1:30–38.

8. Peterson, *New Nation,* p. 90.

9. From Jefferson's original version of the Declaration of Independence, Ford, 1:30.

10. See Peterson, *New Nation,* p. 89.

11. See ibid., p. 94; Malone, 1:175, 227; Chinard, *Commonplace Book,* pp. 18–19, 21–22, 23, 35, 37–38, 41, 57, 105–8; Sowerby, 5:279, 319, 363, 420, 422.

12. TJ to Madison, 30 Aug. 1823, TJ to Henry Lee, 8 May 1825, Ford, 10:267–68, 343.

13. Peterson, *New Nation,* p. 96.

14. TJ to Roger C. Weightman, 24 June 1826, Ford, 10:391–92. Jefferson may have been quoting from his reading the words of Rumbold, a Rye House plotter executed by James II, according to Douglas Adair, "The New Thomas Jefferson," *William and Mary Quarterly,* 3rd ser., 3 (1946): 133.

15. See Daniel J. Boorstin, *The Lost World of Thomas Jefferson* (New York, 1948), pp. 61–62, 59, and Peterson, *New Nation,* pp. 93–94.

16. See Malone, 1:227 and Brown, *Jefferson,* pp. 209–10.

17. Koch, *Philosophy,* p. 143.

18. See Chinard, *Commonplace Book,* pp. 52, 374–76.

19. See Koch, *Philosophy,* p. 136.

20. TJ to William Carmichael, 15 Dec. 1787, TJ to William Stephens Smith, 2 Feb. 1787, TJ to Charles W. F. Dumas, 12 Feb. 1788, TJ to Alexander Donald, 7 Feb. 1788, TJ to James Madison, 20 Dec. 1787, Boyd, 12:425, 558, 583, 571, 440; Peterson, *New Nation,* pp. 100–107.

21. TJ, "Autobiography," Ford, 1:49–50, 58–60; Peterson, *New Nation,* p. 113.

22. TJ to John Adams, 28 Oct. 1813, Ford, 9:425; see also Cappon, 2:478–80.

23. TJ to John Adams, 27 June 1813, Cappon, 2:335; TJ to Judge William Johnson, 12 June 1823, Bergh, 15:440–41.

24. TJ to Gov. John Langdon, 5 March 1810, Bergh, 12:377–78.

25. Koch, *Philosophy,* p. 186.

26. Malone, 1:176.

Chapter IV

1. TJ to Dowse, 19 April 1803, Bergh, 10:378; TJ, "Autobiography," Ford, 1:53.

2. TJ to Miles King, 26 Sept. 1814, TJ to Timothy Pickering, 27 Feb. 1821, Bergh, 14:198, 15:324.

3. TJ, Bill for Establishing Religious Freedom, Ford, 2:237–38.

4. TJ to Charles Thomson, 29 Jan. 1817, Ford, 10:76.

5. TJ, *Notes on the State of Virginia,* Ford, 3:263–64; Chinard, *Commonplace Book,* pp. 377–93; TJ, "Notes on Religion," Ford, 2:92–103.

6. Locke, *A Letter concerning Toleration,* quoted in Chinard, *Commonplace Book,* pp. 380–81.

7. TJ, *Notes on the State of Virginia,* Ford, 3:263; Randall, 3:621.

8. Chinard, *Commonplace Book,* pp. 381, 383; TJ, *Notes on the State of Virginia,* Ford, 3:265, plus similar statements in TJ to Mathew Carey, 11 Nov. 1816, and TJ to Dr. George Logan, 12 Nov. 1816, ibid., 10:67–68.

9. TJ to Horatio Gates Spafford, 17 March 1814, Bergh, 14:119; TJ to Wythe, 13 Aug. 1786, Ford, 4:268–69; TJ to James Madison, 18 June 1789, Bergh, 8:389.

10. Randall, 3:672.

11. TJ to Adams, 1 Aug. 1816, Bergh, 15:58; see also TJ to Edward Rutledge, 2 Feb. 1788, Ford, 5:4–5.

12. Malone, 4:191; TJ to Rev. Thomas Whittemore, 5 June 1822, TJ to John Adams, 5 May 1817, Bergh, 15:373–74, 109; TJ to Horatio Gates Spafford, 10 Jan. 1816, TJ to Edmund Pendleton, 22 April 1799, Ford, 10:12–13, 7:376; TJ to Moses Robinson, 23 March 1801, Bergh, 10:236–37; TJ to Jeremiah Moor, 14 Aug. 1800, TJ to Elbridge Gerry, 29 March 1801, Ford, 7:455, 8:41.

13. Jefferson copied and commented on quotations from Locke and Milton opposing episcopal church organization in his "Notes on Religion," Ford, 2:97–100.

14. TJ, *Notes on the State of Virginia,* Ford, 3:261–62.

15. TJ to Thomas Cooper, 10 Feb. 1814, Bergh, 14:86–87; TJ, "Whether Christianity Is Part of Common Law?", Ford, 1:360–67; TJ to John Adams, 24 Jan. 1814, TJ to Edward Everett, 15 Oct. 1824, Bergh, 14:72–75, 16:80–84; Chinard, *Commonplace Book,* pp. 351–56.

16. TJ to John Cartwright, 5 June 1824, Bergh, 16:50.

17. TJ to Joseph Marx, 1820, and TJ to Dr. Jacob de La Motta, 1 Sept. 1820, quoted in Thomas Jefferson, *Democracy,* ed. and introd. Saul K. Padover (1939, rept. New York, 1969), pp. 178–79, and Saul K. Padover, *Jefferson* (New York, 1942), p. 395.

18. TJ to Adams, 1 Aug. 1816, Bergh, 15:58–59; TJ to Mordecai Manuel Noah, 28 May 1818, Thomas Jefferson, *Basic Writings of Thomas Jefferson,* ed. Philip S. Foner (1944; rept. Garden City, N.Y., 1950), pp. 756–57.

19. TJ to Miles King, 26 Sept. 1814, Bergh, 14:198; TJ, "Notes on Religion," Ford, 2:98–100.

20. TJ to Horatio Gates Spafford, 10 Jan. 1816, Ford, 10:12–13; TJ to Edward Dowse, 19 April 1803, Bergh, 10:378; TJ to Elbridge Gerry, 29 March 1801, and TJ, First Inaugural Address, Ford, 8:41, 2–3.

21. TJ, "Notes on Religion," Ford, 2:102–3.

22. TJ, *Notes on the State of Virginia,* and TJ, "Autobiography," Ford, 3:261–66, 1:52–53.

23. TJ, "Autobiography," and TJ, A Bill for Establishing Religious Freedom, Ford, 1:54, 2:238; Peterson, *New Nation,* pp. 133–45.

24. TJ, *Notes on the State of Virginia*, and TJ, "Notes on Religion," Ford, 3:243, 2:103; TJ, Second Draft of Virginia Constitution of 1776, Boyd, 1:353.

25. Madison to TJ, 9 Jan. 1785 and 22 Jan. 1786, TJ to Madison, 17 Dec. 1786, TJ to William Carmichael, 22 Aug. 1786, Boyd, 7:594, 9:194–95, 10:603–4, 288; TJ to George Wythe, 13 Aug. 1786, TJ to Honoré Gabriel Requetti, comte de Mirabeau, 20 Aug. 1786, Ford, 4:267–68, 283.

26. Jefferson was proud that the Virginia legislature rejected an amendment that would have restricted the act only to "the plan of Jesus Christ" (TJ, "Autobiography," Ford, 1:62).

27. TJ, A Bill for Establishing Religious Freedom, Ford, 2:239.

28. Ibid., pp. 237–39.

29. TJ, "Notes on Religion," Ford, 2:99–102.

30. TJ to Thomas Mann Randolph, 30 May 1790, TJ to Nathaniel Niles, 22 May 1801, Ford, 5:173, 7:24. Jefferson had the complete works of Montesquieu in his library and two commentaries on them (Sowerby, 5:363).

31. Chinard, *Commonplace Book,* pp. 37, 291–93.

32. TJ, "Notes on Religion," Ford, 2:101, 99.

33. Currie to TJ, 17 Oct. 1785, 5 Aug. 1785, Page to TJ, 23 Aug. 1785, Boyd, 8:640, 343, 428–29.

34. William Meade, *Old Churches, Ministers, and Families of Virginia* (Philadelphia, 1861), cited by Peterson, *New Nation,* p. 144.

35. TJ to Moses Robinson, 23 March 1801, TJ to Mrs. Samuel Harrison Smith, 6 Aug. 1816, Bergh, 10:237, 15:60; Randall, 3:676–78.

36. John Page to TJ, 23 Aug. 1785, Hopkinson to TJ, 28 June 1786, Dr. James Currie to TJ, 5 Aug. 1785, Boyd, 8:428, 10:77–78, 8:343; Randall, 3:555.

37. Peterson, *Jefferson Image,* pp. 93–94.

38. TJ to James Madison, 20 Dec. 1787, TJ to Elbridge Gerry, 26 Jan. 1799, Bergh, 6:387, 10:78; TJ, Second Inaugural Address, Ford, 8:344; TJ to Rev. Samuel Miller, 23 Jan. 1808, Bergh, 11:428–29.

39. TJ to a Committee of the Danbury, Conn., Baptist Association, 1 Jan. 1802, TJ to Capt. John Thomas, 18 Nov. 1807, TJ to the General Meeting of Six Baptist Associations at Chesterfield, Va., 21 Nov. 1808, TJ to the Methodist Episcopal Church at New London, Conn., 4 Feb. 1809, Bergh, 16:281–82, 290–91, 320–21, 332.

40. Jefferson to the Methodist Episcopal Church at New London, Conn., 4 Feb. 1809, Bergh, 16:331–32.

41. See TJ to the Republicans of Georgetown, 8 March 1809, Bergh, 16:349; Chinard, *Literary Bible,* pp. 148, 95.

42. See Chinard, *Literary Bible,* pp. 538, 161, 205, 96.

43. TJ to John Lithgow, 4 Jan. 1805, Ford, 3:269–70.

44. Ford, 10:396.

Chapter V

1. TJ to Peter Carr, 19 Aug. 1785, TJ to Thomas Jefferson Randolph, 24 Nov. 1808, Bergh, 5:82, 12:198.

2. Peterson, *New Nation,* pp. 961–75; TJ to John Adams, 28 Oct. 1813, Ford, 9:425.

3. TJ to Short, 31 Oct. 1819, Bergh, 15:219.

4. Koch, *Philosophy,* pp. 2–6; Peterson, *New Nation,* pp. 53–54; Brown, p. 231.

5. Isaac Jefferson, *Memoirs of a Monticello Slave: as Dictated to Charles Campbell in the 1840's by Isaac, One of Thomas Jefferson's Slaves* (Charlottesville, Va., 1951), p. 29.

6. See Peterson, *New Nation,* pp. 658, 720–21; Brown, pp. 232–33. Jefferson's library reflects his broad interests (Sanford, pp. 110–14).

7. TJ to William Short, 31 Oct. 1819, TJ to Thomas Law, 13 June 1814, TJ to Miles King, 26 Sept. 1814, Bergh, 15:223–24, 14:141, 197–98.

8. TJ to Peter Carr, 10 Aug. 1787, TJ to Rutledge, 27 Dec. 1796, Bergh, 6:257, 9:354–55.

9. Brown, p. 5.

10. Koch, *Philosophy,* pp. 1–2; Peterson, *New Nation,* p. 53; Sanford, pp. 116–17.

11. See TJ, Second Inaugural Address, Ford, 8:343; TJ to James Fishback, 27 Sept. 1809, Bergh, 12:316.

12. TJ to Thomas Leiper, 21 Jan. 1809; TJ to James Fishback, 27 Sept. 1809, Bergh, 12:236–37, 315; TJ to Mathew Carey, 11 Nov. 1816, Ford, 10:67–68; TJ to John Adams, 11 Jan. 1817, TJ to Ezra Stiles, 25 June 1819, Bergh, 15:99–100, 203.

13. See Koch, *Philosophy,* p. 2; Chinard, *Literary Bible,* pp. 17–18; Lehmann, p. 33; Samuel Eliot Morison, *The Intellectual Life of Colonial New England* (1936; rept. Ithaca, N.Y., 1965), pp. 32–43.

14. TJ, "Autobiography," and TJ to John Brazer, 24 Aug. 1819, Bergh, 1:3, 15:208–11.

15. Trainer, p. 31; Koch, *Philosophy,* p. 4.

16. Chinard, *Literary Bible,* pp. 12, 18.

17. TJ to Short, 31 Oct. 1819, Bergh, 15:219–20.

18. TJ, "Syllabus of an Estimate of the Merit of the Doctrines of Jesus, Compared with Those of Others," Ford, 8:223–28.

19. Sowerby, 5:415, 292, 268, 410, 242, 349, 305, 439; TJ to William Short, 31 Oct. 1819, Bergh, 15:221.

20. Peterson, *New Nation,* p. 54; Koch, *Philosophy,* p. 5.

21. TJ to Thomas Jefferson Randolph, 24 Nov. 1808, TJ to Martha Jefferson, 28 Nov. 1783, Bergh, 12:201, 4:448; TJ to Peter Carr, 19 Aug. 1785, Ford, 4:428–29.

22. Chinard, *Literary Bible,* p. 16; Koch, *Philosophy,* pp. 4, 7, 1–2; Peterson, *New Nation,* p. 53.

23. See works in Jefferson's library (Sowerby, 5:319, 295, 314, 241, 432, 374–75, 320, 411, 423).

24. Cicero, *Tusc. Quaest.,* Horatius, *Satyr.,* Chinard, *Literary Bible,* pp. 78–79, 120–21.

25. TJ to Adams, 1 Aug. 1816, Bergh, 15:56.

26. Pope's translation of Homer's *Iliad,* Chinard, *Literary Bible,* p. 129.

27. Euripides, *Orestes,* Homer, *Iliad,* Chinard, *Literary Bible,* pp. 90–91, 8.

28. See Horace, epode 2, and Chinard's comments, *Literary Bible,* pp. 184–87, 32–33. For Roman writers in Jefferson's library, see Sowerby, 5:264, 265, 375, 382, 430.

29. Peterson, *New Nation,* pp. 22–27; Lehmann, pp. 51–53, 156–76, 182–88.

30. Peterson, *New Nation,* p. 340–41, 352–53, 543, 968–70, illustration p. 368; Lehmann, pp. 156–88.

31. See Malone, 1:143–49, 391; Lehmann, pp. 74–75, 71; Isaac Jefferson, pp. 27–28; Sowerby, 5:433.

32. TJ to John Adams, 25 March 1826, Cappon, 2:614.

33. Lehmann, pp. 177–87, 252–55; TJ to Thaddeus Kosciuszko, 26 Feb. 1810, Bergh, 12:369.

34. TJ to Alexander Donald, 7 Feb.1788, Bergh, 6:427, TJ, *Notes on the State of Virginia,* and TJ to John Lithgow, 4 Jan. 1805, Ford, 3:268, 270; TJ to John Adams, 11 Jan. 1816, Bergh, 14:395–96.

35. Chinard, *Literary Bible,* pp. 24, 148–50, 180–81, 120–21, 90–95.

36. See TJ to James Monroe, 13 Jan. 1803, TJ to John Adams, 28 Oct. 1813, Ford, 8:191, 9:425; TJ to Maria Cosway, 12 Oct. 1786, TJ to James Madison, 28 Aug. 1789, TJ to Edward Rutledge, 27 Dec. 1796, TJ to John Page, 25 June 1804, TJ to James Breckinridge, 9 April 1822, Bergh, 5:441–45, 7:449–50, 9:354–55, 11:32, 15:363–65.

37. TJ to Judge David Campbell, 28 Jan. 1810, Bergh 12:355–56; Randall, 1:384.

38. TJ to Judge James Sullivan, 21 May 1805, TJ to Judge Spencer Roane, 6 Sept. 1819, Bergh, 11:73, 15:215–16.

39. TJ to Thomas Law, 13 June 1814, Bergh, 14:143.

40. TJ to Thomas Jefferson Smith, 21 Feb. 1825, Bergh, 16:110; TJ to Thomas Jefferson Grotjan, 10 Jan. 1824, TJ for son of Rev. Charles Clay, 12 July 1817, Ford, 10:287, 92–93.

41. TJ to Randolph, 24 Nov. 1808, Bergh, 12:197–19.

42. TJ to Charles Thomson, 11 Nov. 1784, Boyd, 7:518–19.

43. TJ to Cosway, 12 Oct. 1786, Boyd, 10:446–52. Se also Helen C. Bullock, *May Head and My Heart* (New York, 1945); Fawn M. Brodie, *Thomas Jefferson: An Intimate History* (New York, 1974), pp. 221–27.

44. TJ to M. John de Neufville, 13 Dec. 1818, TJ to Dr. Benjamin Waterhouse, 26 June 1822, TJ to Nathaniel Burwell, 14 March 1818, Bergh, 15:178, 383, 167.

45. TJ to Dr. George Logan, 12 Nov. 1816, Ford, 10:68.

46. TJ, "The Anas," Ford, 1:332; TJ to James Madison, 1804, Padover, *Democracy,* p. 255; TJ to Madison, 28 Aug. 1789, Ford, 5:111.

47. TJ, Opinion on French Treaties, 28 April 1793, Ford, 6:220–28.

48. TJ, "Autobiography," Ford, 1:62–63; TJ to Martha Jefferson, 11 Dec. 1783, Boyd, 6:380; TJ to Peter Carr, 10 Aug. 1787, Bergh, 6:257–58; TJ to Washington, 10 May 1798, Ford, 5:96.

49. TJ to Thomas Law, 13 June 1814, TJ to Dr. Benjamin Waterhouse, 28 June 1822, Bergh, 14:142–43, 15:384.

50. See Healey, pp. 19–25.

51. Jefferson wrote of his admiration for these writers to John Adams, 14 Oct. 1816 and 11 Jan. 1817, and had their works in his library (Sowerby, 2:3, 5:282–83).

52. See Koch, *Philosophy,* pp. 15–22, 113–23.

53. TJ to Dupont de Nemours, 25 April 1816, TJ to Peter Carr, 10 Aug. 1787, TJ to Thomas Law, 13 June 1814, Bergh, 14:490–91, 6:257, 14:142; TJ, Opinion on French Treaties, 28 April 1793, Ford, 6:220–21.

54. Trainer, p. 133.

55. TJ to Dr. Benjamin Waterhouse, 13 Oct. 1815, Ford, 9:533; TJ to John Adams, 11 Jan. 1816, Bergh, 14:393–95.

56. Sowerby, 1:286–96, 2:91–148; TJ to Timothy Pickering, 27 Feb. 1821, Bergh, 15:323.

57. Boorstin, pp. 166, 171.

58. TJ to Thomas Law, 13 June 1814, Bergh, 14:141.

59. TJ to Peter Carr, 10 Aug. 1787, Bergh, 6:257–58.

60. See Koch, *Philosophy,* pp. 46–48, 15–16.

61. TJ, *Notes on the State of Virginia,* Ford, 3:268; TJ to Dr. Benjamin Rush, 23 Sept. 1800, Bergh, 10:173; TJ to Francis Gilmer, 7 June 1816, Ford, 10:33.

62. TJ to Thomas Law, 14 June 1814, TJ, "Answers to Questions of Monsieur Jean Nicholas Démeunier, Author of Encyclopédie Méthodique," Bergh, 14:143, 17:80.

63. See Sowerby, 5:320–21; Trainer, pp. 50–80; Koch, *Philosophy,* pp. 15–16.

64. TJ to Adams, 14 Oct. 1816, TJ to Edward Dowse, 19 April 1803, Bergh, 15:76–77, 10:377.

65. TJ to Francis Gilmer, 7 June 1816, Ford, 10:32; TJ to John Adams, 14 Oct. 1816, Bergh, 15:76; Sowerby, 5:318, 3:11.

66. TJ to Francis Gilmer, 7 June 1816, Ford, 10:32.

67. TJ, Opinion on French Treaties, 28 April 1793, Ford, 6:220.

68. TJ to Francis Gilmer, 7 June 1816, Ford, 10:32; see also TJ to Peter Carr, 10 Aug. 1787, and TJ to Thomas Law, 13 June 1814, Bergh, 6:257, 14:142.

69. TJ to Adams, 5 May 1817, Bergh, 15:109.

70. TJ to James Fishback, 27 Sept. 1809, Bergh, 12:315.

71. TJ to Pierre Samuel Dupont de Nemours, 24 April 1816, Ford, 10:24; TJ to Peter Carr, 10 Aug. 1787, Bergh, 6:257–58; TJ to Caesar A. Rodney, 10 Feb. 1810, Ford, 9:271; TJ to John Adams, 14 Oct. 1816; TJ to Miles King, 26 Sept. 1814; Bergh, 15:76, 14:197.

72. TJ to Cosway, 12 Oct. 1786, Bergh, 5:442–44.

73. TJ to Law, 13 June 1814, Bergh, 14:139–44.

74. Sowerby, 5:313, 341, 284, 319, 272–73 (Helvétius, Thomas Law, Denis Diderot, Paul H. d'Holbach, and M. J. A. N. Caritat, the marquis de Condorcet).

75. Koch, *Philosophy*, pp. 17–18, 20, 52, 15; Sowerby, 5:250, 261, 418, 2:7 (Lord Kames, Jeremy Bentham, Pierre Jean Georges Cabanis, and Dugald Stewart); Lehmann, pp. 122, 478.

76. Trainer, pp. 58–80, 169; Sowerby, 5:278, 281, 260 (Lord Shaftesbury, Delisle de Sales, and Burlamaqui).

77. Chinard, *Literary Bible*, pp. 2–4.

Chapter VI

1. TJ to John Adams, 15 Aug. 1820, Bergh, 15:274.

2. TJ to Adams, 11 Jan. 1816, Bergh, 14:393–97; TJ to Adams, 8 April 1816, Cappon, 2:467.

3. TJ to John Adams, 10 Dec. 1819, Cappon 2:549.

4. TJ to Pierre Samuel Dupont de Nemours, 25 April 1816, Bergh, 14:490–91; Adams to TJ, 15 Nov. 1813; TJ to Adams, 28 Oct. 1813; Cappon, 2:400–401, 388–90; TJ to Dr. Benjamin Waterhouse, 3 March 1818, TJ to Miles King, 26 Sept. 1814, TJ to Adams, 14 Oct. 1816, Bergh, 15:164–65, 14:197, 15:76, TJ, Opinion on Treaties, 28 April 1793, Ford, 6:221.

5. See their correspondence edited by Cappon and Peterson, *New Nation*, p. 1008.

6. TJ, "Autobiography," Bergh, 1:152; TJ to John Adams, 25 Feb. 1823, Cappon, 2:589; Jefferson's quote from Cicero, Chinard, *Literary Bible*, pp. 76–79; TJ to Pierre Samuel Dupont de Nemours, 24 April 1816, Bergh, 14:489.

7. TJ, *Notes on the State of Virginia,* Bergh, 2:207–9; TJ to Jeremiah Moor, 14 Aug. 1800, Ford, 7:454.

8. TJ to Peter Carr, 19 Aug. 1785; TJ to Uriah McGregory, 13 Aug. 1800; TJ to John Norvell, 11 June 1807, TJ to DeWitt Clinton, 24 May 1807, TJ to John Adams, 1 June 1822, Bergh, 5:83–84, 10:171, 11:224–26, 208, 15:372.

9. See Boorstin, p. 173, and Jefferson's quotations from Euripides and Pope, Chinard, *Literary Bible,* pp. 84, 88, 94, 96, 98, 100, 102, 106, 130.

10. TJ to George Wythe, 13 Aug. 1786, Bergh, 5:395–97.

11. TJ to Gov. John Langdon, 5 March 1810, Bergh, 12: 377–78.

12. TJ to Samuel Kercheval, 19 Jan. 1810, TJ to Francis A. van der Kemp, 25 April 1816, Bergh, 12:345, 15:2–3; TJ to Dr. George Logan, 12 Nov. 1816, TJ to Dr. Benjamin Waterhouse, 13 Oct. 1815, Ford, 10:68, 9:532–33.

13. See Peterson, *New Nation,* 49–51, and David Harris, *Encyclopedia Britannica* (1973), s.v. "Enlightenment."

14. See Jefferson's quotations from Euripides, Chinard, *Literary Bible,* pp. 82, 86; TJ to Dr. George Logan, 12 Nov. 1816, Ford, 10:68.

15. TJ to John Adams, 10 Dec. 1819, Bergh, 15:233–35; Lehmann, pp. 106–21, 236; Harris, s.v. "Enlightenment," p. 602; Sowerby, 5:307 (Gibbon).

16. TJ to Adams, 28 Oct. 1813, Bergh, 13:397; Adams to TJ, 15 July 1813, Cappon, 2:357–58; TJ to M. Correa de Serra, 28 June 1815, Bergh, 14:331.

17. TJ to Uriah McGregory, 13 Aug. 1800, TJ to William Short, 13 April 1820, TJ to Thomas Cooper, 2 Nov. 1822, TJ to Adams, 11 April 1823, TJ to Dr. Benjamin Waterhouse, 26 June 1822, Bergh, 10:171, 15:246, 403–4, 425, 384.

18. TJ to Ezra Stiles, 25 June 1819, TJ to Dr. Benjamin Waterhouse 19 July 1822, TJ to William Short, 4 Aug. 1820, TJ to John Adams, 22 Aug. 1813, Bergh, 15:204, 392, 258,13:350.

19. TJ to Dr. Benjamin Waterhouse, 19 July, 26 June 1822, TJ to William Canby, 18 Sept. 1813, Bergh, 15:391, 384, 13:378; Sowerby, 5:245 (Athanasius).

20. See Jefferson's quotations from Bolingbroke's *Philosophical Works,* Chinard, *Literary Bible,* pp. 64, 57, 46, 50–51.

21. Quoted in TJ, "Notes on Religion," Ford, 2:93–94, and paraphrased in TJ to Miles King, 26 Sept. 1814, Bergh, 14:198.

22. Chinard, *Literary Bible,* pp. 134–40.

23. See Peterson, *New Nation,* p. 49. Ernst Cassirer has concluded, "The concept of original sin is the common opponent against which all philosophies of the Enlightenment join forces" (*The Philosophy of the Enlightenment* [Princeton, N.J., 1951], p. 141).

24. TJ to John Adams, 22 Aug. 1813, Bergh, 13:352; *The New Schaff-Herzog Encyclopedia of Religious Knowledge* (1956), s.v. "Middleton, Conyers."

25. *The Collegiate Encyclopedia* (1969), s.v. "Rousseau, Jean Jacques"; Sowerby, 5:405 (Rousseau).

26. Cassirer, pp. 157–58.

27. TJ, *Notes on the State of Virginia,* Bergh, 2:82–92.

28. Peterson, *New Nation,* pp. 56–61; TJ to Thomas Cooper, 10 Feb. 1814, TJ to George Wythe, 13 Aug. 1786, Bergh, 14:90–97, 5:396.

29. See writings by Jefferson's friends, Joseph Priestly in *A History of the Corruptions of Christianity* and Dr. Benjamin Rush in a lecture, quoted by Boorstin, p. 148, 149, 276. Jefferson was greatly influenced by Priestley and had 24 of his works and 12 works by Rush in his library (Sowerby, 5:391, 406).

30. TJ to his nephew Peter Carr, 19 Aug. 1785, Bergh, 5:83.

31. Boorstin, pp. 146–48, 150.

32. TJ to John Adams, 8 April 1816, Cappon, 2:467.

33. Thomas Paine, *Age of Reason,* quoted by Boorstin, pp. 151, 276. Jefferson had 13 works by Paine in his library (Sowerby, 5:375).

34. Koch, *Philosophy,* p. 117.

35. See Roy J. Honeywell, *The Educational Work of Thomas Jefferson* (Cambridge, Mass., 1931); Healey; Lehmann, pp. 190–290; Peterson, *New Nation,* pp. 145–52, 961–88.

36. TJ to George Wythe, 13 Aug. 1786, TJ to John Adams, 17 May 1818, Bergh, 5:396–97, 15:170.

37. TJ, A Bill for Establishing a Public Library, Ford, 2:236–37; TJ to John Adams, 4 Sept. 1823, Bergh, 15:465.

38. TJ, "Autobiography," and TJ, *Notes on Virginia,* Bergh, 1:70–72, 2:203. See also Cappon, "The Advantages of Education," in *Adams-Jefferson Letters,* 2:478–80.

39. Cappon, 2:478–83; Ford, 10:396.

40. Peterson, *New Nation,* pp. 963–88.

41. Healey, pp. 205–9.

42. TJ to William Ludlow, 6 Sept. 1824, TJ to John Adams, 12 Sept. 1821, Bergh, 16:75, 15:334.

43. Healey, p. 245.

44. John Adams to TJ, 30 Nov. 1786, Cappon, 1:156; TJ to Katherine Sprowle Douglas, 5 July 1785, Boyd, 8:259–60; TJ to James Madison, 30 Jan. 1787; TJ to William Stephens Smith, 13 Nov. 1787, Bergh, 6:65, 372–73.

45. Adams to TJ, 30 June 1813, Cappon, 2:347.

46. TJ to James Madison, 28 Aug. 1789, TJ, "Autobiography," TJ to Richard Price, 8 Jan. 1789, TJ to François Barbé de Marbois, 14 June 1817, Bergh, 7:445–48, 1:133–34, 103, 127–28, 7:253–54, 15:129–30.

47. John Adams to TJ, 15 July 1813, TJ to Adams, 11 Jan. 1816, Cappon, 2:357–58, 459–60.

48. TJ, "Autobiography," TJ to John Adams, 11 Jan. 1816, TJ to George Hammond, 15 May 1793, Bergh, 1:152, 14:393–94, 9:91–92.

49. See Peterson, *New Nation,* pp. 882–918.

50. TJ to Caesar A. Rodney, 10 Feb. 1810, Bergh, 12:357–58; TJ to Dr. George Logan, 12 Nov. 1816, Ford, 10:68.

51. TJ to Edward Coles, 25 Aug. 1814, Ford, 9:477.

52. See Brodie, pp. 229–33; Peterson, *New Nation,* pp. 705–11.

53. See Koch, *Adams and Jefferson,* p. 106, quoting John Quincy Adams's diary, and Robert McColley, *Slavery and Jeffersonian Virginia,* 2nd ed. (Urbana, Ill., 1972), pp. 4–6.

54. TJ, "Autobiography," Bergh, 1:34–35.

55. William W. Freehling, "The Founding Fathers and Slavery," *American Historical Review* 77 (1972): 87–88; McColley, pp. 125, 92–93.

56. TJ, "Answers to Questions of Monsieur Jean Nicholas Démeunier, Author of Encyclopédie Méthodique," Bergh, 17:98–99, 103.

57. TJ, *Notes on the State of Virginia,* Bergh, 2:227.

58. Ibid., pp. 197–99, 226–27; TJ to Edward Bancroft, 26 Jan. 1789, TJ to Edward Coles, 25 Aug. 1814, Ford, 5:66–67, 9:478.

59. McColley, p. 5; Winthrop D. Jordan, *White over Black: American Attitudes toward the Negro, 1550–1812* (Chapel Hill, N.C., 1968), p. 481.

60. TJ, *Notes on the State of Virginia,* Bergh, 2:226.

61. Ibid., pp. 225–27; TJ to Edward Coles, 25 Aug. 1814, Ford, 9:447.

62. TJ, *Notes on the State of Virginia,* Bergh, 2:200; Isaac Jefferson, pp. 30–32; Malone, 4:495–96.

63. TJ to Frances Wright, 7 Aug. 1825, Bergh, 16:120; TJ to Edward Bancroft, 26 Jan. 1789, Ford, 5:67–68; Isaac Jefferson, p. 37; Peterson, *New Nation,* pp. 536–37.

64. TJ, *Notes on the State of Virginia,* TJ, "Autobiography," Bergh, 2:191–92, 1:72; TJ, "Answers to Questions by Monsieur Démeunier," 24 Jan. 1786, TJ to Edward Coles, 25 Aug. 1814, Ford, 4:185, 9:477–78.

65. TJ to Rev. Jared Sparks, 4 Feb. 1824, Ford, 10:290–92.

66. Ibid.; TJ to Dr. Thomas Humphreys, 8 Feb. 1817, Ford 10:76–77; TJ to Frances Wright, 7 Aug. 1825, Bergh, 16:120–21; Peterson, *New Nation,* pp. 998–99; Foner, p. 803.

67. TJ, *Notes on the State of Virginia,* Bergh, 2:192.

68. TJ to St. George Tucker, 28 Aug. 1797, TJ, "Autobiography," TJ, *Notes on the State of Virginia,* Bergh, 9:418, 1:72–73, 2:192–96, 200–201; TJ to Edward Coles, 25 Aug. 1814, Ford, 9:478.

69. Peterson, *New Nation,* pp. 260–64; Sowerby, 5:428, 259 (Tyson and Buffon).

70. TJ to M. Henri Gregoire, 25 Feb. 1809, TJ to Benjamin Banneker, 30 Aug. 1791, Bergh, 12:254–55, 8:241–42.

71. Peterson, *New Nation,* pp. 705–11; Malone, 4:213, 495; Peterson, *Jefferson Image,* pp. 182–83; Brodie, pp. 229–33; Jordan, pp. 461–69; Virginius Dabney, *The Jefferson Scandals: A Rebuttal* (New York, 1981).

72. Dabney, pp. 23–33; Malone, 4:206–20, 494–98.

73. I. Jefferson, p. 10; Petterson, *Jefferson Image,* pp. 185–86.

74. Peterson, *Jefferson Image,* pp. 182, 186; Malone, 4:496; Brodie, pp. 28–32. I. Jefferson, pp. 10, 56–57; Peterson, *New Nation,* p. 385; Dabney, pp. 45–73.

75. Malone, 4:496–98; Peterson, *New Nation,* p. 244; I. Jefferson, p. 36; Dabney, pp. 74–98.

76. TJ, *Notes on the State of Virginia,* Bergh, 2:192–93, 201, 227; TJ to Edward Coles, 25 Aug. 1814, Ford, 9:478–79.

77. Malone, 4:495–98; TJ, *Notes on the State of Virginia,* Bergh, 2:201.

78. Brodie, p. 187; Peterson, *New Nation,* pp. 246, 295, 405–7, 658; I. Jefferson, pp. 11–12, 31, 33; Randall, 3:671.

79. Peterson, *New Nation,* p. 27.

80. Brodie, pp. 167–68.

81. Peterson, *New Nation,* p. 246; Randall, 1:302.

82. TJ to William Charles Coles Claiborne, 3 May 1810, TJ to Maria Cosway, 12 Oct. 1786, Bergh, 12:385, 5:441.

83. Peterson, *Jefferson Image,* pp. 171–75; Adrienne Koch, *Jefferson* (Englewood Cliffs, N.J., 1971), p. 106.

84. TJ to Edward Coles, 25 Aug. 1814, Ford, 9:447, 479; TJ to Frances Wright, 7 Aug. 1825, Bergh, 16:119.

85. Freehling, p. 9.

86. TJ to William Short, 13 April 1820, Bergh, 15:247–48.

Chapter VII

1. Peterson, *New Nation,* pp. 637–39; TJ to James Monroe, 26 May 1800, Ford, 7:447–48.

2. TJ to Adams, 11 April 1823, TJ to Charles Thomson, 9 Jan. 1816, Bergh, 15:425–26, 14:385–86.

3. John Adams to TJ, 2 March 1816, TJ to Thomas Law, 13 June 1814, TJ to Adams, 8 April 1816, Bergh, 14:438–39, 139–40, 468–69.

4. Gay, pp. 122, 345, 371–72, 376–77, 390–92.

5. Gilbert Chinard, *Thomas Jefferson: The Apostle of Americanism* (Boston, 1929), pp. vii, 215.

6. TJ to Mrs. Samuel Harrison Smith, 6 Aug. 1816, Bergh, 15:60.

7. Koch, *Philosophy,* pp. 27, 37.

8. See Ernst Troeltsch, *The New Schaff-Herzog Encyclopedia of Religious Knowledge* (1958), s.v. "Deism"; Arnold Smithline, *Natural Religion in American Literature* (New Haven, Conn., 1966), pp. 9–13; Gay, pp. 277–80; and TJ to Dr. Benjamin Waterhouse, 26 June 1822, TJ to John Adams, 11 April 1823, 13 Oct. 1813, 22 Aug. 1813, 14 Oct. 1816, TJ to Francis W. Gilmer, 7 June 1816, TJ to Richard Price, 8 Jan. 1789, TJ to Elbridge Gerry, 29 March 1801, TJ to Levi Lincoln, 26 Aug. 1801, TJ to Peter Carr, 10 Aug. 1787, Bergh, 15:384–85, 425–26, 13:389, 352, 15:76, 24–25, 7:252, 10:254, 275, 6:257–58; Sowerby, 5:254, 424, 360 (Blount, Tindal, Middleton).

9. TJ to John Adams, 22 Aug. 1813, 25 Dec. 1813, Bergh, 13:352, 14:34. Compare Chinard, *Literary Bible,* pp. 40–41, 49, and *Joseph Priestley: Selections*

from His Writings, ed. Ira V. Brown (University Park, Pa., 1962), pp. 294–97, and TJ to Adams, 22 Aug. 1813, 11 April 1823, TJ to Miles King, 26 Sept. 1814, TJ to Peter Carr, 10 Aug. 1787, Bergh, 13:352, 15:430, 14:197, 6:259; TJ to John Davis, 18 Jan. 1824, Ford, 10:287–88.

10. TJ to Peter Carr, 10 Aug. 1787, TJ to William Short, 31 Oct. 1819, Bergh, 6:258–59, 15:219–20; TJ to John Davis, 18 Jan. 1824, Ford, 10:288.

11. TJ to John Adams, 5 May 1817, Bergh, 15:109.

12. TJ to John Adams, 8 April 1816, 11 April 1823, Bergh, 14:469, 15:426–27.

13. Chinard, *Literary Bible,* pp. 58–59; Chinard, *Commonplace Book,* pp. 331–32.

14. Healey, pp. 27–28.

15. TJ to John Adams, 8 April 1816, Bergh, 14:469.

16. TJ, *A Summary View of the Rights of British America,* TJ, Declaration of Independence, TJ, Draft of Declaration of Taking Up Arms, TJ, Statute of Religious Freedom, Ford, 1:447, 30, 474, 2:237–38; TJ to James Fishbach, 27 Sept. 1809, Bergh, 12:315.

17. TJ to Thomas Law, 13 June 1814, TJ to James Fishbach, 27 Sept. 1809, TJ to Miles King, 26 Sept. 1814, Bergh, 14:139–42, 12:315, 14:197–98; TJ to William Carver, 4 Dec. 1823; Ford, 10:284–85.

18. TJ to John Adams, 22 Aug. 1813, Cappon 2:368.

19. TJ to Justin Pierre Plumard Derieux, 25 July 1788, Boyd, 13:418; *The Book of Common Prayer* (1867), sect. 16.

20. TJ to Sparks, 4 Nov. 1820, TJ to Smith, 8 Dec. 1822, TJ to Joseph Priestley, 9 April 1803, TJ to Rev. Thomas Whittemore, 5 June 1822, Bergh, 15:288, 408–9, 10:374–75, 15:373.

21. TJ to William Short, 4 Aug. 1820, TJ to John Adams, 22 Aug. 1813, Bergh, 15:258, 13:350.

22. *Priestley,* pp. 285, 298.

23. TJ to John Adams, 11 April 1823, Cappon, 2:593–94.

24. TJ to John Adams, 22 Aug. 1813, Bergh, 15:352; TJ, "Notes on Religion," Ford, 2:92–93.

25. *Priestley,* p. 287; TJ, "Notes on Religion," Ford, 2:96.

26. David Schley Schaff, *The New Schaff-Herzog Encyclopedia of Religious Knowledge* (1958), s.v. "Arianism"; TJ to Rev. Jared Sparks, 4 Nov. 1820, TJ to William Canby, 18 Sept. 1813, Bergh, 15:288, 13:378; *The Book of Common Prayer* (1867), Sec. 11.

27. TJ to William Short, 13 April 1820, TJ to Rev. Jared Sparks, 4 Nov. 1820, TJ to Dr. Benjamin Waterhouse, 26 June 1822, TJ to Smith, 8 Dec. 1822, Bergh, 15:246, 288, 383–84, 408–409.

28. Koch, *Philosophy,* p. 37; Healey, p. 26; Smithline, p. 56; Boorstin, p. 156.

29. Max Heinzet, *The New Schaff-Herzog Encyclopedia of Religious Knowledge* (1958), s.v. "Theism."

30. TJ to John Adams, 8 April 1816, Cappon, 2:467–68; TJ to Joseph Priestley, 9 April 1803, Bergh, 10:375.

31. Heinzet, s.v. "Theism."

32. TJ to Miles King, 26 Sept. 1814, TJ to Ezra Stiles, 25 June 1819, Bergh, 14:197, 15:203–4.

33. Sowerby lists René Descartes in Jefferson's library (5:282).

34. TJ to Adams, 8 April 1816, 11 April 1823, Bergh, 14:469, 15:427.

35. Randall, 3:102, 450–51, 672; TJ to David Barrow, 1 May 1814, Ford, 9:516.

36. TJ, Reply to Massachusetts Citizens, 1809, TJ, Reply to New York Tammany Society, Feb. 1808, John P. Foley, ed., *The Jefferson Cyclopedia,* 2 vols. (1900, rept. New York, 1967), 2:731; TJ, Second Annual Message, 15 Dec. 1802, TJ, Second Inaugural Address, Ford, 8:182, 347–48.

37. TJ to John Adams, 11 April 1823, Cappon, 2:592–94.

38. John Adams to TJ, 4 Oct. 1813, and TJ to Adams, 12 Oct. 1813, Cappon, 2:380–81, 385–86. Jefferson had 40 copies of the New Testament, the Bible, or individual books of the Bible in Greek, Latin, French, and English in his library (Sowerby, 2:91–103, 107–8, 191).

39. Chinard, *Literary Bible,* pp. 25–26, 165, 170, 193, 202–3.

40. TJ, Reply to Address of Republicans of Philadelphia, 25 May 1808, TJ, Reply to Legislature of Orleans, 18 June 1808, TJ, Reply to Legislature of Massachusetts, 14 Feb. 1807, TJ, Reply to Legislature of Georgia, 3 Feb. 1809, Bergh, 16:305, 306, 287, 331; TJ, First Inaugural Address, 4 March 1801, Ford, 8:4.

41. TJ to John Adams, 10 Aug. 1815, 24 Jan. 1814, Cappon, 2:454, 425; TJ to Dr. Walter Jones, 5 March 1810, TJ to Gov. John Langdon, 5 March 1810, Bergh, 12:373, 379; TJ, Second Annual Message, 15 Dec. 1802, Ford, 8:181–82.

42. TJ to John Wayles Eppes, 24 June 1813, TJ to James Madison, 28 Oct. 1785, Ford, 9:390–91, 7:36; TJ to Thomas Earle, 24 Sept. 1823, TJ to Madison, 6 Sept. 1789; Bergh, 15:470, 7:454–61.

43. TJ, Reply to the General Assembly of North Carolina, 10 Jan. 1808, TJ, First Inaugural Address, 4 March 1801, TJ to Benjamin Waring, 23 March 1801, TJ, Reply to Representatives of Massachusetts, 14 Feb. 1807, TJ, Reply to Baltimore Baptist Association, 17 Oct. 1808, TJ, Reply to Ketocton Baptist Association, 18 Oct. 1808, Bergh, 16:301, 3:323, 10:236, 16:290, 318, 320; TJ, First Annual Message, 8 Dec. 1801, TJ, Third Annual Message, 17 Oct. 1803, Ford, 8:108–10, 272.

44. TJ, Reply to Republican Young Men of New London, 24 Feb. 1809, TJ, Reply to Delegates of Massachusetts, 28 March 1809, TJ, Second Inaugural Address, 4 March 1805, TJ to the earl of Buchan, 10 July 1803, Bergh, 16:339–40, 352, 3:383, 10:400.

45. TJ, First Inaugural Address, 4 March 1801, TJ to David Barrow, 1 May 1815, Ford, 8:6, 9:516; TJ to Benjamin Waring, 23 March 1801, TJ to General Assembly of Virginia, 16 Feb. 1809, TJ, Reply to Delegates from Massachusetts, 28 March 1809, Bergh, 10:236,16:234, 352; TJ, Reply to Vermont Address, 1801, Foley, 1:249.

46. TJ, Fifth Annual Message, 3 Dec. 1805, Ford, 8:386–88; TJ to Abigail Adams, 11 Jan. 1817, Cappon, 2:504.

47. Chinard, *Literary Bible,* pp. 59–60.

48. See Jefferson's quotation of Bolingbroke, ibid.

49. TJ to John Adams, 11 April 1823, TJ to Dr. Benjamin Waterhouse, 26 June 1822, Bergh, 15:425–29, 384; Chinard, *Commonplace Book,* pp. 332–33; Chinard, *Literary Bible,* pp. 45, 54–55, 64. See also TJ to John Adams, 12 Oct. 1813, Cappon, 2:383–84; TJ to William Short, 4 Aug. 1820, Bergh, 15:260.

50. Compare Deuteronomy 6:4–5 with Mark 12:28–31.

51. TJ, Address to Gov. Dunmore, 12 June 1775, TJ to Jean Nicholas Démeunier for the *Encyclopédie,* 22 June 1786, TJ to George Thacher, 26 Jan. 1824, Ford, 1:459, 4:185, 10:289; TJ, Address of Congress to Gen. George Washington, 23 Dec. 1783, Foley, 2:731; TJ to François de Marbois, 14 June 1817, Bergh, 15:130.

52. TJ, Reply to Danbury Baptist Association, 1 Jan. 1802, TJ, Reply to Society of Friends, 13 Nov. 1807, Bergh, 16:282, 290; TJ, Opinion on French Treaties, 28 April 1793, Ford, 6:220.

53. TJ, Bill for Establishing Religious Freedom, Ford, 2:237–38.

54. TJ to Miles King, 26 Sept. 1814, Bergh, 14:197; TJ to William Carver, 4 Dec. 1823, TJ to Peter Carr, 10 Aug. 1787, Ford, 10:285, 4:432.

55. TJ to Peter Carr, 10 Aug. 1787, TJ to Thomas Law, 13 June 1814, Bergh, 6:257, 14:142. See also Jefferson's quotation of Bolingbroke, Chinard, *Literary Bible,* pp. 62–64.

56. TJ to Dr. Benjamin Waterhouse, 26 June 1822, TJ to William Short, 4 Aug. 1820, 31 Oct. 1819, Bergh, 15:384, 260, 220.

57. Boorstin, pp. 29, 241–43.

58. Thomas Jefferson Coolidge, "Jefferson in His Family," Bergh, 15:iv.

59. TJ to William Short, 13 April 1820, TJ to James Smith, 8 Dec. 1822, Bergh, 15:246–47, 409.

60. TJ to Timothy Pickering, 27 Feb. 1821, TJ to James Smith, 8 Dec. 1822, Bergh, 15:323, 409.

61. Peterson, *Jefferson Image,* pp. 93, 303.

Chapter VIII

1. TJ to William Short, 31 Oct. 1819, TJ to Francis Adrian van der Kemp, 25 April 1816, and Cyrus Adler, "The Jefferson Bible," Bergh, 15:221, 2, 20:10–11, 19.

2. TJ to Joseph Priestley, 9 April 1803, Bergh, 10:374–76; Boorstin, p. 158.

3. Peterson, *New Nation,* p. 958; TJ to Dr. Benjamin Rush, 21 April 1803, TJ to John Adams, 22 Aug. 1813, TJ to William Short, 13 April 1820, TJ to Francis Adrian van der Kemp, 25 April 1816, Bergh, 10:379–80, 13:351–52, 15:243, 3.

4. TJ to William Short, 31 Oct. 1819, TJ to Charles Thomson, 9 Jan. 1816, Bergh, 15:221, 14:385.

5. O. I. A. Roche, ed., *The Jefferson Bible, with the Annotated Commentaries on Religion of Thomas Jefferson,* "Introduction" by Henry Wilder Foote (New York, 1964), p. 20; Randall, 3:452, 654; Peterson, *New Nation,* p. 960.

6. TJ to Francis Adrian van der Kemp, 25 April 1816, TJ to William Short, 31 Oct. 1819, TJ to Charles Thomson, 9 Jan. 1816, Bergh, 15:2, 221, 14:385–86.

7. TJ to William Short, 13 April, 4 Aug. 1820, Bergh, 15:244–45, 259; Randall, 3:671–72; Adler, "Jefferson Bible," Bergh, 20:10–11, 19. Bergh includes Jefferson's "Bible" in vol. 20; Roche prints the work and includes a facsimile of the original in *Jefferson Bible.*

8. TJ to Francis Adrian van der Kemp, 16 March 1817, Ford, 10:77.

9. Foote, "Introduction," p. 20.

10. TJ to William Short, 31 Oct. 1819, 13 April 1820, TJ to John Adams, 13 Oct. 1813, TJ to Francis Adrian van der Kemp, 25 April 1816, TJ to Timothy Pickering, 27 Feb. 1821, TJ to Samuel Kercheval, 19 Jan. 1810, Bergh, 15:220–21, 245, 13:390, 15:2, 323, 12:345.

11. TJ to William Short, 13 April 1820, 31 Oct. 1819, Bergh, 15:244–45, 219–20.

12. TJ to Joseph Priestley, 8 April 1803, TJ to Francis Adrian van der Kemp, 25 April 1816, TJ to Samuel Kercheval, 19 Jan. 1810, TJ to William Short, 31 Oct. 1819, 13 April 1820, 4 Aug. 1820, Bergh, 10:375, 15:2, 12:345, 15:220, 244, 259; Chinard, *Literary Bible,* p. 50.

13. TJ, "Syllabus," TJ to Joseph Priestley, 9 April 1803, TJ to John Adams, 13 Oct. 1813, TJ to William Short, 31 Oct. 1819, 13 April 1820, 4 Aug. 1820, Bergh, 10:383–84, 375, 13:390, 15:220–21, 244–45, 257–59.

14. TJ to Samuel Kercheval, 19 Jan. 1810, TJ to William Short, 31 Oct. 1819, Bergh, 12:345–46, 15:221; TJ to John Davis, 18 Jan. 1824, Ford, 10:287–88; TJ to Timothy Pickering, 27 Feb. 1821, TJ to James Smith, 8 Dec. 1822, TJ to John Adams, 13 Oct. 1813, Bergh, 15:323, 408, 13:389–90.

15. TJ to William Short, 31 Oct. 1819, 13 April 1820, 4 Aug. 1820, TJ to Moses Robinson, 23 March 1801, TJ to Peter Carr, 10 Aug. 1787, Bergh, 15:220–21, 244–45, 257, 10:237, 6:260–61.

16. Gay, p. 34.

17. He had 627 titles in his library under various types of history. It was the third largest subject area in his library, next to law and science (Sanford, pp. 93–96).

18. See Lehmann.

19. Lehmann, p. 89; TJ to John Brazer, 24 Aug. 1819, TJ to Dr. Benjamin Smith Barton, 21 Sept. 1809, TJ, "Essay on Anglo-Saxon Language," Bergh, 15: 208–9, 12:312–13, 18:359–451.

20. TJ to Adams, 11 April 1823, TJ to Peter Carr, 10 Aug. 1787, Bergh, 15:430, 6:259–60; Chinard, Commonplace Book, pp. 51, 363–64.

21. Carl Friedrich Georg Heinrici, *The New Schaff-Herzog Encyclopedia of Religious Knowledge* (1958), s.v. "Biblical Criticism."

22. Jefferson had in his library 129 works of "Ancient" History which included the early church fathers and Roman and Greek historians, as well as 25 additional works on the Middle Ages and the Reformation (Sowerby, 1:1–61, 286–96). He studied Bolingbroke's account of the canonization of the books of the Bible by "ecclesiastical factions" (Chinard, *Literary Bible,* pp. 51–53) and read "all the histories of Christ, those named Evangelists and those Pseudo-evangelists collected by Fabricus" (TJ to Peter Carr, 10 Aug. 1787, Bergh, 6:261). He had several books by Johann Fabricus on the Bible and the Apocrypha in his library (Sowerby, 5:297).

23. TJ to John Adams, 12 Oct. 1813, Cappon, 2:384.

24. *Priestley,* pp. 297, 287–88.

25. Heinrici, s.v. "Biblical Criticism"; Cassirer, pp. 182–87; Sowerby, 5:282, 352, 417, 293, 310, 284 (Descartes, Malebranche, Spinoza, Erasmus, Grotius, Ernesti, and Diderot).

26. TJ to Carr, 10 Aug. 1787, TJ to Short, 4 Aug. 1820, TJ to Francis Adrian van der Kemp, 25 April 1816, Bergh, 6:258, 15:257, 259, 2; Heinrici, s.v. "Biblical Criticism."

27. TJ to Thompson, 9 Jan. 1816, TJ to Priestley, 29 Jan. 1804, Bergh, 14:385, 10:445–46.

28. See Ernest F. Scott, "The New Testament and Criticism," in *The Abingdon Bible Commentary,* ed. Frederick Carl Eiselen (New York, 1929), p. 888; Ernest Ward Burch, "The Structure of the Synoptic Gospels," ibid., pp. 872–73, and Helmet Heinrich Koester, *Encyclopaedia Britannica* (1973), s.v. "Gospels."

29. TJ to William Short, 4 Aug. 1820, TJ to Joseph Priestley, 9 April 1803, TJ to Rev. Jared Sparks, 4 Nov. 1820, Bergh, 15:259, 10:334, 15:288; TJ to George Thacher, 26 Jan. 1824, Ford, 10:288.

30. TJ to Joseph Priestley, 9 April 1803, TJ to Francis Adrian van der Kemp, 25 April 1816, Bergh, 10:375, 15:2.

31. TJ to George Thacher, 26 Jan. 1824, Ford, 10:288–89; TJ to William Short, 4 Aug. 1820, Bergh, 15:257.

32. TJ to Carr, 10 Aug. 1787, Bergh, 6:260.

33. TJ to John Adams, 11 April 1823, TJ to Benjamin Waterhouse, 26 June 1822, TJ to Short, 31 Oct. 1819, Bergh, 15:430, 383–84, 220–21.

34. *Priestley,* pp. 282–83, 318–20, 308, 285.

35. TJ to John Adams, 12 Oct. 1813, Cappon, 2:384–85; TJ to William Short, 4 Aug. 1820, 31 Oct. 1819, Bergh, 15:258, 219–20.

36. TJ to William Canby, 18 Sept. 1813, TJ to Timothy Pickering, 27 Feb. 1821, TJ to Rev. Jared Sparks, 4 Nov. 1820, TJ to Dr. Benjamin Waterhouse, 26 June 1822, Bergh, 13:378, 15:323, 288, 384.

37. TJ to Timothy Pickering, 27 Feb. 1821, TJ to Rev. Charles Clay, 29 Jan. 1815, TJ to William Canby, 18 Sept. 1813, TJ to Rev. Thomas Whittemore, 5 June 1822, Bergh, 15:323, 14:233, 13:378, 15:374.

38. TJ to William Short, 4 Aug. 1820, Bergh, 15:261.

39. TJ to Carr, 10 Aug. 1787, Bergh, 6:260.

40. See Spinoza's argument, in Jefferson's library (Cassirer, p. 189).

41. Gay, pp. 383–84, 399–400; TJ to Peter Carr, 10 Aug. 1787, Bergh, 6:260.

42. TJ to William Short, 13 April 1820, 4 Aug. 1820, 31 Oct. 1819, TJ to Timothy Pickering, 27 Feb. 1821, TJ to Joseph Priestley, 9 April 1803, Bergh, 15:244, 257, 220–21, 323, 10:375.

43. TJ to Joseph Priestley, 9 April 1803, TJ to William Short, 4 Aug. 1820, TJ to John Adams, 13 Oct. 1813, Bergh, 10:375, 15:261–62, 12:391–92.

44. TJ to Thacher, 26 Jan. 1824, Ford, 10:288–891.

45. TJ to Dr. George Logan, 12 Nov. 1816, Ford, 10:68; TJ to Francis Adrian van der Kemp, 25 April 1816, TJ to Joseph Priestley, 9 April 1803, Bergh, 15:2–3, 10:374–75.

46. TJ to William Short, 4 Aug. 1820, 13 April 1820, TJ to Joseph Priestley, 9 April 1803, TJ to Francis Adrian van der Kemp, 25 April 1816, Bergh, 15:259, 244, 10:374–75, 15:2.

47. TJ to Adams, 11 April 1823, Bergh, 15:430; TJ to George Thacher, 26 Jan. 1824, Ford, 10:288; TJ to William Short, 31 Oct. 1819, TJ to Samuel Kercheval, 19 Jan. 1810, TJ to Short, 4 Aug. 1820, 13 April 1820, TJ to Joseph Priestley, 9 April 1803, TJ to Adams, 12 Oct. 1813, Bergh, 15:220, 12:345, 15:259–60, 244, 10:374, 13:389.

48. TJ to William Short, 4 Aug. 1820, TJ, "Syllabus," Bergh, 15:260–61, 10:382–83.

49. TJ to Francis Adrian van der Kemp, 25 April 1816, TJ to Rev. Charles Clay, 29 Jan. 1815, TJ to Samuel Kercheval, 19 Jan. 1810, Bergh, 15:2, 14:233–34, 12:345–46.

50. Boorstin, p. 158; TJ to Joseph Priestley, 9 April 1803, TJ to Dr. Benjamin Rush, 21 April 1803, Bergh, 10:374–75, 379–85.

51. Boorstin, p. 278. Sowerby lists 13 works of Paine in Jefferson's library (5:375).

52. See Jefferson's quotations from Locke and Bolingbroke, Chinard, *Commonplace Book,* p. 387, and *Literary Bible,* pp. 50–51; TJ to William Short, 13 April 1820, Bergh, 15:244–45.

53. TJ to William Short, 31 Oct. 1819, 4 Aug. 1820, Bergh, 15:221, 260.

54. Chinard, *Literary Bible,* p. 57; TJ to William Short, 13 April 1820, 4 Aug. 1820, Bergh, 15:244, 257.

55. TJ to John Adams, 11 April 1823, TJ to Dr. Benjamin Waterhouse, 26 June 1822, TJ to William Short, 21 Oct. 1819, Bergh, 15:425, 384, 221.

56. TJ to William Short, 4 Aug. 1820, Bergh, 15:260–61.

57. TJ to Richard Price, 8 Jan. 1789, Bergh, 7:252; TJ to John Davis, 18 Jan. 1824, Ford, 10:288.

58. TJ to William Short, 4 Aug. 1820, TJ to Miles King, 26 Sept. 1814, TJ to Alexander Smyth, 17 Jan. 1825; Bergh, 15:261, 14:197, 16:100–101.

59. TJ To William Canby, 18 Sept. 1813, Bergh, 13:377.

60. TJ to Ezra Stiles, 25 June 1819, Bergh, 15:204.

61. TJ to Logan, 12 Nov. 1816, Ford, 10:68, TJ to Mrs. Samuel Hairison Smith, 6 Aug. 1816, TJ to Francis Adrian van der Kemp, 25 April 1816, TJ to

Timothy Pickering, 27 Feb. 1821, TJ to Rev. Jared Sparks, 4 Nov. 1820, TJ to John Adams, 11 April 1823, Bergh, 15:60, 2, 323, 288, 430; TJ to John Davis, 18 Jan. 1824, Ford, 10:287–88.

62. TJ to William Short, 13 April 1820, 4 Aug. 1820, TJ to Francis Adrian van der Kemp, 25 April 1816, Bergh, 15:244–45, 259, 2–3.

63. TJ To Rev. Jared Sparks, 4 Nov. 1820, TJ to John Adams, 5 May 1817, TJ to Charles Thomson, 9 Jan. 1816, TJ to Adams, 13 Oct. 1813, TJ to Samuel Greenhow, 31 Jan. 1814, TJ to William Canby, 18 Sept. 1813, Bergh, 15:288, 109, 14:385, 13:390, 14:81, 13:377–78; TJ to George Thacher, 26 Jan. 1824, Ford, 10:288.

64. TJ to Edward Dowse, 19 April 1803, TJ, "Syllabus," TJ to Joseph Priestley, 9 April 1803, TJ to William Short, 31 Oct. 1819, Bergh, 10:376–77, 381–82, 374, 15:220.

65. TJ to Edward Dowse, 19 April 1803, TJ, "Syllabus," TJ to Ezra Stiles, 25 June 1819, Bergh, 10:377, 385, 15:203.

66. TJ, "Syllabus," Bergh, 10:384.

67. TJ to Charles Thomson, 9 Jan. 1816, TJ to Joseph Priestley, 9 April 1803, Bergh, 14:386, 10:374.

68. TJ to George Thacher, 26 Jan. 1824, Ford, 10:288–89; TJ, "Syllabus," TJ to William Short, 4 Aug. 1820, Bergh, 10:382–85, 15:260.

69. TJ to William Short, 4 Aug. 1820, Bergh, 15:260.

70. TJ to Adams, 13 Oct. 1813, TJ, "Syllabus," Bergh, 13:388–89; 10:385.

71. TJ to George Thacher, 26 Jan. 1824, Ford, 10:289; TJ to William Short, 4 Aug. 1820, 13 April 1820, TJ, "Syllabus," Bergh, 15:260, 244, 10:385.

72. TJ to Joseph Priestley, 9 April 1803, Bergh, 10:374–75.

73. TJ to John Adams, 5 May 1817, Bergh, 15:109; TJ to Thacher, 26 Jan. 1824, Ford, 10:288–89; TJ to Charles Thomson, 9 Jan. 1816, TJ, "Syllabus," TJ to Joseph Priestley, 9 April 1803, Bergh, 14:386, 10:382, 374–75.

74. TJ to William Short, 4 Aug. 1820, TJ to Ezra Stiles, 25 June 1819, TJ to Dr. Benjamin Waterhouse, 26 June 1822, TJ to John Adams, 11 April 1823, TJ, "Syllabus," Bergh, 15:260, 203, 384, 428–29, 10:384.

75. TJ to Ezra Stiles, 25 June 1819, TJ to William Short, 4 Aug. 1820, TJ to Dr. Benjamin Waterhouse, 26 June 1822, Bergh, 15:203, 260, 384.

76. Chinard, *Literary Bible,* pp. 57, 64, 45–46, 68–70.

77. TJ to William Short, 4 Aug. 1820, TJ to Francis Adrian van der Kemp, 25 April 1816, TJ to John Adams, 13 Oct. 1813, Bergh, 15:259, 2, 13:388–89.

78. John Adams to TJ, 22 July 1813, 9 Aug. 1813, 2 Feb. 1816, Cappon, 2:362–63, 364, 462; TJ to Adams, 13 Oct. 1813, 22 Aug. 1813, Bergh, 13:388–89, 351.

79. TJ to George Thacher, 26 Jan. 1824, Ford, 10:288–89; TJ to John Adams, 5 May 1817, TJ to Timothy Pickering, 27 Feb. 1821, Bergh, 15:109, 324.

80. TJ to James Smith, 8 Dec. 1822, TJ to Rev. Jared Sparks, 4 Nov. 1820, Bergh, 15:408, 288.

81. TJ, "Syllabus," TJ to Joseph Priestley, 9 April 1803, TJ to William Short, 4 Aug. 1820, TJ to John Adams, 11 April 1823, Bergh, 10:382, 384, 374–75, 15:260, 425, 428–29; Chinard, *Literary Bible,* pp. 45–46, 56–57, 64, 67–71.

82. See Genesis 22:1–14, Deuteronomy 12:1–3, Leviticus 26:31, Numbers 33:50–53, 2 Kings 23:1–11.

83. See Micah 6:6–8.

84. TJ to Rev. Jared Sparks, 4 Nov. 1820, TJ to John Adams, 11 April 1823, 22 Aug. 1813, TJ to Dr. Benjamin Waterhouse, 26 June 1822, TJ to James Smith, 8 Dec. 1822, TJ to William Canby, 18 Sept. 1813, TJ to Timothy Pickering, 27 Feb. 1821, TJ to William Short, 4 Aug. 1820, 13 April 1820, Bergh, 15:288, 425, 13:350, 15:384, 408–9, 13:378, 15:323, 258–59, 246.

85. TJ to Francis Adrian van der Kemp, 25 April 1816, TJ to Ezra Stiles, 25 June 1819, TJ to William Short, 13 April 1820, TJ to Samuel Greenhow, 31 Jan. 1814, TJ to Charles Thomson, 9 Jan. 1816, TJ to Jacob Engelbrecht, 24 Feb. 1824, Bergh, 15:2, 203, 244, 14:81, 386, 16:16.

86. TJ to Dr. Benjamin Waterhouse, 26 June 1822, TJ to Ezra Stiles, 25 June 1819; TJ to Dr. George Logan, 12 Nov. 1816, Bergh, 15:384, 203, 10:68; TJ to Waterhouse, 13 Oct. 1815, TJ to George Thacher, 26 Jan. 1824, Ford, 9:533, 10:288–89; TJ, "Syllabus," TJ to William Short, 31 Oct. 1819, Bergh, 10:382, 384–85, 15:220.

87. TJ, "Syllabus," TJ to Rev. Charles Clay, 29 Jan. 1815, Bergh, 10:383, 14:233–34.

88. TJ to Rev. Charles Clay, 29 Jan. 1815, TJ to Timothy Pickering, 27 Feb. 1821, TJ to Samuel Kercheval, 19 Jan. 1810, TJ to John Adams, 13 Oct. 1813, TJ to Mrs. Samuel Harrison Smith, 6 Aug. 1816, TJ to Rev. Jared Sparks, 4 Nov. 1820, Bergh, 14:233, 15:323, 12:345, 13:389–90, 15:60–61, 288.

89. TJ. Declaration of Independence, Bergh, 1:29. Jefferson also appealed to the justice and purpose of God in TJ, Draft of Declaration on Taking Up Arms, TJ, Address to Governor Dunmore for the Virginia House of Burgesses, and TJ, Proposed Constitution for Virginia, Ford, 1:476, 459, 3:321.

90. TJ to Mordecai Manuel Noah, 28 May 1818, Foner, pp. 756–57; TJ to Joseph Marx, 1820, TJ to Dr. Jacob de La Motta, 1 Sept. 1820, Padover, *Democracy,* pp. 179, 178; TJ to M. François de Marbois, 14 June 1817, TJ to John Adams, 25 Feb. 1823, Bergh, 15:129–30, 417–18; TJ, Opinion on French Treaties, 28 April 1793, TJ, *Notes on the State of Virginia,* TJ, "Answers to Questions of Monsieur Démeunir," TJ to David Barrow, 1 May 1815, Ford, 6:219–21, 3:267, 4:185, 9:516.

91. TJ to Joseph Priestley, 9 April 1803, TJ to William Short, 4 Aug. 1820, TJ to Dr. Benjamin Waterhouse, 26 June 1822, TJ, "Syllabus," Bergh, 10:374–75, 15:260, 384, 10:385; TJ to George Thacher, 26 Jan. 1824, Ford, 10:288–89.

92. TJ to William Short, 13 April 1820, 31 Oct. 1819, TJ to Judge Augustus B. Woodward, 24 March 1824, TJ to John Adams, 15 Aug. 1820, 11 April 1823, Bergh, 15:244, 219–20, 16:18, 15:274, 429.

93. Boorstin, pp. 157–59.

94. TJ, "Syllabus," Bergh, 10:381.

95. TJ, Second Inaugural Address, 4 March 1805, TJ to the Earl of Buchan, 10 July 1803, Bergh, 3:383, 10:400; TJ to Elbridge Gerry, 29 March 1801, Ford, 8:41; TJ to Maria Cosway, 12 Oct. 1786, TJ to Abigail Adams, 11 Jan. 1817, Bergh, 5:44, 15:96.

96. TJ to John Adams, 13 Oct. 1813, TJ to Smith, 21 Feb. 1825, TJ to Jacob Engelbrecht, 25 Feb. 1824, Bergh, 13:392, 16:110–11, 16.

97. Deuteronomy 6:4–5 and Leviticus 19:18; Matthew 5:5 and Psalm 37:11, Matthew 5:4 and Isaiah 61:2–3, and Matthew 5:8 and Psalm 15:2; Leviticus 19:18 and Tobit 4:15. For an account of modern Jewish religion, see Florence Mary Fitch, *One God: The Ways We Worship Him* (New York, 1945), pp. 22–29.

98. See Gay, p. ix; Foote, *Jefferson: Social Reformer.*

99. Helmet Richard Niebuhr concludes that bringing in the Kingdom of God is the unifying theme of America's religious history (*The Kingdom of God in America* [New York, 1937], pp. x–xiii). Peterson, *Jefferson Image,* pp. 360–64; David Little, "The Social Gospel Revisited," in *The Secular City Debate,* ed. Daniel Callahan (New York, 1966), pp. 69–71. Max L. Stackhouse, "Editor's Introduction," in Walter Rauschenbusch, *The Righteousness of the Kingdom* (Nashville, Tenn., 1968), pp. 14–16, 23, 53; Walter Rauschenbush, *Christianizing the Social Order* (New York, 1916), pp. 48–57, 64–68; Gustavo Gutierrez, *A Theology of Liberation,* trans. and ed. Sister Caridad Inda and John Eagleson (Maryknoll, N.Y., 1973), pp. ix–xi, 34–37, 167–77; Arthur Schlesinger, Jr., "Reinhold Niebuhr's Role in American Political Thought and Life," in *Reinhold Niebuhr: His Religious, Social, and Political Thought,* ed. Charles W. Kegley (New York, 1956), pp. 126–30.

Chapter IX

1. Malone, 1:107; Chinard, *Literary Bible,* pp. 6–7; Peterson, *New Nation,* pp. 960–61; Boorstin, pp. 50, 105, 149, 278; Chinard, *Jefferson,* pp. 519, 527; Randall, 3:540–47; Healey, pp. 30–34, 273–74; Foote, *Champion,* pp. 67–68; Koch, *Philosophy,* p. 38; Chinard, *Commonplace Book,* p. 47.

2. TJ to John Page, 15 July 1763, Bergh, 4:10.

3. TJ to Rev. Isaac Story, 5 Dec. 1801, Ford, 8:107.

4. Chinard, *Literary Bible,* pp. 17, 38, 72–76, 102, 120, 172, 88, 100; TJ to John Brazer, 24 Aug. 1819, TJ to John Adams, 14 March 1820, TJ to Peter Carr, 10 Aug. 1787, TJ, Bill for Proportioning Crimes and Punishments, TJ to Dr. Samuel Brown, 14 July 1813, Bergh, 15:208, 240, 6:260, 1:225–26, 13:310–11.

5. See his notes on Pope's *Elegy* and Edward Young's *Night Thoughts,* Chinard, *Literary Bible,* pp. 143, 171, 202; and Sowerby, 5:441.

6. Chinard, *Literary Bible,* p. 146.

7. TJ, "Notes on Religion," Ford 2:100; TJ to John Adams, 15 Aug. 1820, Bergh, 15:276; TJ to Rev. Isaac Story, 5 Dec. 1801, Ford, 8:107.

8. TJ to Carr, 10 Aug. 1787, TJ to William Short, 31 Oct. 1819, Bergh, 6:260, 15:221.

9. See Jefferson's notes on Bolingbroke, Chinard, *Literary Bible,* p. 57.

10. TJ to Rev. Jared Sparks, 4 Nov. 1820, TJ to Richard Price, 8 Jan. 1789, TJ to Ezra Stiles, 25 June 1819, TJ to John Adams, 11 April 1823, TJ to Dr. Benjamin Waterhouse, 26 June 1822, Bergh, 15:288, 7:252, 15:203, 425, 384; TJ to John Davis, 18 Jan. 1824, Ford, 10:288.

11. TJ to Alexander Smyth, 17 Jan. 1825, Bergh, 16:100–101. He did not include the book or Revelation in his "Bible," see Appendix.

12. TJ to Joseph Priestley, 9 April 1803, Bergh, 10:375; TJ to George Thacher, 26 Jan. 1824, TJ to John Davis, 18 Jan. 1824, Ford, 10:288, 287–88; TJ to John Adams, 22 Aug. 1813, TJ to William Short, 13 April 1820, TJ to James Smith, 8 Dec. 1822, TJ to Benjamin Waterhouse, 26 June 1822, Bergh, 13:350, 15:246, 408–9, 383–84.

13. TJ to Rev. Isaac Story, 5 Dec. 1801, Ford, 7:276; TJ to Page, 15 July 1763, TJ to Carr, 10 Aug. 1787, Bergh, 4:10, 6:260.

14. TJ to Law, 13 June 1814, Bergh, 14:142–43.

15. Peterson, *New Nation,* pp. 14–17.

16. TJ to Thomas Jefferson Smith, 21 Feb. 1825, Bergh, 16:110; TJ to Thomas Jefferson Grotjan, 10 Jan. 1824, Ford, 10:287; TJ to Martha Jefferson, 11 Dec. 1783, Boyd, 6:380–81.

17. TJ to Pierre Samuel Dupont de Nemours, 24 April 1816, Ford, 10:25; John Adams to TJ, 24 Sept. 1821, Bergh, 15:336; Chinard, *Literary Bible,* pp. 50–51, 57–58, 61–64.

18. TJ to Miles King, 26 Sept. 1814, TJ to Mrs. Samuel Harrison Smith, 6 Aug. 1816, Bergh, 14:197–98, 15:60; TJ to Thomson, 29 Jan. 1817, Ford, 10:76; TJ to Dr. Benjamin Waterhouse, 26 June 1822, Bergh, 15:383–84; TJ to George Thacher, 26 Jan. 1824, Ford, 10:288–89.

19. TJ to William Short, 13 April 1820, Bergh, 15:245; TJ, "Syllabus," Ford, 8:228; TJ to John Adams, 8 April 1816, TJ to Short, 4 Aug. 1820, Bergh, 14:470, 15:260; TJ, "Notes on Religion," Ford, 2:94.

20. TJ to Horatio Gates Spafford, 17 March 1814, Bergh, 14:120.

21. Koch states, "It is difficult to determine whether Jefferson approved the argument of immortality only as an extra incentive to moral behavior . . . without literal . . . truth value, or whether he actually believed its promise" (*Philosophy,* p. 33). Boorstin argues, "Jefferson considered the 'doctrine of a future state' primarily as a belief which encouraged a moral life; he thought its truth was not demonstrable (nor even perhaps discussable) and seemed hardly interested in whether it was 'true,' since a belief in it was so undeniably 'useful' " (p. 278).

22. TJ to Carr, 10 Aug. 1787, Bergh, 6:258–61; TJ to Martha Jefferson, 11 Dec. 1783, Boyd, 6:380–81.

23. TJ to William Short, 13 April 1820, Bergh, 15:244.

24. TJ to John Adams, 5 July 1814, 22 Aug. 1813, TJ to William Short, 31 Oct. 1819, 4 Aug. 1820, Bergh, 14:148–49, 13:350, 15:219–20, 258; TJ to John Davis, 18 Jan. 1824, Ford, 10:288.

25. *A Commentary on the Holy Bible,* ed. J. R. Dummelow (New York, 1977), s.v. "St. John's Gospel," p. 774; TJ to John Adams, 11 April 1823, Bergh, 15:429.

26. Adams to TJ, 22 July 1813, 12 May 1820, TJ to Adams, 15 Aug. 1820, Cappon, 2:363, 563–64, 567–69.

27. *Priestley,* pp. 263, 268, 271. Jefferson agreed with Priestley, TJ to Adams, 8 Jan. 1825, Cappon, 2:605–606.

28. TJ to John Adams, 15 Aug. 1820, Cappon, 2:568; TJ to Adams, 14 March 1820, 8 Jan. 1825, Bergh, 15:240, 16:91; Sowerby, 5:239, 261, 284, 299, 348, 391, 418, 282, 313. See also Koch, *Philosophy,* pp. 34–35; Boorstin, p. 118.

29. TJ to John Adams, 14 March 1820, Bergh, 15:240. Jefferson got the idea of comparing thinking with magnetism from the writings of Helvétius (Chinard, *Commonplace Book,* pp. 328–31)

30. See Cyrus Adler, "Jefferson as a Man of Science," in Bergh, 19:iii–x; Sanford, pp. 90–93.

31. *Priestley,* pp. 271–72.

32. TJ to Peter Carr, 10 Aug. 1787; TJ to John Adams, 8 April 1816, Bergh, 6:260, 14:470; Gay, pp. 278–81.

33. TJ to John Adams, 15 Aug. 1820, 14 March 1820, TJ to Thomas Cooper, 14 Aug. 1820, TJ to Judge Augustus B. Woodward, 24 March 1824, Bergh, 15:274, 240–41, 266–67, 16:18–19.

34. TJ to William Short, 13 April 1820, Bergh, 15:244; TJ to John Adams, 15 Aug. 1820, Cappon, 2:568.

35. TJ to Adams, 14 March 1820, 15 Aug. 1820, 11 April 1823, TJ to William Short, 13 April 1820, TJ to Thomas Cooper, 14 Aug. 1820, Bergh, 15:241, 274, 428, 244, 266; TJ to Cooper, 11 Dec. 1823, Ford, 10:285; TJ to Judge Augustus B. Woodward, 24 March 1824, Bergh, 16:18.

36. Chinard, *Commonplace Book,* p. 374; Sowerby, 5:422 (Tertullian); TJ to Thomas Cooper, 14 Aug. 1820, TJ to Judge Augustus B. Woodward, 24 March 1824, TJ to John Adams, 15 Aug. 1820, Bergh, 15:267, 16:18–19, 15:274–75; TJ to Adams, 18 Aug. 1820, 11 April 1823, Cappon, 2:568, 593.

37. Adams to TJ, 22 Jan. 1825, 12 May 1820, Cappon, 2:607, 563–64.

38. Boorstin, pp. 54–55, 136–39.

39. Chinard, *Literary Bible,* pp. 139–40, 182, 114, 88, 100–102; Sowerby, 5:259, 361, 352 (George Buchanan, Milton, David Mallet, Homer, and Euripides); TJ to John Brazer, 24 Aug. 1819, Bergh, 15:208–9.

40. TJ, "Autobiography," Ford, 1:3; Randall, 1:41; Chinard, *Literary Bible,* p. 29.

41. Malone, 1:396–97; TJ to Cosway, 12 Oct. 1786, Boyd, 10:447; Chinard, *Jefferson,* p. 138; TJ, "Autobiography," Ford, 1:71–72; Randall, 1:382; TJ to François Jean, chevalier de Chastellux, 26 Nov. 1782, Ford, 3:64–65.

42. TJ to William Claiborne, 3 May 1810, TJ to Adams, 13 Oct. 1813, Bergh, 12:385, 13:393–94; Randall, 1:384.

43. TJ to Page, 25 June 1804, Bergh, 11:30–31.

44. John Adams to TJ, 2 March 1816, TJ to Adams, 8 April 1816, Cappon, 2:464, 467.

45. TJ to Rush, 23 Sept. 1800, Bergh, 10:173.

46. John Adams to TJ, 3 May, 6 May 1816, Cappon, 2:469–71, 472–73.

47. TJ to John Adams, 1 Aug. 1816, Cappon, 2:483; Chinard, *Literary Bible,* p. 129.

48. TJ to John Adams, 14 Oct. 1816, Cappon, 2:490; Chinard, *Literary Bible,* pp. 206–7.

49. TJ to Page, 15 July 1763, 25 June 1804, Bergh, 4:10, 11:31.

50. TJ to Mrs. Eliza House Trist, 11 Dec. 1783, 25 Dec. 1784, 18 Dec. 1785, Boyd, 6:382–83, 7:583, 8:403; TJ to Adams, 11 April 1823, 8 Jan. 1825, Cappon, 2:594, 606.

51. TJ to Thomson, 29 Jan. 1817, Ford, 10:76; TJ to Adams, 11 April 1823, 14 March 1820, Cappon, 2:594, 562–63; TJ to Canby, 18 Sept. 1813, TJ to King, 26 Sept. 1814, Bergh, 13:377, 14:198.

52. TJ to Abigail Adams, 11 Jan. 1817, TJ to John Adams, 1 June 1822, Adams to TJ, 12 May 1820, TJ to Adams, 8 Jan. 1825, Cappon, 2:504, 577–78, 565, 606.

53. TJ to Thomas Jefferson Grotjan, 12 Jan. 1824, Ford, 10:287; TJ to Thomas Jefferson Smith, 21 Feb. 1825, Bergh, 16:110; TJ to John Adams, 4 Sept. 1823, 17 May 1818, TJ to Abigail Adams, 11 Jan. 1817, Cappon, 2:597, 524, 504.

54. TJ to Cosway, 27 Dec. 1820, Bergh, 18:309–10; TJ to the marquis de Lafayette, 14 Feb. 1815, Ford, 9:510.

55. TJ to John Adams, 1 June 1822, Cappon, 2:578; TJ, "A Death-bed Adieu from Th. J. to M.R.," *The Wisdom of Thomas Jefferson,* ed. Edward Boykin (New York, 1941), p. 212.

56. Adams to TJ, 20 Oct. 1818, TJ to Adams, 13 Nov. 1818, Cappon, 2:529.

57. Randall, 3:342–43.

58. TJ to Martha Jefferson, 28 March 1787, Ford, 4:374; TJ to John Page, 25 June 1804, Bergh, 11:31.

59. TJ to John Adams, 28 Oct. 1814, Cappon, 2:387; Chinard, *Literary Bible,* p. 74.

60. TJ to Cosway, 27 Dec. 1820, Bergh, 18:309.

61. TJ, First Inaugural Address, 4 March 1801, and Second Inaugural Address, 4 March 1805, TJ to Page, 25 June 1804, TJ, Reply to John Thomas, 18 Nov. 1807, TJ, Reply to Legislature of Vermont, 10 Dec. 1807, Bergh, 3:322–23, 383, 11:31, 16:291, 294.

62. Chinard, *Literary Bible,* p. 18.

63. See TJ to James Monroe, 13 Jan. 1803, Ford, 8:191, and Jefferson's quotation from Edward Young, Chinard, *Literary Bible,* p. 177.

64. TJ to Mrs. Samuel Harrison Smith, 6 Aug. 1816, Bergh, 15:60–661.

65. TJ to John Adams, 14 March 1820, 21 Jan. 1812, 11 April 1823, 11 Jan. 1816, 25 March 1826, Cappon, 2:562, 292, 594, 458–59, 614. Jefferson, Adams, and Charles Carroll were the last survivors of those who signed the Declaration of Independence (ibid., p. 292).

66. TJ to Madison, 17 Feb. 1826, Bergh, 16:155–59; Peterson, *New Nation,* p. 992. The grandson wrote of paying Jefferson's bequests (Randall, 3:561, 672).

67. Randall, 3:549–50; TJ to Madison, 17 Feb. 1826, Bergh, 16:156–57.

68. It was Madison who succeeded in getting the Virginia General Assembly to pass Jefferson's act establishing religious freedom (Madison to TJ, 22 Jan. 1786, Boyd, 9:194–95).

69. TJ to Archibald Thweatt, 19 Jan. 1821, Bergh, 15:306–307.

70. TJ to Dr. Benjamin Rush, 17 Aug. 1811, TJ to James Madison, 6 Sept. 1789, TJ to John Cartwright, 5 June 1825, Bergh, 13:76–77, 7:454–55, 459–60, 16:48.

71. Randall, 3:549.

72. TJ to Roger C. Weightman, 24 June 1826, Bergh, 16:181–82.

73. TJ to Rev. Isaac Story, 5 Dec. 1801, Bergh, 10:299; see also Healey, p. 33.

74. TJ to John Adams, 14 March 1820, Bergh, 15:240–41; Adams to TJ, 12 May 1820, 22 Jan. 1825, TJ to Adams, 14 March 1820, 8 Jan. 1825, Cappon, 2:563–65, 607, 563, 606.

75. TJ to John Page, 25 June 1804, TJ to Short, 31 Oct. 1819, Bergh, 11:31, 15:221.

76. TJ to John Adams, 14 March 1820, Cappon, 2:563; TJ to John Page, 25 June 1804, Bergh, 11:31–32; Chinard, *Literary Bible,* pp. 147–48.

77. TJ to Archibald Thweatt, 19 Jan. 1821, Bergh, 15:306–307; TJ to John Adams, 1 Aug. 1816, Cappon, 2:484.

78. TJ to M. François de Marbois, 14 June 1817, Bergh, 15:131; TJ to John Adams, 1 Aug. 1816, Cappon, 2:485.

79. TJ to Cosway, 27 Dec. 1820, TJ to John Page, 25 June 1804, TJ to Henry Dearborn, 17 Aug. 1821, TJ to John Adams, 1 June 1822, Bergh, 18:309–10, 11:31, 15:329, 371; TJ to Adams, 1 Aug. 1816, Cappon, 2:484.

80. TJ to John Adams, 21 Jan. 1812, Cappon 2:292; Randall, 3:538; TJ to Adams, 5 July 1814, 12 Oct. 1823, Cappon, 2:430–31, 599.

81. Ecclesiastes 12:1 and 3:1–2 (Revised Standard Version).

82. TJ to John Adams, 1 June 1822, Cappon, 2:577–78; Chinard, *Literary Bible,* p. 175.

83. TJ to John Adams, 27 June 1822, Cappon, 2:580–81; Randall, 3:342.

84. Quoting from Milton, *Paradise Lost,* in Chinard, *Literary Bible,* pp. 138–39; John Adams to TJ, 11 June 1822, Cappon, 2:579.

85. Edward Young, *Night Thoughts,* quoted in Chinard, *Literary Bible,* p. 142; TJ to Abigail Adams, 11 Jan. 1817, Cappon, 2:504.

86. See Koch, *Philosophy,* pp. 34–35, and Boorstin, p. 118. Government, politics, law, history, and science comprised the largest sections in Jefferson's library (Sanford, pp. 99, 11–12).

87. TJ to John Adams, 13 Nov. 1818, Cappon, 2:529.

88. TJ, epitaph, Boykin, pp. 212–13; facsimile of Jefferson's epitaph and his design for his tombstone, Bergh, 1:262.

89. *The Book of Common Prayer* (1867), sect. 10; Randall, 3:545–47; Boykin, p. 212.

90. Randall, 3:542–45.

Chapter X

1. See Peterson, *Jefferson Image,* pp. 92–98.

2. See Randall, 2:567, 3:620–22; J. T. Adams, pp. xv–xvi; Shulz, p. 279.

3. TJ, "Autobiography," Bergh, 1:3. Jefferson's library contained some 650 titles on religion, ethics, Bible study, church history, philosophy (Sanford, pp. 94, 116–18, 141–42).

4. TJ to John Adams, 11 April 1823, TJ to William Short, 31 Oct. 1819, Bergh, 15:430, 220–21.

5. TJ to Peter Carr, 10 Aug. 1787, TJ to Joseph Priestley, 9 April 1803, TJ to William Short, 31 Oct. 1819, Bergh, 6:260, 10:375, 15:220–21.

6. Thomas Jefferson Collidge, "Jefferson in His Family," Bergh, 15:iv.

7. TJ to John Adams, 15 Aug. 1820, Bergh, 15:273–74.

8. TJ, Opinion on French Treaties, 28 April 1793, Ford, 6:220–21; TJ, *Notes on the State of Virginia,* and TJ to Thomas Law, 13 June 1814, Bergh, 2:227, 14:141–42.

9. TJ to Dr. George Logan, 12 Nov. 1816, Ford, 10:68.

10. TJ, "Notes on Religion," TJ, *Notes on Virginia,* TJ, Bill for Establishing Religious Freedom, TJ to William Carver, 4 Dec. 1823, Ford, 2:95, 101, 3:265, 2:237–38, 10:284–85.

11. TJ to Danbury Baptist Association, 1 Jan. 1802, Bergh, 16:281–82; Randall, 3:555.

12. TJ to Thomas Law, 13 June 1814, Bergh, 14:142–43; TJ to George Wythe, 13 Aug. 1786, Ford, 4:268–69; TJ to Dr. Benjamin Rush, 23 Sept. 1800, Bergh, 10:174–75.

13. TJ to John Adams, 28 Oct. 1813, Cappon, 2:388.

14. TJ, "Syllabus," Bergh, 10:383–85. See discussion by Schlesinger in *Niebuhr,* ed. Kegley, pp. 126–30.

15. TJ to John Adams, 15 Aug. 1820, Bergh, 15:273–74.

16. Chinard, *Literary Bible,* pp. 74, 76, 120, 171–72, 189, 202; TJ to John Page, 25 June 1804, TJ to John Adams, 15 Aug. 1820, Bergh, 11:31, 15:274–76.

17. Peterson, *Jefferson Image,* p. 14.

18. Healey, pp. 1–10.

19. TJ to Roger C. Weightman, 24 June 1826, Ford, 10:391.

20. Peterson, *Jefferson Image,* pp. 3–5.

Selected Bibliography

Collections of Jefferson's Writings

Cappon, Lester J., ed. *The Adams-Jefferson Letters*. 2 vols. Chapel Hill, N.C., 1959.

Jefferson, Thomas. *Basic Writings of Thomas Jefferson*. Ed. Philip S. Foner. 1944; rept. Garden City, N.Y., 1950.

——. *The Commonplace Book of Thomas Jefferson: A Repertory of His Ideas on Government*. Ed. Gilbert Chinard. Baltimore, 1926.

——. *The Complete Jefferson*. Ed. Saul K. Padover. New York, 1943.

——. *Democracy*. Ed. and Introd. Saul K. Padover. 1939; rept. New York, 1969.

——. *The Family Letters of Thomas Jefferson*. Ed. Edwin Morris Betts and James Adams Bear, Jr. Columbia, Mo., 1966.

——. *Index to the Thomas Jefferson Papers*. (Presidential papers index series.) U.S. Library of Congress. Manuscript Division. Washington, D.C., 1976. Lists by name of correspondent all the writings of Thomas Jefferson on microfilm in the Library of Congress.

——. *The Jefferson Bible, with the Annotated Commentaries on Religion of Thomas Jefferson*. Ed. O. I. A. Roche. Foreword by Donald S. Herrington. Introd. Henry Wilder Foote. New York, 1964.

——. *The Jefferson Cyclopedia*. Ed. John P. Foley. 2 vols. 1900; rept. New York, 1967.

——. *A Jefferson Profile*. Ed. Saul K. Padover. New York, 1956.

——. *Jefferson Reader*. Ed. Francis Coleman Rosenberger. New York, 1953.

——. *The Literary Bible of Thomas Jefferson: His Commonplace Book of Philosophers and Poets*. Ed. Gilbert Chinard. 1928; rept. New York, 1969.

——. *The Papers of Thomas Jefferson*. Ed. Julian P. Boyd et al. 20 vols. to date. Princeton, N.J., 1950– .

——. *The Wisdom of Thomas Jefferson, including the Jefferson Bible, "The Life and Morals of Jesus of Nazareth."* Ed. Edward Boykin. New York, 1941.

——. *The Writings of Thomas Jefferson*. Definitive Edition. Ed. Albert Ellery Bergh. 20 vols. Washington, D.C., 1907.

——. *The Writings of Thomas Jefferson*. Ed. Paul Leicester Ford. 10 vols. New York, 1892–99.

Monographs on Jefferson's Life

Brodie, Fawn M. *Thomas Jefferson: An Intimate History*. New York, 1974.

Brown, Stuart Gerry. *Thomas Jefferson*. 1963; rept. New York, 1966.

Bullock, Helen C. *My Head and My Heart*. New York, 1945.

Chinard, Gilbert. *Thomas Jefferson, the Apostle of Americanism*. Boston, 1929.

Dabney, Virginius. *The Jefferson Scandals: A Rebuttal*. New York, 1981.

Jefferson, Isaac. *Memoirs of a Monticello Slave: As Dictated to Charles Campbell in the 1840's by Isaac, One of Thomas Jefferson's Slaves*. Charlottesville, Va., 1951.

Koch, Adrienne. *Adams and Jefferson: Posterity Must Judge*. Chicago, 1963.

——. *Jefferson*. Englewood Cliffs, N.J., 1971.

——. *Jefferson and Madison*. New York, 1950.

Malone, Dumas. *Jefferson and His Time*. 6 vols. Boston, 1948–81.

Padover, Saul K. *Jefferson*. New York, 1942.

Peterson, Merrill D. *The Jefferson Image in the American Mind*. New York, 1960.

——. *Thomas Jefferson and the New Nation*. New York, 1970.

Randall, Henry Stephens. *The Life of Thomas Jefferson*. 3 vols. New York, 1858.

Monographs Pertaining to Aspects of Jefferson's Religious Beliefs

Adams, James Truslow. *Jefferson Principles and Hamiltonian Principles*. Boston, 1932.

Boorstin, Daniel J. *The Lost World of Thomas Jefferson*. New York, 1948.

Bowers, Claude Gernade. *Civil and Religious Liberty: Jefferson, O'Connell*. Worcester, Mass., 1930.

Callahan, Daniel, ed. *The Secular City Debate*. New York, 1966.

Cassirer, Ernst. *The Philosophy of the Enlightenment*. Princeton, N.J., 1951.

Cousins, Norman. *In God We Trust: the Religious Beliefs and Ideas of the American Founding Fathers*. New York, 1958.

Foote, Henry Wilder. *Thomas Jefferson: Champion of Religious Freedom, Advocate of Christian Morals*. Boston, 1947.

——. *Thomas Jefferson: Social Reformer*. Boston, 1947.

Gay, Peter. *The Enlightenment: An Interpretation*. New York, 1967.

Gutierrez, Gustavo. *A Theology of Liberation*. Trans. and ed. Sister Caridad Inda and John Eagleson. Maryknoll, N.Y., 1973.

Healey, Robert M. *Jefferson on Religion in Public Education*. 1962; rept. Hamden, Conn., 1970.

Honeywell, Roy John. *The Educational Work of Thomas Jefferson*. Cambridge, Mass., 1931.

Jordan, Winthrop D. *White over Black: American Attitudes toward the Negro, 1550–1812*. Chapel Hill, N.C., 1968.

Kegley, Charles W., ed. *Reinhold Niebuhr: His Social, Religious, and Political Thought*. New York, 1956.

Koch, Adrienne. *The Philosophy of Thomas Jefferson*. 1943; rept. Gloucester, Mass., 1957.

Lehmann, Karl. *Thomas Jefferson: American Humanist*. 1947; rept. Chicago, 1965.

McColley, Robert. *Slavery and Jeffersonian Virginia.* 2d ed. Urbana, Ill., 1972.

Morison, Samuel Eliot. *The Intellectual Life of Colonial New England.* 1936 (as *The Puritan Pronaus*); rept. Ithaca, N.Y., 1965.

Niebuhr, Helmet Richard. *The Kingdom of God in America.* New York, 1937.

Priestley, Joseph. *Joseph Priestley: Selections from His Writings.* Ed. Ira V. Brown. University Park, Pa., 1962.

Rauschenbusch, Walter. *Christianizing the Social Order.* 1912; rept. New York, 1916.

——. *The Righteousness of the Kingdom.* Ed. and introd. by Max L. Stackhouse. Nashville, Tenn., 1968.

Sanford, Charles B. *Thomas Jefferson and His Library: A Study of His Literary Interests and of the Religious Attitudes Revealed by Relevant Titles in His Library.* Hamden, Conn., 1977.

Schulz, Constance Bartlett. "The Radical Religious Ideas of Thomas Jefferson and John Adams: A Comparison." Ph.D. diss., University of Cincinnati, 1973.

Smithline, Arnold. *Natural Religion in American Literature.* New Haven, Conn., 1966.

Sowerby, E. Millicent, comp. *Catalogue of the Library of Thomas Jefferson.* 5 vols. Washington, D.C., 1952–59.

Stevens, William Arnold, and Ernest DeWitt Burton. *A Harmony of the Gospels.* New York, 1932.

Swancara, Frank. *Thomas Jefferson versus Religious Oppression.* New York, 1969.

Thomas, Elbert D. *This Nation under God.* New York, 1950.

Trainer, M. Rosaleen. "Thomas Jefferson on Freedom of Conscience." Ph.D. diss., St. John's University, 1966.

Williams, Kenneth Raynor. "The Ethics of Thomas Jefferson." Ph.D. diss., Boston University, 1962.

Articles on Jefferson and Aspects of His Religion

Adair, Douglas. "The New Thomas Jefferson." *William and Mary Quarterly,* 3d ser., 3 (1946): 122–33.

Adler, Cyrus. "Jefferson as a Man of Science." In *The Writings of Thomas Jefferson,* Definitive Edition, ed. Albert Ellery Bergh, 19:iii–x. Washington, D.C.: 1907.

——. "The Jefferson Bible: Introduction." Ibid., 20:7–19.

Bryan, William Jennings. "The Statute for Establishing Religious Freedom." Ibid., 8:i–xi.

Calish, Edward M. "Jefferson's Religion." Ibid., 17::i–xi.

Coolidge, Thomas Jefferson. "Jefferson in His Family." Ibid., 15:i–vii.

Freeling, William W. "The Founding Fathers and Slavery." *American Historical Review* 77 (1972): 87–88.

Foote, Henry Wilder. "Introduction." In *The Jefferson Bible.* Ed. O. I. A. Roche. New York, 1964.

Gould, William D. "The Religious Opinions of Thomas Jefferson." *Mississippi Valley Historical Review* 20 (1933): 191–208.

Hall, J. Leslie. "The Religious Opinions of Thomas Jefferson." *Sewanee Review* 21 (1913): 163–76.

Little, David. "The Social Gospel Revisited." In *The Secular City Debate*. Ed. Daniel Callahan (New York, 1966), pp. 69–71.

Schlesinger, Arthur, Jr. "Reinhold Niebuhr's Role in American Political Thought and Life." In *Reinhold Niebuhr: His Religious, Social, and Political Thought*. Ed. Charles W. Kegley. New York, 1956.

Vest, George Graham. "Jefferson's Passports to Immortality." In *The Writings of Thomas Jefferson,* Definitive Edition, ed. Albert Ellery Bergh, 12:i–xxxviii. Washington, D.C., 1907.

Index